PROSTITUTION

GARLAND REFERENCE LIBRARY
OF SOCIAL SCIENCE
(VOL. 670)

PROSTITUTION
A Guide to Sources, 1960–1990

Edited by
Vern L. Bullough
Lilli Sentz

Co-Editors
Nancy Henry
Kathleen Quinlivan
Dorothy Tao

Assistant Editors
Lisa Sentz
Kari Sentz

Special Contributing Editor
Ruth Mazo Karras

GARLAND PUBLISHING, INC. • NEW YORK & LONDON
1992

Library of Congress Cataloging-in-Publication Data

Prostitution : a guide to sources, 1960–1990 / edited by Vern L.
Bullough and Lilli Sentz ; co-editors, Nancy Henry ... [et al.].
    p.   cm. — (Garland reference library of social science ;
v. 670)
    Includes bibliographical references.
    ISBN 0–8240–7101–8
    1. Prostitution—Bibliography.   I. Bullough, Vern L.
II. Sentz, Lilli. III. Series.
Z7164.P95P76   1992
[HQ111]
016.30674—dc20   92–5112
                                       CIP

Printed on acid-free, 250-year-life paper
Manufactured in the United States of America

PREFACE

This compilation of recent works on prostitution continues an earlier bibliography edited by Vern Bullough and others which was published in 1976. Although there have always been studies on prostitution, the number of serious scholarly efforts has exploded in the past fifteen or twenty years. Major contributing factors to this trend include the influence of feminist scholarship and a greater willingness on the part of scholars to deal with such subjects as homosexuality and homosexual prostitution. While prostitution has been linked to sexually transmitted diseases throughout history, the appearance and spread of AIDS has furthermore led to a renewed interest.

The bibliography includes books and articles from many perspectives covering all facets of prostitution. We have organized these works under various subheadings and have provided a cross-reference index since many items could belong in more than one category. There is also a separate listing by authors.

Though we have attempted to be as comprehensive as possible, we have not cited titles in non-European languages unless English abstracts were available. There are, for example, a large number of studies in Japanese which are not listed. Studies in major European languages are included, but usually without abstracts. In the section on AIDS, we have exercised considerable discretion and only included studies which deal with the subject extensively. In spite of these limitations, we hope that this bibliography, particularly when combined with the earlier one, gives the most complete and comprehensive guide to prostitution available.

Since Vern Bullough was the initiator of the project, he is listed as the first author, but the contributions of Lilli Sentz were equally important. Nancy Henry was responsible for the sections on psychology and area studies. Kathleen Quinlivan compiled the legal section. Ruth Mazo Karras completed the historical references dealing with the medieval period. Much of the editing and compilation was done by Lisa Sentz and Kari Sentz. Particularly important to the project were members of the library staff of the State University of New York at Buffalo. They include Donald Hartman of Lockwood Memorial Library, Patricia A. Webster of the National Center for Earthquake Engineering Research, and Sharon Keller and Annette Williams of the Health Sciences Library. We would like to extend a special note of appreciation to Carol Lelonek who guided us all through WordPerfect. Last but not least, we thank Phyllis Korper and Gary Kuris of Garland for their help and assistance.

Vern L. Bullough and Lilli Sentz

CONTENTS

Prostitution

GENERAL SOURCES

BIBLIOGRAPHIES

1. Brewer, J.S., and R.W. Wright. *Sex Research: Bibliographies from the Institute for Sex Research.* Phoenix: Oryx, 1979.

   Classified but unannotated list of 4267 items selected from the holdings of the Alfred C. Kinsey Institute, Indiana.

2. Bullough, V.L., B. Elcano, M. Deacon, and B. Bullough. *A Bibliography of Prostitution.* New York: Garland, 1977.

   This was a pioneering attempt to cover prostitution. It has some 6494 references to world literature with geographical and topical approaches including history, fiction, public health, and psychiatry. Includes an author index. It is not particularly critical and it has a number of misprints, particularly in the foreign language sections. Most of the material listed in this bibliography is not listed in the previous one and the interested reader should consult both editions.

3. Bullough, V.L., W.D. Legg, B.W. Elcano, and J. Kepner. *An Annotated Bibliography of Homosexuality.* 2 vols. New York: Garland, 1976.

   This is a monumental work of some 13,000 entries, and was the first attempt to cover, without limitations of country or time period, the entire ensemble of relevant fields--scholarly, scientific, and creative. Comparatively few titles are annotated, and misprints abound, particularly in the foreign language citations. Each volume has an author index, which is helpful since some entries are misassigned in the topical index. Includes references to male prostitutes and prostitution.

4. Dynes, W.R. *Homosexuality: A Resource Guide.* New York: Garland, 1987.

   This is an update to the Bullough, Legg, Elcano, Kepner bibliography mentioned above. It includes considerable discussion on male prostitution.

1

It is extremely well organized with valuable comments.

5.　*Federation Abolitioniste.* Library in Geneva, Switzerland.

In 1947 they had 7850 volumes in their library and 728 periodical volumes. They also had a file of 18000 cards about other books. Many of the references are only of peripheral interest but many others are valuable.

6.　Gay, J. *Bibliographie des ouvrages relatifs à l'amour, aux femmes, au marriage.* Paris: 1863. Also published in Turin and London, 1871. Several other editions.

An early bibliography which also had some references to prostitution.

7.　Goodland, R. *A Bibliography of Sex Rites and Customs.* London: George Rutledge, 1931.

Hard to use, but useful for some anthropological materials and references.

8.　Hawley, D.L. "Prostitution in Canada: A Bibliography." *Resources for Feminist Research,* 14 (1985-86):61-63.

9.　Jacobs, S.E. *Women in Perspective: A Guide for Cross-Cultural Studies.* Urbana: University of Illinois Press, 1974.

Lists some 82 books published on prostitution between 1857 and 1971.

10.　Joardar, B. *Prostitution: A Bibliographical Synthesis.* New Delhi: Inter-India Publications, 1984.

We have not been able to see this bibliography to examine it. Joardar, however, has written other books on prostitution.

11.　Kantha, S.S. *Prostitutes in Medical Literature: An Annotated Bibliography.* Westport, CT: Greenwood, 1991.

Lists some 1274 items. Is somewhat broader than the title indicates and includes general and history, anthropology, sociology, psychology and mental health. Particularly good on sexually transmitted diseases. Has some items in foreign languages not included in this bibliography. Not all items are annotated.

12. Kearney, P.J. *The Private Case: An Annotated Bibliography of the Private Case Erotica Collection in the British (Museum) Library*. London: Jay Landes, 1981.

   Definitive catalogue of the special collection. Some entries are pertinent.

13. Library of Congress. *List of references on the history and suppression of prostitution*. Washington, DC: Library of Congress, 1917.

   This is but one of the lists issued by the Library of Congress. Others include Select List of References On the Social Evil (1910, 1911); White Slave Act, 1930, and many others.

14. Pia, P. *Les livres de l'enfer: bibliographie critique des ouvrages érotiques dans leurs différentes éditions du XVIe siècle à nos jours*. 2 vols. Paris: C. Colulet et A. Faure, 1978.

   A Bibliography of the *enfer* (private case) of the Bibliothèque Nationale, Paris. Alphabetically arranged by title. Lacks an author index. Still it has useful information.

15. [Rose, A.] "Rolf. S. Reade." *Registrum librorum eroticorum*. 2 vols., London: Privately printed, 1936.

   A pioneering, though disorganized and often inaccurate, list of over 1000 erotic works in major European languages. Reprinted New York: Jack Brussel, 1965. Includes some of the erotic works associated with prostitution.

16. Seligman, E.R.A., ed. *List of Books on the Social Evil, Including Pamphlets and Leaflets Published in the United States and Foreign Countries*. New York: American Social Hygiene Association, n.d.

The American Social Hygiene Association was active in pointing out the evils of prostitution and was the publisher of the Journal of Social Hygiene.

17.   Seroya, F.C., et al. *Sex and Sex Education: A Bibliography.* New York: Bowker, 1972.

A balanced selection with some annotation.

18.   Shore, D.A. *An Annotated Resource Guide to Periodicals in Human Sexuality.* Chicago: The author, 1978.

Discusses 53 periodicals, some of which are no longer published.

19.   Surgeon General's Office, United States Army. *Index-Catalogue of the Library.* Washington, DC: U.S. Government Printing Office, 1880-1955.

Contains references to medical and psychiatric books and articles in many languages. Collection is now part of the National Library of Medicine.

STUDIES ON FEMINISM

20.   Alexander, P. *Working on Prostitution.* Rockville, MD: National Institute of Justice, 1983.

Reviews historical, legal, and cross-cultural aspects of prostitution. Examines decriminalization and legalization, the policy of the National Organization of Women (NOW), and suggests activities for feminists to promote the policy.

21.   Barry, K., C. Bunch, and S. Castley, eds. *International Feminism: Networking Against Female Sexual Slavery: Report of the Global Feminist Workshop to Organize Against Traffic in Women, Rotterdam, The Netherlands, April 6-15, 1983.* New York: International Women's Tribune Centre (777 U.N. Plaza, NY 10017), 1984.

A 141 page report with bibliography dealing with prostitution, sex crimes, violent crimes, and victims of crimes.

22.   Basow, S.A., and F. Campanile.   "Attitudes Toward Prostitution as a
Function of Attitudes Toward Feminism in College Students: An
Exploratory Study."   *Psychology of Women Quarterly* 14(10) (March
1990):135-41.

Eighty-nine undergraduates completed a questionnaire on attitudes toward
feminism and attitudes toward prostitutes. Those who were pro-feminist
were found to be more likely to view prostitution as reflecting exploitation
and subordination of women and less likely to believe that women became
prostitutes out of economic necessity.

23.   Bell, L., ed.   *Good Girls/Bad Girls: Feminists and Sex Trade Workers
Face to Face*.   Seattle, WA: Seal, 1987.

Papers from a conference entitled *Challenging Our Images: The Politics
of Pornography and Prostitution* held in Toronto, Canada, Nov. 22-24,
1984, and sponsored by the Ontario Public Interest Research Group.

24.   Blackwell, E.   *Purchase of Women: The Great Economic Blunder*.
London: John Kensit, 1887.

This is a classic study by Elizabeth Blackwell, the first woman to be
educated as a physician in the United States, and a pioneer in the feminist
movement.

25.   Caplan, J.   "Male Vice and Feminist Virtue: Feminism and the Politics
of Prostitution in Nineteenth Century Britain."   *History Workshop Journal*
13 (1982):77-93.

Though this is an historical study, there is a brief introduction on "The
Politics of Prostitution" summarizing current controversy in the women's
movement in the United States with regards to prostitution.

26.   Cooper, B.   "Prostitution: A Feminist Analysis."   *Women's Rights Law
Reporter* 11 (1989):98-119.

27.   Dominelli, L.   "The Power of the Powerless: Prostitution and the
      Reinforcement of Submissive Femininity." *The Sociological Review*
      34(1) (February 1986):65-92.

      Examines prostitutes' attempt to rally in support of decriminalization in
      Great Britain through the formation of the Programme for the Reform of
      the Laws on Soliciting. Uses Liazos's paradigm of power. Considers
      significance of the gender base of power for social work intervention.
      Concludes that by organizing women become more powerful but do not
      change the existing power/gender relationships.

28.   Ericsson, L.O.   "Charges Against Prostitution--An Attempt at a
      Philosophical Assessment." *Ethics* 90(3) (1980):335-366.

      This attempt at what has been called a contractarian and formalist defense
      of prostitution led to such a strong feminist reaction that it is included
      here. See entry numbers 41 and 44.

29.   Fernand-Laurent, J.   *Activities for the Advancement of Women: Equality,*
      Development and Peace: Report of Jean Fernand-Laurent, Special
      Rapporteur on the Suppression of the Traffic in Persons and the
      Exploitation of the Prostitution of Others.   New York: United Nations,
      1985.

      Summarizes U.N. data on the prostitution of women and children.
      Examines prostitution as a universal and interdisciplinary question, and
      describes the principal international routes of prostitution traffic. Suggests
      policies and proposals for international cooperation in controlling
      prostitution.

30.   Goldman, E.   *The Traffic in Women and Other Essays on Feminism.*   New
      York: Times Change, 1970.

      A reprint by militant left-wing radical of the late nineteenth and first part
      of the twentieth century.

31.   Gordon, L., and E. Du Bois.   "Seeking Ecstasy on the Battlefield: Danger
      and Pleasure in Nineteenth-Century Feminist Sexual Thought." *Feminist*
      Studies 9 (Spring 1983):7-26.

A historical look at the two trends of sexual politics in feminist thought. The major trend emphasized the dangers and ignored the pleasures of sex for women while the lesser tradition encouraged women to seek sexual adventure without recognizing the dangers. Prostitution was the central feminist symbol of danger in contrast to rape which fills that ideological role today. The result of the emphasis on dangers was to limit women's sexual possibilities.

32.   Kaplan, M. "Prostitution, Morality Crusades and Feminism: German-Jewish Feminists and the Campaign Against White Slavery." *Women's Studies International Forum* 5(6) (1982):619-27.

33.   Maillard, C. *Les prostituées: ce qu'elles disent quand elles parlent "a une femme."* Paris: R. Laffont, 1975.

A collection of statements and responses by prostitutes.

34.   McLean, A. "Snuffing Out Snuff: Feminists React." *Canadian Dimension* 12(8) (1978):20-23.

A brief review of feminist responses in 1975 to the government crackdown on prostitution related offences in Toronto.

35.   McLeod, E. "Feminist Action Research and the Criminal Justice System: Lessons From the PROS Campaign on Prostitution." *Resources for Feminist Research* 14(4) (December/January, 1985/86):40-41.

Relates the experiences of the Program for Reform of the Law on Soliciting (PROS) in Birmingham, England, in 1976. The PROS campaign successfully encouraged legislative action to stop the imprisonment of prostitutes.

36.   Messerschmidt, J. "Feminism, Criminology and the Rise of the Female Sex 'Delinquent'." *Contemporary Crises* 11 (1987):243-63.

Examines relationship between social feminists, social purists, and criminologists in the period 1880 to 1930 in the United States. Argues that feminists joined in a coalition with the conservative social purity movement to raise the age of sexual consent in United States in order to protect young females from allegedly being forced into prostitution. Emphasizes the end result was not a decrease in sexual exploitation of young females but a denial of the right of females to engage in heterosexual activity when they pleased, and the creation of a new class of female offenders, the teenage sex delinquents.

37.   Millett, K. *The Prostitution Papers: "A Quartet for Female Voice."* New York: Ballantine, 1976.

38.   Miner, M.E.   *Slavery of Prostitution: A Plea for Emancipation.* New York: Garland, 1987.

       This is a reprint of a classic work with an early feminist perspective. Book originally appeared in 1916.

39.   Morris, M.H. "Sex, Marriage and Feminism." *Religious Humanism* 19 (Autumn 1985):174-80, 194-97.

       A letter replying to an earlier article by A. York, and a rejoinder by York.

40.   Musheno, M., and K. Seeley. "Prostitution Policy and the Women's Movement: Historical Analysis of Feminist Thought and Organization." *Contemporary Crises* 10(3) (1986):237-55.

       Traditionally, feminists in United States supported severe state repression of prostitution while contemporary feminists join prostitutes in support of decriminalization of the activity. Suggests that this contradiction in policy positions is due to shifts in feminist thought about the role of the state as well as organizing strategies.

41.   Pateman, C. "Defending Prostitution: Charges Against Ericsson." *Ethics* 93(3) (April 1983):561-65.

       Feminist argument against L.O. Ericsson's contractarian and reformist analysis of prostitution mentioned above. Challenges the claim that prostitution constitutes the sale of sexual services and is comparable to other forms of contractual exchange.

42. *Promoción cultural creatividad y cambio.* A pamphlet series on microfilm in Princeton University Library, 1984.

Twenty-nine pamphlets dealing with women's issues in Peru including prostitution.

43. Shaver, F.M. "The Feminist Defense of the Decriminalization of Prostitution." *Resources for Feminist Research* 14 (1985-86):38-39.

44. Shrage, L.I. "Should Feminists Oppose Prostitution." *Ethics* 99(2) (1989):347-361.

The ongoing debate over prostitution initiated by Ericsson's article. See number 41.

45. Smart, C. "Researching Prostitution: Some Problems for Feminist Research." *Humanity and Society* 8(4) (November 1984):407-13.

Argues that prostitution has been a political issue for feminists in the United Kingdom since the nineteenth century. Argues that prostitution should remain an important topic for research which should aim towards the elimination of larger social forces fostering and maintaining the practice of sexual inequality and oppression of women.

46. Walkowitz, J.R. "Male Vice and Feminist Virtue: Feminism and the Politics of Prostitution in Nineteenth-Century Britain." *History Workshop Journal* 13 (1982):77-93.

Argues that the attempts of the feminists to use "purity crusades" to extend women's rights were impeded by the hierarchy of power in Victorian England.

47. Walkowitz, J.R. "The Politics of Prostitution." *Signs* 6(1) (1980):123-35.

Found that some women in the United Kingdom supported the right of working class women to adopt prostitution as a career but were ambivalent about sexuality. This led them to engage in a campaign against white slavery and ultimately to support a single standard of chastity. Argues

there is a tendency for feminist campaigns against commercial sex to be
transformed into repressive state policy.

STUDIES ON SEXUALITY AND PROSTITUTION

48.   Barry, K. *Female Sexual Slavery*. Englewood Cliffs, NJ: Prentice-Hall,
       1979.

       Argues that prostitution is a crime against women. See entry number 49.

49.   Barry, K. "Social Etiology of Crimes Against Women." *Victimology* 10
       (1985):164-73.

       Argues that prostitution is a crime against women because it is a form of
       female sexual slavery and for the aggressor (customer) sex is rendered
       into a commodity for purchase. This purchased sex is the same as that
       sought and seized in rape and other crimes of sexual violence.

50.   Chaneles, S., ed. *Gender Issues, Sex Offences, and Criminal Justice:
       Current Trends*. New York: Haworth, 1984. Also published as a
       combined issue of the *Journal of Offender Counseling, Services, and
       Rehabilitation* 9(1/2) (1984).

       Includes 11 studies which examine criminal justice issues related to gender
       and sex offenses. Makes program recommendations.

51.   Chelala Aguilera, J.M. *Cinco ensayos sobre la vida sexual*. Havana,
       Cuba: Universidad de la Havana, 1959.

       Discusses prostitution, homosexuality, sex hygiene, and sexual ethics and
       includes references and bibliography.

52.   Cross, H.U. *The Lust Market*. New York: Citadel, 1963.

       Includes a discussion of prostitution.

53. Francoeur, R.T., ed. *Taking Sides: Clashing Views on Controversial Issues in Human Sexuality.* Guilford, CT: Dushkin, 1987.

A series of arguments and statements, by articulate advocates on opposite sides, of a variety of sexual questions including prostitution.

54. Holmes, R.M. *Sexual Behavior: Prostitution, Homosexuality, Swinging.* Berkeley, CA: McCutchan, 1971.

55. James, J. "Friendship Between Prostitutes and Homosexuals." *Medical Aspects of Human Sexuality* 10(3) (March 1976):123.

Briefly looks at friendships between prostitutes and homosexuals and argues that they have common interests in avoiding the police and surviving the condemnation of society; they share common business interests on the streets and in bars, and because the gays are neither pimps nor customers, they can relate to the prostitute's problems.

56. Janus, S., B. Bess, and C. Saltus. *A Sexual Profile of Men in Power.* Englewood Cliffs, NJ: Prentice-Hall, 1972.

Looks at sexual behavior of "statesmen" in U.S., and includes a discussion of prostitution.

57. Langone, J. *Life, Love, Lust: A View of Sex and Sexuality.* Boston, MA: Little, Brown, 1980.

Examines the ethics of sex and love including such topics as prostitution, pornography, marriage, and living together as well as homosexuality, and jealousy. Aimed at a juvenile market.

58. Roberts, N. *The Front Line.* London: Grafton, 1986.

Women in the "sex industry," including prostitution, talk about their experiences.

59. Whittaker, P. *The American Way of Sex.* New York: Berkley, 1974.

Case studies of prostitution in the United States including massage parlors.

STUDIES ON VIOLENCE AND CRIME

60. Ardilla, A. *Psicología y problemas sociales en Colombia.* Tunja: Universidad Pedagógica y Tecnológica de Colombia, 1971.

Examines violence in Columbia, social conditions, and prostitution.

61. Datesman, S.K., and J.A. Inciardi. "Female Heroin Use, Criminality and Prostitution." *Contemporary Drug Problems* 8 (1979):455-73.

62. Engelstein, L. "Gender and the Juridical Subject: Prostitution and Rape in 19th-Century Russian Criminal Codes." *Journal of Modern History* 60(3) (1988):458-95.

63. File, K.N., T.W. McCahill, and L.D. Savitz. "Narcotics Involvement and Female Criminality." *Addictive Diseases: An International Journal* 1(2) (1974):177-88.

Analyzed 227 women arrested for narcotic related issues and found that some were also prostitutes and some were not and that among the prostitutes some had a history of serious crimes while others did not.

64. Flowers, R.B. *Violent Women: Are They Catching Up to Violent Men or Have They Surpassed Them?* (Position Paper) 1987.

Argues that gang activities including muggings of customers of prostitutes, as well as thefts, have increased, as has physical abuse by women of children and partners. Cites four reasons for increase in female violence including premenstrual syndrome, women's liberation, economic pressures, and substance abuse.

65. Greenblatt, M. "Is Prostitution a Victimless Crime?" *Medical Aspects of Human Sexuality* 12(8) (August 1978):106, 109.

The answer is yes. A similar answer is given by D.E.J. McNamara in the same issue, pp. 101, 106, and by J. Marmor, pp. 101. M. Symonds argues that since the prostitute and the customer are both victims, it is not a victimless crime (pp. 94), as does A.S. Wallace (pp. 109).

66. Hatty, S. "Violence Against Prostitute Women: Social and Legal Dilemmas." *Australian Journal of Social Issues* 24(4) (1989):235-48.

Examines the various legal approaches to prostitution in Australia and evaluates the impact on the lives of the prostitutes. Argues that the law plays a critical role in determining the physical vulnerability of prostitute women.

67. Hirsch, M.F. *Women and Violence*. New York: Van Nostrand Reinhold, 1981.

Analyzes conscious and unconscious manifestations of abuse of women from a variety of viewpoints. Includes discussion of prostitution and criminal behavior of women. Looks at interplay of violence with a number of societal factors.

68. Lief, V.F. "Prostitution and Crime." *Medical Aspects of Human Sexuality* 3(10) (October 1969):94.

Argues that prostitutes commit only minor crimes.

69. Nelligan, M. *Mujeres que matan: prostitución y homicidio femenil en Mexico*. Mexico: Edamex, 1988.

Looks at women murderers in Mexico including prostitutes.

70. Powell, H. *Lucky Luciano: His Amazing Trial and Wild Witnesses*. Secaucus, NJ: Citadel, 1975. A reprint of *Ninety Times Guilty* (New York: Harcourt, Brace, 1939).

Includes a discussion of Luciano's efforts to control prostitution.

71. Schnitzler, P. *Issues in Sexual Behavior: Prostitution*. New York: Harper & Row, 1976. 80 2x2 slides with cassette and script.

Examines the issues of prostitution as seen by law enforcement officials, psychiatrists, pimps, madams, clients, and prostitutes themselves.

72.   Silbert, M.H.   "Prostitution and Sexual Assault: Summary of Results." *International Journal for Biosocial Research* 3(2) (1982):69-71.

Claims that common viewpoints on prostitutes are contradicted by questionnaire data from 200 women street prostitutes in the San Francisco Bay area. Pictures prostitutes as women who have suffered excessive victimization, physical and sexual abuse, and who have learned helplessness. They are trapped in their lifestyle which they do not want and yet feel unable to leave. See other entries for Silbert.

73.   Silbert, M.H.   *Sexual Assault of Prostitutes*.   San Francisco, CA: Delancey Street Foundation, 1982.

Explores the nature and extent of the problem of rape and juvenile exploitation among 200 female prostitutes, both prior to and since becoming prostitutes. Reports on the development, implementation, and evaluation of an intervention model as a demonstration project.

74.   Silbert, M.H., and A.M. Pines.   "Pornography and Sexual Abuse of Women." *Sex Roles* 10(11-12) (June 1984):857-68.

Based on responses to questionnaire by 200 current and former female prostitutes in San Francisco Bay Area, authors report that most have been raped (73%), are victims of juvenile abuse (60%), and that in 25% of these instances the abuser had made references to pornographic films, literature, or other material. Argues that pornography serves as an "imitation model" for sexual abuse.

75.   Walkowitz, J.R.   "Jack the Ripper and the Myth of Male Violence." *Feminist Studies* 8(3) (1981):543-74.

Argues that the sexual mutilation of five prostitutes in a 10 week period in London in 1888 both reflected and exacerbated class, ethnic, and sexual tensions. Lurid newspaper reporting strengthened male authority over females emphasizing that women in deviant roles are threatened with Ripper-like punishment.

76. Zdinak, P. *Bessie's House.* New York: Carlton, 1976.

   Prostitution and its involvement in a murder trial.

ASSOCIATIONS

77. Johns and Call Girls United Against Repression (Sexual Freedom) (Jacguar)
   P.O. Box 02101
   Brooklyn, NY 11202-0022

   Founded in 1978, this organization seeks to dispel the notion that there is anything reprehensible or immoral in being a prostitute and to instill in adult prostitutes and their adult customers a sense of self-respect. Works to safeguard civil rights, and to repeal laws criminalizing prostitution.

78. National Task Force on Prostitution (Civil Rights and Liberties) (NTFP)
   Formerly known as Coyote
   333 Valencia St., Suite 101
   San Francisco, CA 94103

   Founded in 1973, seeks to decriminalize prostitution and remove stigmas associated with female sexuality. Offers referrals to competent lawyers and social aids for arrested prostitutes. Lobbies state legislature, conducts research and prepares position papers on topics related to prostitution. There are also various local groups such as P.O.N.Y. (Prostitutes of New York), which go in and out of existence. The National Task Force is probably the best source.

AREA STUDIES

AFRICA

79. Bakwesegha, C.J. *Profiles of Urban Prostitution: A Case Study from Uganda.* Nairobi: Kenya Literature Bureau, 1982.

80. Bondestam, L. *Prostitution in Addis Ababa.* Addis Ababa: Bondestam, 1972.

Discusses prostitution as an economic problem facing women in Addis Ababa, and looks for positive solutions to changing existing patterns of prostitution through short and long-term goals. Presents socio-economic and demographic statistics related to prostitution in this area, and concludes that there are few voluntary prostitutes. Prostitutes are forced into this lifestyle because of the patriarchal nature of the society and the lack of job opportunities for women.

81. Bovin, M. *Frie Piger i Mangaland: Kønsroller, Ægteskab og Prostitution i Vestafrika.* Edited by Henning Nielsen. København: Nationalmuseet, 1975.

82. Bujra, J.M. "Production, Property, Prostitution--Sexual Politics in Atu." *Cahiers d'Études Africaines* 17(1) (1977):13-39.

This is a case study of "institutional weapons" used by women in Atu to expand their freedoms within a male dominated social order and an evaluation of the effectiveness of such measures. Since divorce is a frequent occurrence in this polygamous society, women often find it necessary to support themselves financially. Prostitution has become a lucrative means of providing women with economic stability but often involves migration to a neighboring town. Without equivalent access to productive resources, and participation in the economy, women cannot gain equality and are forced into using sexuality as a commodity. Although prostitution serves as a temporary solution, it does not elevate the status of women within the Atu society.

83. Dirasse, L. "The Socio-economic Position of Women in Addis Ababa:

16

The Case of Prostitution." (Thesis) Boston University, 1978.

Examines characteristics of prostitution in Addis Ababa, Ethiopia, in an attempt to determine the reasons for the high incidence in the city. This study covers a one year period and uses in-depth interviews, a stratified sample survey, and social interaction with prostitutes for research methodology. Concludes that increased economic opportunities would decrease, and possibly eradicate, prostitution but that such intervention would require drastic socio-economic changes within the country.

84. Igbinovia, P.E. "Prostitution in Black Africa." *International Journal of Women's Studies* 7(5) (November-December 1984):430-449.

Analyzes several dimensions of prostitution in Africa, including origins, meaning, nature, extent, functions, and characteristics.

85. Minnaar, G.G. *'n Psigodinamiese Verkenningstudie van 'n Aantal Blanke Prostitute in Johannesburg.* Pretoria: Raad vir Geesteswetenskaplike Navorsing, Suid-Afrikaanse Instituut vir Sosiologiese, Demografiese en Kriminologiese Navorsing, 1980.

86. Muga, E. *Studies in Prostitution: East, West, and South Africa, Zaire, and Nevada.* (Addresses, lectures and essays) Nairobi: Kenya Literature Bureau, 1980.

87. Oleru, U.G. "Prostitution in Lagos: A Sociomedical Study." *Journal of Epidemiology and Community Health* 34(4) (December 1980):312-5.

Studies 150 hotel prostitutes in Lagos, to determine their socio-economic identity, health knowledge, attitudes and practices which may affect public health. Suggests that the attitude of the subjects to health care may provide an opportunity for the control of disease among prostitutes, if prostitution is organized.

88. Schurink, W.J. *"Seks-te-koop in diensorganisasies": 'n sosiologiese verkenning van prostitusie in masseersalonne en eskortagentskappe.* Pretoria: Suid-Afrikaanse Raad vir Geesteswetenskaplike Navorsing, Instituut vir Sosiologiese, Demografiese en Kriminologiese Navorsing, 1979.

89.   Shomba, K. *La prostitution, son vrai visage au Zaire.* Lubumbashi,
      République du Zaire: Africa, 1987.

90.   Songue, P. *Prostitution en Afrique: l'exemple de Yaounde.* Paris:
      L'Harmattan, 1986.

91.   Tshibanda, W.B. *Femmes libres, femmes enchaînées: la prostitution au
      Zaire.* Lumbumbashi: Saint Paul Afrique, 1986.

ASIA

92.   Lewis, N.B. "The Connection of Uneven Development, Capitalism and
      Patriarchy: A Case of Prostitution in Asia." *Women, Work and Poverty.*
      Edited by E. Fiorenza and A. Carr. Edinburgh: T.& T. Clark, 1987.

      Explores the exploitation of female labor in Asia and the Third World,
      focusing on prostitution and the influences of uneven development,
      capitalism, and patriarchy on this enterprise. Suggests that unless this
      correlation is dealt with, the feminization of poverty will continue to
      worsen women's well being.

93.   Snyder, P. "Prostitution in Asia." *Journal of Sex Research* 10(2) (May
      1974):119-127.

      A discussion of prostitution in several noncommunist countries of Asia.

94.   Truong, T.D. *Sex, Money and Morality in South-east Asia.* London:
      Zed, 1990.

Bangladesh

95.   Siddiqui, K., and S.R. Qadir, et al. *Prostitutes of Dhaka City; Socio-
      economic Profile of Dhaka City Study Project; No.2., 1986.* (Working
      Paper)

      This study is based on in-depth case studies of 15 prostitutes in Dhaka city, utilizing the interview technique to determine the socio-demographic characteristics and economic conditions of this population. Several conclusions are offered regarding this population from the resultant statistical data.

China

96. Wolfe, B. *The Daily Life of a Chinese Courtesan: Climbing up a Tricky Ladder: With a Chinese Courtesan's Dictionary.* Hong Kong: Learner's Bookstore, 1980.

India

97. Awachat, A. "Prostitution in Pune and Bombay--A Report." *Economic and Political Weekly* 21(12) (1986):478-482.

Examines the socio-economic and political aspects of prostitution in Pune and Bombay and offers suggestions for improving the system to benefit women who find it necessary to work in this environment.

98. Bennet Chandra Kumar, T. *Sociology of Prostitution.* Trivandrum: Kerala Historical Society, 1978.

99. Chandra, M. *The World of Courtesans.* Delhi: Vikas, 1973.

100. Children's Aid Society, Bombay. *Study of Kidnapped Children in the City of Bombay.* Bombay: The Society, 1973.

This report describes the characteristics of kidnapped children, their families, and the accused kidnappers; includes investigation of the motivating factors behind kidnapping and relationship to juvenile prostitution.

101. Hooja, S.L. "Prostitution in Rajasthan: Then and Now." *The Indian Journal of Social Work.* 31(2) (July 1970):183-90.

Explores the history of prostitution in Rajasthan from the medieval period to the contemporary situation, including the cultural and socio-economic aspects.

102.   India. Central Bureau of Correctional Services.   *Implementation of Suppression of Immoral Traffic in Women and Girls Act: A Statistical Analysis, 1965-1969.* (Microform) New Dehli: The Bureau, 1973.

Presents statistical data dealing with the administration of prostitution laws in India. The legislation in India is designed to control prostitution as a commercialized vice and provides for the creation of non-official advisory bodies to assist the police.

103.   India Central Bureau of Correctional Services.   *Social Defense--A Statistical Handbook.* New Delhi: The Bureau, 1976.

A compilation of statistical information on all social defense programs currently in operation in the states and union territories of India, including those dealing with prostitution.

104.   Kapur, P. "Sex in Trade." *Readings in Social Defense.* Edited by Navin Chandra Joshi and Ved Bhushan Bhatia. India: A.H. Wheeler, 1981, pp. 37-45.

Attempts to present a comprehensive, unbiased study of the call girl in India utilizing an interdisciplinary approach. Includes results of interviews with 150 call girls, over a period of several years. Concludes by focusing on rehabilitative efforts to eradicate prostitution in India.

105.   Kumar, P. "Prostitution: A Socio-Psychological Analysis." *Indian Journal of Social Work* 21(4) (March 1961):425-430.

Uses a questionnaire to study the mental health of 136 registered prostitutes of Basia and Guthla, two prostitute villages in Agra, and makes recommendations to suppress the immoral trafficking of women within these districts.

106.   Mark, M.E. *Falkland Road: Prostitutes of Bombay: Photographs and Text.* New York: Knopf, 1981.

A photographic study of prostitutes on Falkland Road in Bombay, taken between October 1978 and January 1979. Depicts the social order of prostitution in this setting.

107. Mukherji, S.K. *Prostitution in India.* New Delhi: Inter-India Publications, 1986.

Studies the social, political, and medical problems associated with prostitution in India. The methodologies employed include personal investigation, government sources, and contact with associations and persons actively combatting the trafficking of women.

108. Nanda, S. "The Hijras of India: Cultural and Individual Dimensions of an Institutionalized Third Gender Role." *Journal of Homosexuality* 11(3-4) (Summer):35-54.

Discusses religious meanings of the "hijra" (eunuch/transvestite), an institutionalized third gender role in India, and their involvement in prostitution which leads to a conflict in their culturally valued sacred role.

109. Oommen, T.K. "Women in Prostitution." *Readings in Social Defense.* Edited by Navin Chandra Joshi and Ved Bhushan Bhatia. Allanhabad, India: A.H. Wheeler, 1981, pp. 59-67.

This paper provides a classification of prostitutes in India, referring to them as "victims" or "offenders," depending on the circumstances and motivations that have led to their becoming prostitutes. Concludes that different approaches should be utilized to deal with the various categories of prostitutes and their clients.

110. Patil, B.R. "The Devadasis." *Indian Journal of Social Work* 35(4) (January 1975):377-389.

The original meaning of the term "Devadasi" referred to women who served the temple as dancers and courtesans but has come to be equated with prostitution. This article discusses the positive and negative contributions of the Devadasis to Indian culture.

111. Pillai, T.V. "Prostitution in India." *Indian Journal of Social Work* 43(3) (October 1982):313-320.

Attempts to ascertain the socio-economic background of prostitutes in India and their reasons for becoming prostitutes. Data is gathered from personal interviews with 50 prostitutes in Delhi; conclusions drawn for reasons of entry into prostitution include poverty, ignorance, unrealistic expectations, mistreatment by family and a generally unhealthy environment.

112.   Punekar, S.D. *A Study of Prostitutes in Bombay, with Reference to Family Background.* Bombay, India: Lalvani, 1967.

Studies prostitution in "tolerated areas" of Bombay City. Tolerated areas are limited areas within which the existence of prostitutes is tolerated by the general public and even by the police and local authorities. Includes statistics on age, hours of employment, health, family background, and sect. Analyzes causes of prostitution and makes recommendations for the prevention of this problem.

113.   Raghuramaiah, K.L. "Law and Immoral Traffic." *Readings in Social Defense: a Study of Crimes and Corrections in Indian Society.* Edited by N.C. Joshi, and V.B. Bhatia. Allahabad: A.H. Wheeler, 1981.

Reviews the Indian law of 1956 to control prostitution.

114.   Ramachandran, P. "Research Reports and Notes on the Problems of Beggars and Prostitutes." *Indian Journal of Social Work* 24(1) (April 1963):35-39.

Critiques studies done on the problems of beggars and prostitutes in India, focusing on methodology. Concludes that serious evaluative efforts have not been made and that the methods of data collection, as well as statistical reporting, have been inefficient.

115.   Ranga Rao, M. *The Prostitutes of Hyderabad; A Study of the Sociocultural Conditions of the Prostitutes of Hyderabad.* Hyderabad: Association for Moral and Social Hygiene in India, Andhra Pradesh Branch, 1970.

116.   Ross, A.V. *Vice in Bombay.* London: Tallis, 1969.

Describes prostitution and sex customs in Bombay, India.

117. Rozario, M.R. *Trafficking in Women and Children in India: Sexual Exploitation and Sale.* New Delhi: Uppal, 1988.

118. Sharma, K.K., P.S. Dubey, et al. "Prostitution." *Indian Sociologist* 3(4) (March 1961):33-39.

119. Sikka, K.D. "Prostitution: Indian Perspectives and Realities." *Indian Journal of Social Work* 45(2) (July 1984):213-231.

Explores aspects of prostitution in India, including societal control, health implications, and whether paticipants experience distress as a result of this activity.

120. Singh, A., and S. Singh. "Psychological Correlates of Prostitution." *Indian Journal of Criminology* 10(1) (January 1982):24-29.

Examines the psychosocial backround and personality traits that contribute to the prostitute's choice of lifestyle. Utilizes the PEN inventory (Eysenck and Eysenck, 1968) and Lanyon's Psychological Screening Inventory (1970), administered to a prostitute and a nonprostitute group. Sample size consisted of two groups of 100 subjects. Results show lower socio-economic status of the prostitute group and a middle child status in the family. Additionally, prostitutes show a higher level of personal disturbance and interpersonal difficulties.

121. Singh, S. "The Problem of Prostitution in Contemporary Indian Society." *Social Defence* 11(44) (April 1976)16-21.

Discusses the causes and socially harmful effects of prostitution in India and advocates the cultural restoration of dignity to femaleness, as well as the establishment of socio-economic equality between the sexes.

122. Srivastava, S.P. "Rehabilitation of Fallen Women and Girls--Need For a New Outlook." *Indian Journal of Criminology* 10(1) (January 1, 1982):16-23.

Examines reasons for the failure of preventative and rehabilitative efforts to eradicate prostitution in India. Offers suggestions for additional measures that might prove more successful. Advocates the replacement of traditional approaches with an interdisciplinary methodology, which includes therapy, education, vocational training, and aftercare.

123. Trivedi, H.R. *Scheduled Caste Women: Studies in Exploitation with Reference to Superstition, Ignorance, and Poverty.* Delhi: Concept, 1977.

A two-part sociological study on the status of women within the caste system and the exploitation of scheduled caste women for the purposes of prostitution. The study specific to prostitution was undertaken in three regions: Bijapur district at Karnataka, Raipur of Madhya Pradesh and Uttar Kashi of Uttar Pradesh. Focuses on cultural, social, and economic variables that contribute to prostitution, and suggests preventative as well as curative measures.

Japan

124. Harris, S. *House of the 10,000 Pleasures; A Modern Study of the Geisha and of the Street-Walker of Japan.* New York: Dutton, 1962.

Describes the roles of women in Japanese society and their interrelatedness. Focuses on the life of the Geisha and pan-pans, or streetwalkers and societal attitudes.

125. Iga, M. "Socio-cultural Factors in Japanese Prostitution." *Journal of Sex Research* 4(2) (May 1968):127-146.

126. Ito, F. "A Study on Female Juveniles' Sexual Misconducts: I. Relationships Between the Extent of Deviance in Lifestyle and the Types of Sexual Misconducts." *Reports of National Research Institute of Police Science* 28(1) (July 1987):52-62.

A 3-month survey conducted of 570 female Japanese children and adolescents (age eleven to over seventeen years), to determine the relationship of lifestyle to the type of sexual misconduct exhibited.

127. Ito, F. "A Study on Female Juveniles' Sexual Misconduct: II. An Analysis of the Background of Sexual Misconducts." *Reports of the National Research Institute of Police Science* 28(1) (July 1987):63-71.

Studies the contributing factors of sexual misconduct. Delinquent and nondelinquent female Japanese children and adolescents were administered a questionnaire. This is Part II of a 2-part paper.

128. "Japanese Men's Prostitution Tours in Asia." *Japan Quarterly* 28(2) (1981):149-152.

Protests by Asian and Japanese women's groups have resulted in the control of group prostitution tours by Japanese men to Korea, Taiwan, the Philippines, and Thailand.

129. Kaplan, D.E., and A. Dubro. *Yakuza: The Explosive Account of Japan's Criminal Underworld.* Reading, PA: Addison Wesley, 1986.

Traces the history of Yakuza, the principal organized crime society in Japan, to its current worldwide network and considers aspects of its involvement in prostitution.

Philippines

130. Moselina, L.M. *Olongapo's R.& R. Industry: A Sociological Analysis of Institutionalized Prostitution.* Manila: Asian Social Institute, 1982.

131. Niesner, E. *Prostitution auf den Philippinen.* Berlin: Express, 1988.

A series of interviews with six female prostitutes in the Philippines.

132. Olsson, G. *Pretence and Contempt: Life in a Filipino Brothel.* Stockholm, Sweden: SIDA'S Office of Women in Development, 1985.

A personal account of what it's like to live in a brothel for three months. The author interviews several prostitutes during this period of time, gaining insight into their innermost thoughts, and their socialization process to this lifestyle. She concludes that the only escape is through education and legitimate economic opportunities.

133.   West, L.A.   "Philippine Feminist Efforts to Organize Against Sexual
       Victimization."   *Response to the Victimization of Women and Children*
       12(2) (1989):11-14.

       Describes efforts by the General Assembly Binding women for Reforms,
       Integrity, Equality, Leadership, and Action (GABRIELA) against
       prostitution, sexual harassment, rape and battering in the Philippines. It
       is an attempt to combat prostitution among women workers and male
       children and to organize against rape, pornography, and mail-order brides.

Singapore

134.   Mak, L.F.   "Professionals of the Third Sexual Category: A Study of the
       Pondans in Singapore."   *National Taiwan University Journal of Sociology*
       17 (November 1985):173-88.

       Describes 10 transvestites in Singapore, known locally as "pondan," who
       support themselves through prostitution. Interviews provide insight into
       this subculture, including pondan attitudes about society and family. It
       suggests that their subcultural environment may compensate for
       deficiencies in family life.

Taiwan

135.   McCaghy, C.H., and C. Hou.   *Aspirations and Career Onsets of
       Taiwanese Prostitutes.*   (Association Paper) *Society for the Study of Social
       Problems.*   Bowling Green State University, 1989.

       Examines the characteristics and experiences of Taiwanese women before
       entering prostitution, based on 89 interviews with individuals detained at
       a training center, police station, and a youth court. Results highlight the
       need for culturally based theories of prostitution.

136.   Pan, M.   "The Attitudes of Businessmen Toward the Entertaining Girls
       of the City of Taipei."   (Ph.D. Thesis) University of Michigan at Ann

Arbor, 1973.

Studies the history of the "entertaining girls" of Taipei and relates it to the current hierarchichal structure of the industry; with a major focus on attitudes of businessmen towards the women who participate in this industry. Entertainment includes prostitution but is perceived as one aspect of a total package which "entertaining girls" elevate to an art form. Concludes by making suggestions which may benefit the continued support of this industry in Taipei.

137. Tsung, S.F. "Moms, Nuns and Hookers: Extrafamilial Alternatives for Village Women in Taiwan." (Ph.D. Dissertation) University of California, San Diego, 1978.

Studies traditional and non-traditional female roles within family systems in Taiwanese society. Defines possible role models, including prostitution and discusses the resulting conflicts between assuming "family" or "unfamily" values.

Thailand

138. Cohen, E. "Lovelorn Farangs: The Correspondence between Foreign Men and Thai Girls." *Anthropological Quarterly* 59(3) (July 1986):115-127.

Explores cross-cultural cognitive mapping from a Schuetzian perspective using images formed by farangs (white foreigners) of Thai girls engaged in tourist-oriented prostitution. The analyses of personal letters suggests that some of the women are skilled in manipulating their absent boyfriends. Exemplifies the problems of cross-cultural definitions and identification of prostitution.

139. Cohen, E. "Sensuality and Venality in Bangkok: The Dynamics of Cross-Cultural Mapping of Prostitution." *Deviant Behavior* 8(3) (1987):223-234.

Argues that the relationships between white foreigners and Thai girls engaged in tourist-oriented prostitution constitute a vague area lying between full-fledged prostitution and straight sexuality and that the newcomer initially refuses to label the girls as prostitutes.

140. Malee. *Tiger Claw and Velvet Paw*. St. James's, London: Arlington, 1986.

Descriptive narrative of the life of a prostitute in Thailand based on her diary.

141. Pasuk Phongpaichit. *From Peasant Girls to Bangkok Masseuses*. Geneva: International Labour Office, 1982.

142. Thiemann, H. *Frauenrolle und Prostitution in Thailand*. Köln: Pahl-Rugenstein, 1987.

AUSTRALIA, NEW GUINEA, AND NEW ZEALAND

143. Buckley, K. *Vagrancy and Prostitution*. Melbourne: Victorian Council for Civil Liberties, 1968.

144. Hasleton, S. "Permissiveness in Australian Society." *Australian Journal of Psychology* 27(3) (December 1975):257-267.

Studies attitudes of permissiveness using a questionnaire presented to the Australian electorate and a stratified random sample selection method.

145. *Inquiry into Prostitution*. Melbourne: F.D. Atkinson, 1985.

146. MacFarlane, D.F. "Transsexual Prostitution in New Zealand: Predominance of Persons of Maori Extraction." *Archives of Sexual Behavior* 13(4) (August 1984):301-309.

Studies 27 male to female transsexual prostitutes in New Zealand, utilizing interviews and questionnaires. Although the Maori constitute only 9% of the population, they account for approximately 90% of transsexual prostitutes in Wellington. This study attempts to identify the reasons for the high representation of the Maori population in this lifestyle.

147. Nash J. "Sex, Money and the Status of Women in Aboriginal South Bougaineville." *American Ethnologist* 8(1) (February 1981):107-26.

Compares three societies of aboriginal South Bougainville, Papua, New Guinea, where there is an increasing exchange value placed on the sexual services of women. Proposes that this increase is in direct relation to the development and use of general-purpose money which may have implications for the comparative status of women and the evolution of society.

148. Perkins, R., and G. Bennett. *Being a Prostitute*. Boston, MA: Allen and Unwin, 1985.

Addresses prostitution among women and homosexual men in Sydney, Australia, focusing on the comparison of the two types. Analyzes backgrounds, family, class, practices, geography, motivations, hazards, medical and legal aspects. Includes individual case histories.

149. Winter, M. *Prostitution in Australia: A Sociological Study Prepared by a Qualified Research Team under the Supervision of Marcel Winter*. Balgowlah, Australia: Purtaboi, 1976.

Provides an analysis of female prostitution in Australia, from the viewpoint of the male customer. Proposes some procedures that would control prostitution but does not advocate its legalization. Additionally, advocates the formation of trade unions for prostitutes and owner associations to advance the interests of the profession.

EUROPE

Austria

150. Girtler, R. *Der Strich: Erkundungen in Wien*. Wien: Âge d'Homme, Karolinger, 1985.

Belgium

151. Haacht, A. *La prostituée; statut et image*. Bruxelles: Éditions de

l'Université de Bruxelles, 1973.

152. Vincineau, M. *La débauche en droit et le droit à la débauche.* Bruxelles: Éditions de l'Université de Bruxelles, 1985.

Denmark

153. Hartmann, G. *Boliger og bordeller. Oversigt over prostitutionens former og tilholdssteder i København til forskellige tider.* København: Rosenkilde og Bagger, 1967.

154. Henriksen, S.V.D., and S. Springborg. *Prostituerede kvinder: seks livshistorier.* København: De Sociale Højskolers Årskursus, 1986.

155. Koch, I. *Prostitution: om truende unge og socialt arbejde.* København: Munksgaard, 1987.

France

156. Alexandre, J. *L'argot de la prostitution du XIXe siècle à nos jours.* Clichy: N. Gauvin, 1987.

157. Aziz, G., and M.O. Delacour. *Cinq femmes à abattre: récit véridique d'un fait divers.* Paris: Stock, 1981.

158. Chantal, J.B. *Nous ne sommes pas nées prostituées.* Moulin, Paris: Éditions Ouvrières, 1978.

159. Dallayrac, D. *Dossier prostitution.* Paris: Laffont, 1966. (Reprinted in 1973)

160. Jaget, C. *Prostitutes, Our Life.* Bristol, England: Falling Wall, 1980.

161. Morin, E., B. Paillard, et al. *Rumour in Orleans.* New York: Pantheon, 1971.

Examines the nature of a rumor about the disappearance of women in Orleans, France. It was believed by many in the town that a white slave trafficking network was being run through several local Jewish dress shops, although there were no cases of disappearance actually reported to the police. This study investigates the validity of the rumor that women were, in fact, being sold into prostitution and focuses on aspects of anti-Semitic feeling in Orleans.

162. Paoleschi, M. *Le milieu et moi.* Paris: Fanval, 1987.

163. Philippon, O. *Visage actuel de la traite dans quelques pays et le relèvement de ses victimes, témoignages.* Paris: P. Téqui, 1966.

164. Richard-Molard, G. "La prostitution en France, aujourd'hui: un signe de mépris, un temps d'hypocrisie." *Études* (May 1974):713-26.

165. Romi. *Maisons closes dans l'histoire, l'art, la littérature et les moeurs.* Paris: Éditions Serg, 1965.

166. Sacotte, M. "How to Humanize the Situation of French Prostitutes." (French with English Abstract) *Revue Internationale de Criminologie et de Police Technique* 31(2) (April-June 1978):131-148.

Discusses the demands of prostitutes for rights and professional recognition, as well as their dissatisfaction with legal controls, resulting from international and national legislation seeking to halt the moral and physical degradation of women.

167. Scelles, J. "Procuring in France-- Profits, Cost of Repression, Fresh Profits." (French with English Abstract) *Revue Internationale de Criminologie et de Police Technique* 31(2) (April-June 1978):123-130.

Correlates the economic and legal costs of prostitution in France.

Germany

168.   Alexander, R.B.   *Die Prostitution in Deutschland.*   München:
        Lichtenberg, 1969.

169.   Alexander, R.B.   Prostitution in Sankt Pauli.   München: Lichtenberg,
        1968.

170.   Anina Report.   *Call Girls, Liebe per Telefon.*   Hamburg: Konkret Verlag,
        1970.

171.   Fichte, H.   *Interviews aus dem Palais d'Amour* . . .   Reinbek b.
        Hamburg: Rohwohlt Taschenbuch-Verlag, 1973.

172.   Giesen, R.   *An der Front des Patriachats: Bericht vom langen Marsch
        durch das Prostitutionsmilieu.*   Bernsheim: Pad-Extra-Buchverlag, 1980.

173.   Kahmann, J.   *Weibliche Prostitution in Hamburg.*   Heidelberg:
        Kriminalistik Verlag, 1981.

174.   Lipka, S., and E. Niesner.   "Über die Arbeit der AGISRA gegen
        Sextourismus und Frauenhandel."   *Beitrage zur Feministischen Theorie
        und Praxis* 11(23) (1988):27-37.

175.   Niss, A.   *Das Strich-Buch. 500 Adressen von Bordellen, von
        einschlagigen Lokalen vom Strassenstrich, Preistab* . . .   Frankfurt am
        Main: Zero, 1971.

176.   Offergeld, D.   *Erscheinungsformen, Ursachen und Auswirkung der
        Prostitution in Bochum.*   Düsseldorf: R. Stehle, 1965.

177.   Ohse, U.   *Forced Prostitution and Traffic in Women in West Germany.*
        Edinburgh, London: Human Rights Group, 1984.

Reports on the trafficking of persons for the purpose of forced prostitution; based on information obtained from German police, public prosecution authorities, and newspaper archives. Demonstrates the reality of the continued existence of such activity in West Germany.

178. Reiser, A. *Domenica und die Herbertstrasse.* Frankfurt am Main: Eichborn, 1981.

179. Ritter-Rohr, D. "Prostitution in Frankfurt." Giesen: s.n., 1971. (Thesis.)

180. Schmidt, H.G. *Der neue Sklavenmarkt: Geschäfte mit Frauen aus Übersee.* Basel: Lenos, 1985.

181. Stuemper, A. "Measures For an Effective Fight Against Pandering." (German with English Abstract) *Kriminalistik* 28(3) (March 1974):97-104.

Italy

182. Bianchi, P. *Le signorine di Avignone.* Milano: Ferro, 1967.

183. Carrer, and F. Pallanca. "Cultural Transmission of Deviance in Genoa (Italy) Investigation of the Distribution of 1000 Dangerous Persons According to Law No 1423 of 27 December 1956." *Rassegna Di Criminologia* 8(1 and 2) (1977):181-196.

184. Casagrande di Villaviera, R. *Le cortigiane veneziane nel cinquencento.* Milano: Longanesi, 1968.

185. Cutrera, A. *Storia della prostituzione in Sicilia.* Palermo: Editori stampatori associati, 1971.

186. *Le servitù sessuali: 19 autobiografie di donne scritte col registratore.* Edited by M. Quaini and P. Maggiani. Milano: Bompiani, 1976.

187.   Leone, F. *Delitti di prossenetismo ed adescamento.* Milano: Giuffrè, 1964.

188.   Macrelli, R. *L'indegna schiavitù: Anna Maria Mozzoni e la lotta contro la prostituzione di Stato.* Roma: Editori Riuniti, 1981.

189.   Miccinesi, M. *Prostituzione segreta.* Milano: Edizioni il quadrato, 1963.

190.   Protettì, E. *Offesa al pudore e all'onore sessuale nella giurisprudenza.* Padova: CEDAM, 1972.

191.   Santini, A. *Madama Sitrì, che vergogna: geografia, costumi e aventure di quelle "case" livornesi.* Livorno: Belforte Editore Libraio, 1982.

Netherlands

192.   Groothuyse, J.W. *De arbeidsstructuur van de prostitutie.* Deventer: Loghum Slaterus, 1970.

193.   Groothuyse, J.W. *Het menselijk tekort van de pooier.* Amsterdam: Wetenschappelijke Uitgeverij, 1973.

194.   Haan, H. *Het leven met regels: de aanpak van de prostitutie in 's-Gravenhage.* Haarlem: Architext, 1988.

195.   Punch, M. *Policing the Inner City--A Study of Amsterdam's Warmoesstraat.* London: Macmillan, 1979.

Reports on the quality of order in the red-light district of Amsterdam, Holland.

196.   Rensen, T. *Alles uit . . . behalve de radio. Gesprekken met Rosse Alie.* Amsterdam: Montelbaen, 1969.

197. Uschi, B. *Onderwerp: Jeugdprostitutie.* Amsterdam: De Bezige Bij, 1971.

198. van der Werff, C., and A. van der Zee-Nefkens. *Commercial Sex Shops in the Netherlands.* (Dutch) The Hague: Ministry of Justice Research and Documentation Centre, 1977.

Examines operations which exploit sex commercially, including window and street prostitution, highway prostitution, sex clubs, etc., in order to assist in formulating a national policy.

199. van der Werff, C. *De commerciele sexbedrijven in Nederland: een inventarisatie van verschijnselen en nevenverschijnselen.* 's-Gravenhage: Wetenschappelijk Onderzoek- en Documentatiecentrum, Ministerie van Justitie, 1977.

Norway

200. Finstad, L., L. Fougner, and V.L. Holter. *Prostitusjon i Oslo.* Oslo: Pax, 1982.

Poland

201. Kojder, A. "The Phenomenon of Social Psychology in Poland in the Light of Empirical Research." *Studia Socjologiczne* 1(60) (1976):171-202.

A collation of findings from government reports and research studies on the degree of social deviation in Poland, including the problem of prostitution.

Portugal

202. Afonso, M.G. *Estudo de casos: prostituição e espaço social: o caso do intendente.* Lisboa: Universidade Nova de Lisboa, Faculdade de Ciências Sociais e Humanas, Departamento de Communicaç˜ao Social, 1984.

203. Carmo, I. do, and F. Fráguas. *Puta de prisão: a prostituição vista em*

Custóias. Lisboa: Regra do Jogo, 1982.

Soviet Union

204. Ahlberg, R. "Prostitution in the Soviet-Union." Free University Berlin, Osteuropa Institute, Berlin.

205. "Soviet Prostitution: A Candid Look." *Current Digest of Soviet Press* 39 (November 18, 1987):11-13.

Provides brief abstracts of articles on prostitution in the Soviet Union; most of which present case scenarios as warnings to the dangers of engaging in such activity. Focuses on venereal disease as a major deterrent to engaging in illicit sex.

Spain

206. Caudet, F. *Mis conversaciones con 10 prostitutas.* Barcelona: Producciones Editoriales, D.L., 1977.

207. Cebrián Franco, J.J. *Prostitución y sociedad.* Barcelona: A.T.E., 1977.

208. Cela, C.J. *Izas, rabizas y colipoterras: drama con acompañamiento de cachondeo y dolor de Corazón.* Barcelona: Editorial Lumen, 1964. (Reprinted in 1971 and 1984).

209. Draper Miralles, R. *Guía de la prostitución femenina en Barcelona.* Barcelona: Martínez Roca, 1982.

210. Jiménez Asenjo, E. *Abolicionismo y prostitución; justificación y defensa del Decreto-ley de 3 de Marzo de 1956.* Madrid: Instituto Editorial Reus, 1963.

211. Juliette. *Porqué yo?: confesiones de una mujer libre de hoy.* Barcelona: Martínez Roca, 1988.

212. Mora, E. *Nuestra prostitución*. Lugo: Alvarellos, 1980.

213. Otero Pizarro, G., and O. Natucci. *Las prostitutas y yo*. Barcelona: Bruguera, 1978.

214. Pomar, A. *La prostitución vista de cerca*. Palma de Mallorca: J. Mascaró Pasarius, 1976.

215. *La prostitución de las mujeres*. Madrid: Ministerio de Cultura, Instituto de la Mujer, 1988.

216. Yale. (i.e. F. Navarro García) *Las mujeres de la Vida*. Barcelona: Ediciones Zeta, 1976.

Sweden

217. Åslund, R. *Svenska bordeller: en kartläggning av establissemang i Sverige till tjanst for resande och turister*. Stockholm: Williams, 1967. (microform)

218. Danielsson, S. *Ömhetens kaniner: män, kvinnor, prostitution*. Stockholm: Bonnier, 1980.

219. Larsson, S. *Könshandeln: om prostituerades villkor*. Älvsjö: SkeabFörlag, 1983.

Summary in English.

220. Lind, B.I. *Kärlek för pengar? en bok om prostitutions-projectet i Malmö 1976-80*. Stockholm: Ordfront, 1980.

221. Månsson, S.A. *Könshandelns främjare och profitörer: om förhållandet mellem hallick ock prostituerad*. Lund: Doxa, 1981.

222. Persson, L.G.W. *Horor, hallicker och torskar: en bok om prostitutionen i Sverige.* Stockholm: Norstedt, 1981.

223. *Prostitution: beskrivning, analys, förslag till åtgärder? Prostitutionsutredningen.* Edited by A. Borg. Stockholm: LiberFörlag, 1981.

224. *Prostitutionen i Sverige: en rapport.* Stockholm: Socialdepartementet: LiberFörlag, 1980.

225. *Prostitutionen och samhället: rapport från ett forskningsseminarium anordnat av Delegationen för Social Forskning (DSF).* Stockholm: Socialdepartementet: LiberFörlag, 1984.

226. Verlag, W.R. "New Bill on Sexual Crime in Sweden." (German with English Abstract) *Schriftenreihe der Polizei-Führungsakademie* 4(1) (1977):66-73.

Describes a bill developed by seven experts in various fields regarding the abrogation of certain criminal laws against adultery, sodomy, homosexual relations, pimping, and prostitution.

227. Winquist, T. *Bordeller i Sverige? Framsteg eller nederlag.* Stockholm: Natur och Kultur, 1972.

United Kingdom

228. Carmichael, K. "A City and Its Prostitutes." *New Society* 59(1000) (January 14, 1982):53-55.

Provides a descriptive analysis of prostitition in Glasgow, Scotland. Critiques the legal aspects and provides possible alternatives to the current system of control.

229. Great Britain. Committee on Homosexual Offences and Prostitution. *The Wolfenden Report.* New York: Stein and Day, 1963.

A committee report examining the extent to which homosexual behavior and female prostitution should come under the jurisdiction of criminal law; an official document prepared for the British Parliament. It is an attempt to determine which acts ought to be punished by the State, taking into account the relationship between public opinion and the law. Recommendations are made for penalizing offensive acts.

230. McLeod, E. *Women Working: Prostitution Now.* London, England: Croom Helm, 1982.

Explores features of contemporary heterosexual prostitution in London, including working conditions, client expectations, the workplace, and forms of legal control. Includes a discussion on the decriminalization of prostitution.

231. Roberts, H. *"Trap the Ripper." New Society* 44(809) (April 6, 1978):11-12.

Highlights attitudes of the local press, police, church, and other "experts" toward victims of a series of vicious rapes and murders that occurred in Yorkshire, England. Most of the victims were prostitutes.

232. Russell, K.V. *"Prostitution in Leicester." Police Journal* 52(1) (January-March 1979):48-56.

Examines the number of convictions recorded against prostitutes in England and Wales since passage of the Street Offenses Act in 1959.

233. Thomas, H. "Prostitution in Great Britain Today." *Social Defense* 8(30) (October 1972):14-26.

Advocates changing laws related to sexual offenses. Describes previous laws and present legislation, and offers suggestions for effecting change.

234. Turner, E.B., and R. Morton. "Prostitution in Sheffield." *British Journal of Venereal Disease* 52(3) (June 1976):197-203.

Reviews prostitution in Sheffield, including legal, social, and medical aspects. Indicates a need for the regular monitoring of the social phenomenon of prostitution.

235. Woolley, P.D., C.A. Bowman, et al. "Prostitution in Sheffield: Differences between Prostitutes." *Genitourinary Medicine* 64(6) (December 1988):391-393.

A comparative study to assess the use of barrier methods for disease prevention between street walking prostitutes and sauna girls. Both groups were seen at a clinic during 1986 and 1987; results indicate less use of protective measures by the street walking prostitutes. Therefore, they represent a potential pathway for the heterosexual spread of HIV to the region, and prostitutes should be advised to undergo cytology testing yearly.

LATIN AMERICA AND THE CARIBBEAN

236. Abreu, W. de *O submundo da prostituição, vadiagem e jôgo do bicho; aspectos sociais, jurídicos e psicológicos.* Rio de Janeiro: Freitas Bastos, 1968.

237. Acuña, M.O., C. Denton, and F. Naranjo. *La prostitución en San José: estudio socioeconómico de un problema costarricense.* (Spanish with English Abstract) San José, Costa Rica: Ministerio de Cultura, Juventud y Deportes, 1982.

Includes results of a questionnaire survey of 348 prostitutes in the metropolitan area of San Jose.

238. Altamirano Guevara, J.G. *En pueblos subdesarrollados, las prisiones y la prostitución?* Lima, Perú: [s.n., 1973?].

239. Ardiles Gray, J. *Memorial de los infiernos; Ruth Mary, prostituta.* Buenos Aires: Ediciones La Bastilla, 1972.

240. Bacelar, J.A. *A família da prostituta.* São Paulo: Editora Atica, 1982.

241. Bourgonje, F. *La luna se desangra por el otro costado: testimonios sobre la prostitución en Caracas.* Caracas, Venezuela: Editorial Ateneo de Caracas, 1980.

242. Calvany, C. *Yo fuí una de ellas: el tenebroso mundo de la prostitución en América Latina.* 3rd ed. México: B. Costa-Amic, 1977.

243. Cavalcanti, C., C. Imbert, and M. Cordero. *Prostitución: esclavitud sexual femenina.* Santo Domingo, R.D.: Centro de Investigación para la Acción Femenina, 1985.

244. Cuevas, J. *Prostitución en Nicaragua: una experiencia de reeducación: Proyecto INSSBI-CAV, 1983-1986.* Managua, Nicaragua: Centro de Documentación de la Mujer, 1987.

245. de Gallo, M.T., and H. Alzate. "Brothel Prostitution in Colombia." *Archives of Sexual Behavior* 5(1) (January 1976):1-7.

Discusses brothel prostitution in several Colombian cities. Concludes that prostitution shows many sociocultural variations and that theoretical generalizations regarding it do not apply to different cultural milieus.

246. del Olmo, R. "The Cuban Revolution and the Struggle Against Prostitution." *Crime and Social Justice* 12 (Winter 1979):38-40.

Studies prostitution in Cuban society since the Revolution and discusses successful organized efforts to eradicate the problem.

247. Espinheirs, G. *Divêrgencia e prostituição: uma análise sociológica da comunidade prostitucional do Maciel.* Rio de Janeiro-RJ-Brasil: Tempo Brasileiro com a participação da Fundação Cultural do Estado da Bahia, Secretaria de Educação e Cultura, 1984.

248. Freitas, R.S. "Bordel, bordéis: negociando identidades." (Portuguese with English Abstract) (Master's Thesis) Instituto Universitario de Pesquia do Rio de Janeiro. Petrópolis: Vozes, 1985.

Includes a study of Belo Horizonte prostitutes, from 1980-1982, examining self-image, social values, and their relationships.

249. Gaspar, M.D. *Garotas de programa: prostituição em Copacabana e identidade social.* Rio de Janeiro: J. Zahar, 1985.

250. Grisanti de Luigi, I.C. *La prostitución y el juego como anomalías sociales.* Valencia: Universidad de Carabobo, Dirección de Cultura, 1973.

251. Harter, C.L., and W.E. Bertand. "Live-in Maids and Prostitutes in Cali, Colombia: Social Demographic Similarities and Dissimilarities." *Human Mosaic* 9(1) (Fall 1975):17-31.

Compares the socio-demographic characteristics of maids and prostitutes, in Cali, using interview techniques. Includes 8 tables.

252. Ielpi, R.O., and H.N. Zinni. *Prostitución y rufianismo.* Buenos Aires: Editorial Encuadre, 1974.

253. Kalm, F. "The Two 'Faces' of Antillean Prostitution." *Archives of Sexual Behavior* 14(3) (June):203-217.

A comparative study of two different categories of prostitutes who operate in the refinery town of St. Nichiolas. They include temporary migrants from Colombia and permanent residents from the Dominican Republic. Addresses aspects of economic competition, ethnicity, length of employment, and Antillian perception of these two groups.

254. Lagenest, J.P. Barruel de. *Mulheres em leilão: um estudio da prostituição no Brasil.* Petrópolis: Editora Vozes, 1977.

255. Lorenzi, M. *Prostituição infantil no Brasil e outras infâmias.* Porto alegre, RS, Brasil: Tchê, 1987.

256. Lúcia, A. *A difícil vida fácil: a prostituta e sua condição.* Petrópolis:

Vozes, 1984.

257. Mayorca, J.M. *Introducción al estudio de la prostitución.* Caracas, 1967.

258. Meniconi, T. *Contribuição para o estudo de alguns aspectos médico-legais e médico-sociais da menor na prostituição.* São Paulo: [s.n.], 1969.

259. O'Callaghan, S. *Damaged Baggage: The White Slave Trade and Narcotics Trafficking in the Americas.* New York: Roy, 1969.

Investigates the socio-cultural and economic aspects of providing prostitutes to brothels in South America, from other countries including France, Italy and the Middle East.

260. Pereira, A. *Bandidos e favelas: uma contribuição ao estudo do meio marginal carioca.* Rio de Janeiro: Livraria Eu e Você Editora, 1984.

261. Prats-Ramírez de Pérez, I. *La prostitución: aspectos educativos.* Santo Domingo, R.D.: Departamento de Publicaciones, Universidad Autónoma de Santo Domingo, 1977.

262. Primov, G., and C. Kieffer. "The Peruvian Brothel as Sexual Dispensary and Social Arena." *Archives of Sexual Behavior* 6(3) (May 1977):245-253.

Presents an ethnographic description of a Peruvian brothel, including stratification process of services afforded to clientele according to social class.

263. Rivanera Carlés, F. *Los judíos y la trata de blancas en Argentina.* Buenos Aires, Argentina: Instituto de Investigaciones sobre la Cuestión Judía, 1986.

264. Robaina, T.R. *Recuerdos secretos de dos mujeres publicas.* Ciudad de

La Habana, Cuba: Editorial Letras Cubanas, 1984.

Attempts to come to terms with prostitutes whose existence had been previously denied by Cuban authorities.

265. Rodriquez Molas, R., J.C. Giusti, and E. Goldar. *Lugares y modos de diversión.* Buenos Aires: Centro Editor de América Latina, 1985.

266. Romero A., L., and A.M. Quintanilla E. *Prostitución y drogas: estudio psicológico de la prostitución en México y su relación con la farmacodependencia.* México: Editorial Trillas, 1976.

267. Sepúlveda Niño, S. *La prostitución en Colombia: una quiebra de las estructuras sociales.* Bogotá: Editorial Andes, 1970.

268. Werner, D. "Paid Sex Specialists Among the Mekranoti." *Journal of Anthropological Research* 40(3) (Fall 1984):394-405.

Explores the non-stratified society of the Mekranoti Indians of Central Brazil and the practice of having kupry, or unmarried women with children, who provide sexual services to men in the community in return for gifts of beads, meat, and other items. Examines the social status, characteristics, and family background of the kupry.

MIDDLE EAST

269. Cnaan, R.A. "Notes on Prostitution in Israel." *Journal of Sociological Inquiry* 52 (Spring 1982):114-121.

The increase of tourism and free movement between the occupied territories and Israel, by the end of 1970, resulted in an increase in prostitution in Israel. Explores the reasons for this increase, and concludes that it is the price a society pays for political and economic independence.

270. Kellner, J. *Zwiesprache mit Ziwjah: das Werden e. neuen Identität; Tagebuch der Behandlung.* Freiburg: Lambertus-Verlag, 1972.

Translated from Hebrew.

271. Philipp, D. "Frauenkriminalität in Israel: Prostituierte und Diebinnen im Langzeitvergleich." (Thesis) Universität Bremen, 1983.

NORTH AMERICA

272. West, J.M. *La prostitución clandestina en Norteamérica.* Barcelona: Petronio, 1975.

Canada

273. Crook, N. *Prostitution in the Atlantic Provinces.* (Microform) Ottawa: Department of Justice Canada, Policy, Programs and Research Branch, Research and Statistics Section, 1984. Reproduction of original in the Rutgers University Library. Ann Arbor, MI: University Microfilms International, 1986.

274. Fleischman, J. *Prostitution in Ontario: An Overview.* Ottawa: Dept. of Justice Canada, Policy, Programs and Research Branch, Research and Statistics Section, 1984.

Working papers on pornography and prostitution in Canada; examines the economic and legal aspects of the problem.

275. Fulford, R. "Sex for Sale: The Fraser Committee, Which Examined Prostitution and Pornography in Canada." *Saturday Night* 100 (August 1985):3-5.

Provides commentary on the two-volume report, "Pornography and Prostitution in Canada," prepared by a committee.

276. Lautt, M.L. *Project T.A.P. Towards an Awareness of Prostitution: An Empirical Study of Street Prostitution in the Prairie Region.* Ottawa: Dept. of Justice Canada, Policy, Programs and Research Branch, Research and Statistics Section, 1984.

Working papers on pornography and prostitution in the Prairie Provinces of Canada; includes statistics.

277. Layton, M. *Prostitution in Vancouver 1973-1975: Official and Unofficial Reports.* Vancouver: B.C. Police Commission, 1975.

278. Limoges, T. *La prostitution à Montréal; comment, pourquoi certaines femmes deviennent prostituées.* Montréal: Les Éditions de l'homme, 1967.

279. Lowman, J. "Prostitution in Canada." *Resources for Feminist Research* (Canada) 13(i.e., 14) (4) (1985-6):35-7.

Determines the characteristics and identity of prostitutes and clientele. Discusses the relationship between prostitutes, customers, and the police. Identifies the power behind the prostitution trade.

280. Lowman, J. "Prostitution in Vancouver: Some Notes on the Genesis of a Social Problem." *Canadian Journal of Criminology* (Canada) 28(1)(1986):1-16.

Focuses on a discussion of the effects of the 1972 Canadian soliciting law, and the manner of police enforcement on the incidence of prostitution in Vancouver, British Columbia.

281. Lowman, J. *Vancouver Field Study of Prostitution: Appendices to Research Notes.* (Microform) Ottawa: Department of Justice Canada, Policy, Programs, and Research Branch, Research and Statistics Section, 1984. Reproduction of original in the Rutgers University Library. Ann Arbor, MI: University Microfilms International, 1986.

282. O'Brien, M. *Plaisirs sans frontière.* Montréal: Domino, 1983.

283. Texier, C., and M.O. Vezina. *Profession, prostituée: rapport sur la prostitution au Québec.* Montréal: Libre Expression, 1978.

Mexico

284. Fonseca, J. *La prostitución en México: epidemiología psicosocial descriptiva: (investigación).* San Luis Potoi: Universidad Autónoma de San Luis Potosí, 1977.

285. García Durán, A. *Mis 7 amadas mujeres públicas.* Mexico, D.F.: Editorial Diana, 1981.

286. Gomezjara, F.A., E. Barrera, and N. Pérez. *Sociología de la prostitución.* México: Ediciones Nueva Sociología, 1978.

287. Roebuck, J., and P. McNamara. "Ficheras and Free-Lancers: Prostitution in a Mexican Border City." *Archives of Sexual Behavior* 2(3) (June 1973):231-244.

    Focuses on prostitution in a large Mexican city bordering the United States, where prostitution is a stable, lucrative industry. Prostitutes are registered, protected from police harassment, receive regular medical checkups, and meet in a situation which minimizes risks of being cheated or robbed.

United States

288. Additon, H.S. *City Planning for Girls: A Study of the Social Machinery for Case Work with Girls in Philadelphia...* Chicago: University of Chicago Press, 1928.

289. Budros, A. "The Ethnic Vice Industry Revisited." *Ethnic and Racial Studies* (Great Britain) 6(4) (1983):438-456.

    Studies the widespread ethnic-group participation in U.S. prostitution.

290. Campbell, A. "The Call Girls of Manhattan." *New Society* 70(1142) (November 8, 1984):203-205.

    This article reviews prostitution from a business point of view, through the eyes of a receptionist involved in the daily operations of a call girl service. Concludes that this particular operation flourished because of greed on the part of the prostitutes and not because of any psychological inadequacies. Most of these call girls simultaneously pursued other careers.

291.   Carlson, B. *Some Awfully Tame, but Kinda Funny Stories about Iowa Ladies-of-the-Evening.* Sioux City, Iowa: Quixote, 1989.

292.   Cohen, B. *Deviant Street Networks: Prostitution in New York City.* Lexington, MA: D.C. Heath, 1980.

Examines the social and ecological structures of visible street deviance in thirteen separate locations: includes deviant street network profiles, characteristics and patterns of visible street deviance and recommendations to alter deviant patterns.

293.   Diana, L. *The Prostitute and Her Clients: Your Pleasure Is Her Business.* Springfield, IL: Charles C. Thomas, 1985.

Creates a profile of the prostitute and her clientele within American society, by means of personal interviews with members of the profession.

294.   Esselstyn, T.C. "Prostitution in the United States." *The Annals of the American Academy of Political and Social Science* 376 (March 1968):123-135.

In developing areas, large-scale international tourism often offers a market for illegal goods and services. Curtailment of competitive street markets for prostitution may lie in applying enforcement against firms in the hotel/agency market.

295.   Freund, M., T.L. Leonard, and N. Lee. "Sexual Behavior of Resident Street Prostitutes with Their Clients in Camden, New Jersey." *Journal of Sex Research* 26(4) (1989):460-478.

Studies the sexual behaviors of 20 resident street prostitutes in Camden, New Jersey, including number of client contacts per day, typical work-week, and the use of condoms. Results indicate the development of long-term relationships between some clients and prostitutes.

296. Gladden, S.C. *Ladies of the Night*. Boulder, CO: S.C. Gladden, 1979.

Includes a compilation of conversations with prostitutes in the New York City area; explores the legal, psychological, and socio-economic aspects of prostitution.

297. Jordan, P.D. *Prostitution: An American Dilemma*. St. Louis, MO: Forum, 1979.

Traces the history of prostitution in America; presents arguments for and against the legalization of prostitution.

298. Klausner, P.R. "Politics of Massage Parlor Prostitution: The International Traffic in Women for Prostitution into New York City, 1970-present." (Dissertation) University of Delaware, 1987.

Investigates the trafficking of Latin American and Korean women into New York City for massage parlor prostitution. Explores the socio-economic and political conditions that exist to contribute to this situation.

299. Lila. *Black Bait as Told to Leo Guild*. Los Angeles: Holloway, 1975.

300. Miller, E.M. *Street Woman*. Philadelphia, PA: Temple University Press, 1986.

A sociological study of prostitution in Milwaukee, Wisconsin; includes aspects of criminality, runaway youths, recruitment techniques, ethnic participation, drug use, living conditions, and results of interviews with prostititutes. Concludes by suggesting that further studies are needed related to female criminality and opportunities for legitimate work as well as studies of the political economy of women's labor force participation in illegal work.

301. Murtagh, J.M., and S. Harris. *Cast the First Stone*. Westport, CT: Greenwood, 1978. (Reprint of the 1957 edition)

302. Nwankwo, A. "Self Esteem Maintenance and Social Construction of Occupation: Bar Prostitutes in a Small Midwestern City." (Ph.D. Thesis) Michigan State University at Ann Arbor, 1988.

Utilizes the self-investment theory to examine the effects of a low-status occupation on the self-esteem of its participants. Examines prostitution as a low-status occupation and how it has become an economic option for women. Concludes that prostitution does not produce low self-esteem and notes average or above average self-esteem in prostitutes, possibly indicating their ability to avoid negative evaluations or effectively use coping mechanisms.

303. Packer, H., S. Glassco, and C. Konigsberg. "Prostitution in Memphis: Then and Now." *Journal of the Tennessee Medical Association* 76(2) (February 1983):86-8.

Examines the role of the prostitute as a major contributing source of venereal infection within the Memphis community. Includes statistics on syphilis and gonorrhea and a program that includes a cooperative agreement by the prostitute to undergo examination for the presence of venereal disease when she faces arrest for soliciting.

304. Potterat, J.J., J. Phillips, et al. *Female Prostitutes in Colorado Springs: A Case-Control Pilot Study.* (Association Paper) Society for the Study of Social Problems, El Paso Community Health Dept., 1979.

A comparative study of fourteen female prostitutes and 15 controls who had attended a clinic for sexually transmitted diseases to determine patterns of socialization, adolescent experiences, and illness episodes. Results indicate few differences. Suggests that prostitution is a process of socialization that requires involvement with a given subculture to encourage entrance into this lifestyle.

305. Powell, H. *Ninety Times Guilty.* New York: Arno, 1974. (Reprint of the 1939 edition).

306. Reckless, W.C. *Vice in Chicago.* Montclair, NJ: Patterson Smith, 1969. (Reprint of the 1933 edition).

307. Silbert, M.H., and A.M. Pines. "Entrance into Prostitution." *Youth and Society* 13(4) (1982):471-500.

Questionnaires were administered to a cross-sectional sample of 200 prostitutes in the San Francisco Bay area to systematically investigate the causes for their entrance into prostitution. Results indicate entrance was often due to abuse problems at home, lack of socio-economic support, survival needs, a negative self-concept, and deviant social networks.

308. Stopp, G.H. "The Distribution of Massage Parlors in the Nation's Capital." *Journal of Popular Culture* 11(4) (1978):989-997.

Discusses the licensure of massage parlors in Washington, D.C., which actually serve as fronts for prostitution. The validity of the licensure process generally precludes these establishments from harassment or control by local law enforcement agencies.

309. Symanski, R. "Prostitution in Nevada." *Annals of the Association of American Geographers* 64(3) (1974):357-377.

Studies thirty-three brothels in rural and small-town Nevada, with a prostitute population between 225-250, and examines the effect of legal and quasi-legal restrictions.

310. B., Nathalie. *Call Girl*. Montreal: Quebecor, 1982.

A biography of Nathalie B. (1946-).

311. Bailey, P. *An English Madam: The Life and Work of Cynthia Payne*. London: Cape, 1982.

312. Barnes, R. *[Madame Sherry] Pleasure Was My Business. Told to S.R. Tralins*. New York: Paperback Library 1963.

Prostitution in Miami, FL.

313. Barrows, S.B., (and W. Novak) *Mayflower Madam: The Secret Life of Sydney Biddle Barrows*. Santa Barbara, CA: ABC Clio, 1987. Large print edition.

There are several printings of this autobiography, and it was made into a movie. This edition is an interesting and seemingly honest portrayal.

314. Bell, E.M. *Josephine Butler, Flame of Fire*. London: Constable, 1963.

Biography of the Josephine Butler (1828-1906), who led the campaign against involuntary prostitution in nineteenth-century England.

315. Billy, Madame. *La maîtresse de "maison": les dessous roses de trois républiques*. Paris: La Table ronde, c. 1980.

A biography of Madame Billy (1901-) in Paris.

316. Blumir, G., and A. Sauvage. *Donne di vita: vita di donne*. Milan: A. Mondadori, 1980.

Interviews with prostitutes.

317. Brown, P.L. "The Problem with Miss Laura's House." *Historical Preservation* 32(5) (1980), 16-19.

Examines the hesitation of some preservationists to restore Laura Sargeant's house in Fort Smith, Arkansas, originally built as the Riverfront Commercial Hotel shortly after the Civil War. It later became a notorious house of prostitution.

318. Burford, E.J. *Queen of the Bawds; or, the True Story of Madame Britannica Hollandia and Her House of Obscenities, Hollands Leaguer.* London: Spearman, 1973.

319. Butler, J.E.G. *Personal Reminiscences of a Great Crusade.* Westport, CN: Hyperion, 1976. This is a reprint of the 1911 edition: London: H. Marshall, 1911.

Butler was one of the great women of the nineteenth century. Her efforts to end regimentation led to an international movement. She never lost sight of the fact that prostitutes were real people and always had great compassion for them.

320. Chavez, J. (with J. Vitek). *Defector's Mistress: The Judy Chavez Story.* New York: Dell, 1979.

321. *Christiane F., Autobiography of a Girl of the Streets and Heroin Addict.* Edited by K. Hermann and H. Rieck. Translated by Susanne Flatauer from German, *Wir Kinder vom Bahnhof Zoo.* Toronto: Bantam Books, 1982.

There are also translations in French and Italian. The original German edition was published in 1979. Tells the story of a thirteen-year-old West German child prostitute and heroin addict.

322. Cordelier, J., and M. Leroche. *La Dérobade.* Paris: Hachette, 1976. (Translated into English by H. Mathews. New York: Viking, 1978. Also a Spanish edition. Barcelona: Noquer, 1978.)

323. Cousins, S. *To Beg I Am Ashamed.* Reprinted New York: Garland,

1979.

A reprint of a 1938 biography.

324.   Duncan, D.   *Here Is My Hand: The Story of Lieutenant Colonel Alida Bosshardt of the Red Light Area, Amsterdam.* London: Hodder and Stoughton, 1977.

A biography of a Salvation Army officer who dealt with prostitutes in Amsterdam.

325.   Eagle, K. (with Leo Guild). *Black Streets of Oakland.* Los Angeles: Holloway House, 1977.

Biography of an Oakland (California) prostitute.

326.   Erwin, C. (with F. Miller). *The Orderly Disorderly House.* London: Souvenir, 1961.

An American prostitute writes her memoirs.

327.   Francis, L. *Hollywood Madam.* Los Angeles: Hollywood House, 1987.

Originally published as *Ladies on Call.*

328.   Francis, S. *Sara: Her Own Story of Life and Times in Australia's Red Light District.* South Melbourne: Macmillan, 1984.

329.   French, D. (with L. Lee). *Working: My Life as a Prostitute.* New York: Dutton, 1988.

330.   Genini, R. "Red Light Lady with a Heart of Gold: Will the Real Julia Bulette Please Step into the Parlor?" *Californiana* 4(4) (1986):23-29.

Julia Bulette, a Virginia City prostitute, nursed victims of an influenza epidemic and tended to injured miners, actions which gave her an important role and status in the community. She was murdered in 1867 and her assailant, John Millein, was executed.

331. Graham, V. *How I Became Hollywood's Favorite Party Girl.* New York: Pinnacle, 1975. Also published under title *The Joy of Hooking.*

332. Hecke, R. *Love Life: Scenes with Irene.* New York: Rogner and Bernhard, 1982. Translated by Christopher Doherty.

Prostitution in Zurich, Switzerland and Rome, Italy, as reported by Irene.

333. Hollander, X. (with R. Moore and Y. Dunleavy). *The Happy Hooker: My Own Story.* New York: Dell, 1973.

Hollander became a publishing phenomenon as her collaborators built a business upon her life and advice. Personally, we are suspicious of many of the things she recounts although her first book is probably the most accurate. There are several translations of her work into other languages. Among her other titles are:

334. Hollander, X. *Fiesta of the Flesh.* London: Panther, 1984.

335. Hollander, X. *The Inner Circle.* London: Granada, 1983.

336. Hollander, X. *The Knights in the Garden of Spain.* London: Grafton, 1988.

337. Hollander, X. *Xaviera's Magic Mushrooms.* Sevenoaks, Kent: New English Library, 1984.

338. Horvath, C. (with M. Castellano). *The Madame Celeste: A True Story.* Bloomington, MN: Landmark, 1981.

Prostitution in New York City and the story of a conversion of a prostitute.

339.   Ignoto, B. *Confessions of a Part-Time Call Girl.* New York: Dell, 1986.

A New York City call girl.

340.   Jones, M.T. *Maxine, "Call Me Madam."* Little Rock, AK: Pioneer, 1983.

Prostitution in Hot Springs, Arkansas.

341.   Julie. *My Nights and Days.* New York: Putnam, 1973. Also a Spanish translation by José María Cañas. Mexico City: Rocu, 1975.

Autobiography of a prostitute.

342.   Kale, S. *The Fire Escape.* London: Putnam, 1960.

Autobiographical.

343.   Kapur, P. *The Life and World of Call-Girls in India. A Socio-psychological Study of the Aristocratic Prostitute.* New Delhi: Vikas, 1978.

Offers solutions to the problem of prostitution as well as describes the socio-economic implications.

344.   Kimball, N. *Nell Kimball: Her Life as an American Madam.* New York: Berkley, 1980. Edited by Stephen Longstreet.

Nell Kimball (1854-1934) wrote her reminiscences from her preserved correspondence. This is a reprint of an earlier edition.

345.   Leah. *Leah.* Old Tappan, NJ: F. H. Revell, 1973.

An autobiography of a prostitute. Also deals with her drug abuse.

346.   Lee, L.J. "The Social World of the Female Prostitute in Los Angeles." (Ph.D. Thesis) San Diego: U.S. International University, 1981. University

Microfilms, 1985.

347. Levine, J., and L. Madden. *Lyn: A Story of Prostitution.* London: Women's Press, 1988.

A prostitute in Dublin.

348. Little, C. J. "Paulina Luisi: Uruguayan Feminist and Reformer of Morals." *Transactions of the Conference Group for Social and Administrative History* 6 (1976), 91-104.

Examines the efforts of Uruguayan physician and feminist in her campaign against the prostitution laws in Montevideo and Buenos Aires from the early 1900s until her death in 1950.

349. Lovatt, G., and P. Cockerill. *A Nice Girl Like Me: The Autobiography of Gloria Lovatt.* London: Columbus, 1988.

350. Luchetts, V. "The Fate of Julia Bulette." *Westways* 68 (9) (1976), 31-33, 69-70.

Another account of the Virginia City prostitute, Julia Bulette. See entry number 330.

351. Madame Claude. *Allô, oui; ou, Les mémoires de Madame Claude.* Edited by Jacques Quoirez. Paris: Stock, 1975.

352. *Madeleine: An Autobiography.* New York: Persea, 1986.

Originally published by Harper and Brothers in 1919, this autobiography became a center of political controversy in New York City.

353. Martin, M.C. *Chinatown's Angry Angel: The Story of Donaldina Cameron.* Palo Alto, CA: Pacific, 1986.

Donaldina MacKenzie Cameron (1869-1968) did social work in San Francisco including working with Chinese prostitutes in the Chinese

Presbyterian Girls Home.

354. McDonald, D. *The Legend of Julia Bulette and the Red Light Ladies of Nevada.* Edited by Stanley Paher. Las Vegas, NV: Nevada, 1980.

Still another account of Julia Bulette. See Luchetts and Genini above.

355. Melissa. *The Harlot's Room.* London: Chatto and Windus, 1987.

Biography of a prostitute.

356. Michèle. *La vie continue: histoire de Michèle.* Paris: Fayard, 1976.

357. Miranda, R.E. *Cuando las mariposas aprenden a volar: relato biográfico de una muchacha de los bajos fondos, para ser leído por personas adultas y concientizadas.* Caracas, Venezuela: Publicaciones Seleven, 1980.

Venzuelan prostitutes tell their story. Also discusses narcotic addiction.

358. Misomastropus. *The Bawds Trial and Execution; also, A Short Account of Her Whole Life and Travels.* London: Printed for L.C., 1679. Microfilm, Ann Arbor, MI., University Microfilms International, 1980.

359. Mol, A. *Greta, Amsterdam Streetwalker Talks to Albert Mol.* Introduction by A. Ellis. London: Tandem, 1968.

360. Mote, J. *The Flesh.* Nairobi: Comb Books, 1975.

Prostitution in Kenya.

361. Myers, R.C. "An Inning for Sin: Chicago Joe and Her Hurdy-Gurdy Girls." *Montana* 27(2) (1977), 24-33.

Brief account of Mary Josephine Welch (1844-1899) known as Chicago Joe because she imported young women from Chicago to staff her businesses in Helena including hurdy gurdy houses, brothels, and saloons.

She became one of Helena's major property owners.

362. Myriama. *Mon nom est plaisir.* Paris: La Pensée moderne, 1972.

Discusses prostitution in Algeria through the correspondence and reminiscences of Myriama.

363. Phonpaicht, P. *From Peasant Girls to Bangkok Masseuses.* Geneva: International Labor Office, 1982.

364. Picard, R. *Ma vie dans les bordels.* Montréal: Éditions Quebecor, 1985.

Rita Picard (1927-) and her life as a prostitute in Quebec.

365. Pinzer, M. *The Maimie Papers.* Edited with a historical introduction by Ruth Rosen. Old Westbury, N.Y.: Feminist, 1977.

Includes a discussion of prostitutes in Philadelphia using correspondence and reminiscences. Letters chiefly written to Fanny Quincy Howe.

366. Rollman, H. *Erowina: Zwei Jahre mit Heroin.* Gumligen: Zytglogge Verlag, 1981.

Prostitution and heroine, a biographical study.

367. Sandford, J. *Prostitutes: Portraits of People in Sexploitation.* London: Seeker & Warburg, 1975; revised Abacus, 1977.

368. *Sex Work: Written by Women in the Sex Industry.* Edited by Frederique Delacoste and Priscilla Alexander. Pittsburgh: Cleis, 1987.

Includes personal observations, correspondence, and reminiscences.

369. Smith, R., and D. Boutland. *The Professional: A Day in the Life of a Prostitute.* Sydney: Free, 1972.

370.   Stanford, S. *The Lady of the House: The Autobiography of Sally Stanford.*
       New York: Putnam, 1966.

       The autobiography of a prominent West Coast madam.

371.   Stuck, G. *Annie McCune: Shreveport Madam.*   Baton Rouge, LA.:
       Moran, 1981.

       Annie McCune died in 1920.

372.   Susan. *Diary: Peace and the Puta and the Day of the Beautyful Jail.*
       Santa Fe: s.n., 1970.

373.   Symonds, N. (with Thelma Sangster). *The Secret Rose.* Basingstoke,
       Hants, England: Marshall Pickering, 1987.

       A prostitute and narcotic addict who changed her lifestyle through
       conversion.

374.   Tabor, P. *Pauline's.* Illustrated by D.S. Martin. Louisville, KY:
       Touchstone, 1972; reprinted Greenwich, CN, 1973.

       A popular madam and her house in Louisville.

375.   Thompson, B. *Madam Bell Brezing.* Lexington, KY: Buggy Whip, 1983.

       A biography of a Lexington, Kentucky, prostitute.

376.   Thompson, P. *The Midnight Patrol: The Story of a Salvation Army Lass
       Who Patrolled the Dark Streets of London's West End on a Midnight
       Mission of Mercy.* London: Hodder and Stoughton, 1974.

       An account of Mary Scott and her work with the Salvation Army and
       prostitution.

377.   Ulla. *Ulla.* Albertville, France: Ch. Denu., 1976. Also Barcelona:
       Grijalbo, 1977.

378. Virginie. *Virginie, Prostitutuée.* Montreal: Éditions Quebecor, 1979.

Republished in 1982 as *Un tendre amour de Virginie* by the same publisher. Prostitution in Quebec.

379. Williams, G. *Rosa May: The Search for a Mining Camp Legend.* Riverside, CA: Tree by the River, 1980.

Rosa May (1855-1912) was a Nevada prostitute.

380. Williamson, J. *Friends of Father Joe: Pages From His Diary.* London: Hodder and Stoughton, 1965.

Father Joe and his church work with prostitutes.

381. Williamson, J. *Josephine Butler, The Forgotten Saint.* Leighton Buzzard: Faith, 1977.

An account of the social reformer Josephine Elizabeth Grey Butler (1828-1906). One of the most significant women of the nineteenth century.

382. Wilson, A. *The Female Pest: An Expose of Misogynist Mythology.* London: The author, 1985.

Listed as in memoriam to Nancy Bouverie and includes discussion of prostitution.

383. Wilson, R. *The Wendy King Story.* Introduction by Laurier LaPierre. Vancouver, BC: Langen, 1980.

A biography of a Vancouver prostitute.

384. Yamazaki, T., and S. W. Kohl. *The Story of Yamada Waka: From Prostitute to Feminist Pioneer.* Translated from Japanese by W. Hironaka and A. Kostant. Tokyo: Kodansha, 1985. Originally published in Bungei Shunju issues of April, July, Oct., and Nov., 1977 in Japanese.

An account of Waka Yamada (1879-1957) prostitute and feminist on U.S.

West Coast.

385.   Zausner, M. *The Streets: A Factual Portrait of Six Prostitutes as Told in Their Own Words.* New York: St. Martin's, 1986.

386. Brinck, G., and H. Sjögren. *Guide til Europas natteliv.* Kolbotn: Jaforlaget, 1972.

    Lists restaurants, lunch rooms, music halls, and prostitutes in directory form.

387. The Covent Garden Jester. *Harris's List of Covent-Garden Ladies.* New York: Garland, 1986.

    Many editions under slightly different titles during the last four decades of the eighteenth century.

388. Erickson, B. *Nevada Playmates: A Guide to Cathouses.* 4th ed. San Francisco: Bangkok, 1985.

    This is periodically updated. Continues a long tradition of guides to brothels.

389. Erickson, B. *San Francisco Streetwalkers Sex Guide.* 3rd ed. San Francisco: Bangkok, 1973.

    Erickson has done a series of guides.

390. Friedman, J.A. *Tales of Time Square.* New York: Delacourte, 1986.

    Prostitution in Times Square.

391. Hutson, J. *The Chicken Ranch: The True Story of the Best Little Whorehouse in Texas.* South Brunswick, NJ: A.S. Barnes, 1980.

    The whorehouse in LaGrange, Texas, located just outside of Houston, which is featured in the Broadway musical was one of the oldest, continually operating brothels in America.

392. Johansson, L. *Sex är inte nagon känsla längre.* Stockholm: Liber, 1979.

Prostitution in Sweden.

393. Röhrmann, C. *Der sittliche Zustand von Berlin nach Aufhebung der geduldeten Prostitution des weiblichen Geschlechts.* Heidelberg: Kriminalistik Verlag, 1981. (Also published: Leipzig: Zentralantiquariat, 1987.)

This was originally published in 1846 as a description of prostitution in Berlin.

394. Schwartz, J.R. *The Traveller's Guide to the Best Cat Houses in Nevada; Everything You Want to Know About Legal Prostitution in Nevada.* Los Altos, CA: Straight Arrow, 1985.

395. St. Agnès, Y. de. *Le sexe qui vient du froid.* Paris: Presses de la Cité, 1975.

A directory to prostitutes and a description of European sex customs.

396. *Sex in Benelux.* Berlin: Dulk, 1973.

Prostitution, including directories, for Benelux countries.

397. *Sexikon Helveitkuss.* Berlin: Dulk, 1971.

Prostitution and sex customs in Switzerland.

398. Tytler, J. *Ranger's Impartial List of the Ladies of Pleasure in Edinburgh.* Edinburgh: P. Harris, 1978.

This is a facsimile of the original edition privately published in 1775 in Edinburgh. It is not absolutely certain that Tytler is the author.

ECONOMICS

399. Aguilar, D.M. "Women in the Political Economy of the Philippines." *Alternatives* (Centre for the Study of Developing Societies). 12 (October 1987):511-26.

Discusses the exploitative working conditions, the prevalence of prostitution, and the plight of the women migrant workers.

400. Aleman, J.L. "La Prostitución: Seus Determinantes Economicos. (Prostitution: Its Economic Determinants)." *Estudios Sociales* (Dominican Republic) 7(4) (1974):201-10.

Defines the problem of prostitution in Santo Domingo during the 1960s and 1970s. Stresses the economic factors contributing to prostitution in the Dominican Republic as well as in the rest of Latin America.

401. Alexander, C.L. "Job, John, or Joint--Three Alternatives for Prostitution." *Crime and Corrections* 3(1) (1975):31-5.

402. Barnett, H.C. "Political Economy of Rape and Prostitution." *Review of Radical Political Economy* 8(1) (1976):59-69.

Examines social and legal precedents in rape and prostitution which reinforce attitudes toward women as the property of men.

403. Chapman, J.R. "Economics of Women's Victimization." *Victimization of Women*, by J.R. Chapman and M. Gates. Newbury Park, CA: Sage, 1978.

Assesses the economic factors contributing to prostitution and various crimes against women. Finds prostitution has its roots in limited economic opportunities for women.

404. "Fast Growth of the Underground Economy--Views of P.M. Guthman."

Business Week (March 13, 1978):73-5.

Discusses the growth of various illegal underground activities, including prostitution. Estimates that about ten percent of the recorded gross national product is generated by illegal income. Also finds that the figure for unemployment is probably overstated, since many of these occupations are not recorded.

405.   Frey, J.H., L.R. Reichert, and K.V. Russell. "Prostitution, Business and Police--The Maintenance of an Illegal Economy." *Police Journal* 54(3) (July-September 1981):239-49.

Analyzes the role of prostitution in Las Vegas. Finds that, in view of economic characteristics, prostitution is considered acceptable behavior here, as in other urban areas. Discusses the role of the hotel network in soliciting and particularly controlling prostitution to enable law enforcement to concentrate in other areas.

406.   Harrop, D. "Taking It Easy." *Saturday Evening Post* (May/June 1981):61-3, 112.

Considers the profit-making aspects of criminal activity, including prostitution.

407.   Heyl, B.S. *The Madam as Entrepreneur: Career Management in House Prostitution.* New Brunswick, NJ: Transaction Books, 1979.

Compares the running of a brothel to the management of a legitimate commercial establishment. Examines movement from legitimate occupations and culture to deviant ones and back again. Critically reviews the sociological and psychological literature on pimping, hustling, and prostitution.

408.   Karch, C.A., and G.M.S. Dann. "Close Encounters of the Third World." *Human Relations* 34(4) (April 1981):249-68.

Analyzes role reversal encounters in Barbados between white female guests and black male hosts with payment for sexual services.

409. Lowe, K. "Travel Arranged, Bodies Sold: A Tourism Sex Saga." *One World* (December 1980).

410. Lynch, T., and M. Neckes. "Cost Effectiveness of Enforcing Prostitution Laws." San Francisco: Unitarian Universalist Service Committee, 1978.

Advocates the decriminalization of prostitution, finding that present methods of enforcing the laws and controlling prostitution in San Francisco are too expensive. Recommends decriminalization and development of viable economic alternatives be developed nationwide.

411. Miyoshi, A. "Women and Social Transformation in the Philippines." *Crossing Boundaries: Stories from the Frontier Internship in Mission Programme.* Edited by K.Todd. Geneva: World Council of Churches, 1985.

412. Morgan, T. "The Gross Project: The Business Side, Updated, of a Very Old Business (Establishments Known as Massage Parlors in New York City)." *Across the Board* 14(May 1977):66-8+.

413. Munín, A., and R.G. Schlúter. *Turismo y sexo: aproximación a un estudio sobre prostitución y turismo en Argentina.* Buenos Aires: Centro de Investigaciones en Turismo, 1985.

414. O'Malley, J. "Sex Tourism and Women's Status in Thailand." *Loisir et Societe/Society and Leisure* 11(1) (Spring 1988):99-114.

Analyzes the disproportionate growth of the prostitute population in Bangkok, Thailand. Identifies a series of political, economic, and social conditions that account for this as well as the exploitative nature of this industry. Finds that transformation of gender relations and development strategy is a necessary part of a larger solution.

415. Peretiatkowicz, J.A. "The Effect of Being Out of Work on Young People in Chile." Translated by P. Burns. *Youth Without a Future.* Edited by J. Coleman and G. Baum. Edinburg: T. & T. Clark, 1985.

416. Petrick, P. "Capitalists with Rooms: Prostitution in Helena, Montana, 1865-1900." *Montana* 31(2) (1981):20-41.

      Shows how prostitution in Helena, Montana, was the largest means of employment for women outside the home between 1865 and 1900. Traces the decline of this phenomenon resulting from changes in economic conditions and social values.

417. "A Report from South Korea (Tourists and Prostitution; Kisaeng Houses)." *IDOC Bulletin* 1982.

418. Reynolds, H. *Cops and Dollars--The Economics of Criminal Law and Justice.* Springfield, IL: Charles C. Thomas, 1981.

      Presents criminal law and justice from an economic perspective. Discusses the application of economic principles to legal and illegal markets, including prostitution.

419. Reynolds, H. *The Economics of Prostitution.* Springfield, IL: Charles C. Thomas, 1986.

      Uses the principles and tools of economics to analyze prostitution. Develops four models of prostitution: (1) laissez faire where prostitution is illegal but tolerated; (2) regulated where prostitution is lawful but closely monitored; (3) controlled by rigorous law enforcement which suppresses obvious prostitution, and (4) zoning where illicit prostitution is allowed within a circumscribed area. Discusses incentives for prostitution.

420. Rothstein, D. *Hooking in Olongapo: Economic and Cultural Factors in Primary and Secondary Deviation.* (Association Paper) University of Alabama: Mid-South Sociological Association, 1978.

      Examines prostitution in one city in the Philippines to determine the economic and cultural factors that allow this to become a way of life for some women. Finds the primary deviation to be the loss of virginity. The secondary deviation occurs when prostitution arises as a reasonable occupation and forces the woman to choose among a limited list of possibilities.

421. Schurink, W.J., and T. Levinthal. "Business Women Exchanging Sex for Money: A Descriptive Study." *Suid-Afrikaanse Tydskrif vir Sosiologie/The South African Journal of Sociology* 14(4) (November 1983):154-63.

     Questions environment and background as determining factors resulting in prostitution. Argues this excludes those who voluntarily adopt prostitution as an occupation. Adopts an occupational perspective.

422. Simon, C.P., and A.D. Witte. *Beating the System--The Underground Economy.* Washington, DC: US Department of Justice National Institute of Justice, 1982.

     Provides a microeconomic analysis of the underground economy, including prostitution. Finds that prostitution is one of the largest sectors in the illegal goods and service market. Makes policy recommendations.

423. Simon, C.P., A.D. Witte, K. Eakin, et al. *Underground Economy-- Estimate of Size, Trends and Structure; Executive Summary.* Raleigh, NC: Osprey Company, 1975?.

     Discusses the income produced by the underground economy, including prostitution. Recommends a better understanding of the nature and extent of the underground economy to aid economic policymaking.

424. Tabet, P. "From Gift to Commodity, Sexual Relations for Compensation (Prostitution and Beyond)." *Temps Modernes* 42 (1987):1-53.

425. Tansey, R. "Prostitution and Politics in Antebellum New Orleans." *Southern Studies* 18(4) (1979):449-79.

     Discusses prostitution as a major industry, with considerable economic profit, in New Orleans during the antebellum period. Describes the unsuccessful attempts to reform prostitution in the mid-1850s.

426. Vanelderen, M.J. "Third World People and Tourism." *One World* (May 1986).

     Includes a discussion of prostitution.

427.   Walkowitz, J.R., and D.J. Walkowitz.   "We Are Not the Beasts of the
       Field: Prostitution and the Poor in Plymouth and Southampton under the
       Contagious Diseases Acts."   *Clio's Consciousness Raised; New
       Perspectives on the History of Women*. Edited by M.S. Hartman and L.W.
       Banner. New York: Harper & Row, 1974.

428.   Yayori, M.   "Sexual Slavery in Korea."   *Frontiers* 2(1) (1977):22-30.

       Discusses Japanese guided prostitution tours to South Korea since 1910
       and continued Korean government support since 1945.

HISTORY

GENERAL

429. Acton, W. *Prostitution*. Edited with an introduction and notes by Peter Fryer. New York: Praeger, 1969.

   This is a classic nineteenth-century study of prostitution by a physician.

430. Addams, J. *A New Consciousness and an Ancient Evil*. New York: Arno, 1972.

   Reprint of a classic work by the famed Jane Addams.

431. Apruzzi, I.,ed. *La moglie e la prostituta: due ruoli, una condizione*. Rimini; Firenza: Guaraldi, 1975.

432. Barclay, S. *Sex Slavery: A Documentary Report on the International Scene Today*. London: Heinemann, 1968. (American edition, *Bondage: the Slave Traffic in Women Today*. New York: Funk and Wagnalls, 1968.)

433. Bassermann, L. *The Oldest Profession*. Translated from the German by James Cleugh. London: A. Barker, 1967.

434. Bauer, W. *Geschichte und Wesen der Prostitution, verfasst unter Mitarbeit von Richard Waldeff, mit Beitragen von Werner Heinz. Eine geschichtliche und sozialethische Darststellung der Prostitution in Wort und Bild und ihrer Folgen im Zeitraum von uber 4000 Jahren*. 3. völlig erneuerte Aufl. Stuttgart: Weltspiegel-Verlag, 1960.

435. Bernheimer, C. "Of Whores and Sewers--Parent Duchâtelet, Engineer of Abjection (The Fascination of a Nineteenth Century Public Health Official for Foul Odors, Waste and Prostitution)." *Raritan-A Quarterly Review*

6(3) (1987):72-90.

Parent-Duchâtelet is the founder of modern studies of prostitution.

436. Biermann, P. *"Wir sind Frauen wie andere auch!": Prostituierte und ihre Kämpfe.* Reinbeck bei Hamburg: Rowohlt, 1980.

437. Bullough, V.L. *The History of Prostitution.* New Hyde Park, NY: University Books, 1964.

An early attempt by a professional historian to survey the field.

438. Bullough, V.L. "Women: Birth Control, Prostitution, and the Pox." *Transactions of the Conference Group for Social and Administrative History* 6 (1976):20-8.

Examines late nineteenth-century and early twentieth-century movements to abolish prostitution in relation to sexually transmitted diseases and changing attitudes towards women.

439. Bullough, V.L., and B. Bullough. *An Illustrated Social History: Prostitution.* New York: Crown, 1978.

A totally revised and updated study. More sophisticated than the earlier effort.

440. Bullough, V.L., and B. Bullough. *Women and Prostitution--A Social History.* Buffalo, NY: Prometheus, 1987.

A 1987 update, based mainly on the 1978 study but without illustrations. Probably the best one-volume survey.

441. Butler, J.E.J. *Truth Before Everything.* London: Pewtress, 1897. (Microform: New Haven, CT: Research Publications, 1977. 1 microfilm reel, 35 mm.)

Josephine Butler's response to prostitution.

442. Chaleil, M. *Le corps prostitué: essai.* Paris: Galilée, 1981.

443. Cortés Conde, R., and E.H. Cortés Conde. *Historia negra de la prostitución: su pasado, su presente, esbozo de una solución.* Buenos Aires: Plus Ultra, 1978.

History of prostitution and possible solutions.

444. Cutrufelli, M.R. *Il cliente: inchiesta sulla domanda di prostituzione.* Roma: Editori riuniti, 1981.

445. De Wulf, L.M.L. *Faces of Venus: The History of Prostitution Through the Ages.* New York: Books in Focus, 1981.

446. Evans, H. *Harlots, Whores & Hookers: A History of Prostitution.* New York: Taplinger, 1979.

Has a somewhat different viewpoint than Bullough and Bullough.

447. Evans, H. *The Oldest Profession: An Illustrated History of Prostitution.* Newton Abbot, England: David & Charles, 1979.

Illustrated version of the above book.

448. Flexner, A. *Prostitution in Europe.* Reprinted Montclair, NJ: Patterson Smith, 1969.

A reprint of the 1914 study sponsored by the Bureau of Social Hygiene and the Rockefeller interests. A significant study of prostitution in Europe.

449. Freund der Menschheit. *Das Dirnentum und der Dirnengeist in der Gesellschraft (microform); ein Reformbuch der Sittlichkeit, von einem Freunde der Menschheit . . . 2.,* vom Verfasser verm. Aufl. Leipzig: Spohr, 1894. Microfilm, New York: Columbia University Libraries, 1985.

450. Geis, G. *Not the Law's Business? An Examination of Homosexuality,*

Abortion, Prostitution, Narcotics, and Gambling in the United States. Rockville, MD, National Institute of Mental Health, Center for Studies of Crime and Delinquency. Washington, DC: U.S. Government Printing Office, 1972.

A cross-cultural discussion of homosexuality, abortion, prostitution, narcotics, and gambling, including legal, moral, social, and medical aspects.

451.   Geis, G. *One Eyed Justice: An Examination of Homosexuality, Abortion, Prostitution, Narcotics and Gambling in the United States.* New York: Drake, 1974.

Examines the legal, psychological, and social effects of victimless crimes and their legal sanctions. Questions whether such crimes actually have damaging social consequences of continued criminalization of these behaviors.

452.   Gerin, C. *Aspetti medico-sociali della prostituzione; con particolare riferimento alle attuali norme di legge.* Roma: Istituto italiano di medicina sociale, 1964.

453.   Groothuyse, J.W. *De arbeidsstructuur van de prostitutie.* Deventer: Van Loguhum Slaterus, 1970.

454.   Hall, S. *Ladies of the Night.* New York: Trident, 1973.

455.   Henriques, F. *Modern Sexuality.* London: McGibbon & Knee, 1968.

The third volume of Henriques' three-volume history. See entry number 456. This volume deals mostly with the twentieth century and is independent of the two others.

456.   Henriques, F. *Prostitution and Society, a Survey.* New York: Citadel, 1962.

American edition of the first volume of this comprehensive study has the subtitle *Primitive, Classical and Oriental.* Also published as a three-volume set by McGibbon & Kee, 1962-68. Includes extracts of documents.

457. Henriques, F. *Prostitution in Europe and the Americas.* New York: Citadel, 1965.

Second volume of Henriques' comprehensive history which has the subtitle *Prostitution in Europe and the New World* in the complete British edition. See entry number 456.

458. Hervas, R. *Historia de la prostitución.* Barcelona: Ediciones Telsrar, 1969.

459. *History of Women.* New Haven, CT: Research Publications, 1975-1979.

Microfilm of selected materials on women before 1920 in libraries of various institutions: Radcliffe College, Smith College, N.Y. Public Library, etc. Includes materials on prostitution.

460. Hughes, V. *Ladies' Mile.* Bristol: Abson, 1977.

461. Hunold, G. *Hetaren, Callgirls und Bordelle: Geschichte u. Erscheinungsformen d. Prostitution.* München: Heyne, 1979.

462. Hunold, G. *Prostitution in Vergangenheit und Gegenwart.* München: Heyne, 1970.

463. Husain, M. *The Suppression of Immoral Traffic in Women and Girls Act, 1956.* Lucknow: Eastern Book, 1978.

464. Inciardi, J.A., and C.E. Faupel. *History and Crime: Implications for Criminal Justice Policy.* Beverly Hills, CA: Sage, 1980.

Includes historical and cross-cultural perspectives divided into four sections: theory and methodology, historical analysis of crime, historical analysis of criminal legislation and policy, and historical analysis of law enforcement and corrections. Discusses the policies of prohibition, regulation, and decriminalization of prostitution in the United States and Europe.

465. Lebel, J.J. *L'amo(u)r et l'argent: traversée de l'institution prostitutionnelle.* Paris: Stock, 1979.

466. Matthew, R. "Prostitution and Social Structure: Towards a Materialist Analysis." (Dissertation) University of Essex, England, 1984.

Includes a section on historiography.

467. Mulder, W.G. *De wereld van de prostitutie.* Gravenhage: N.V.S.H., 1969.

468. Murphy, E. *Great Bordellos of the World: An Illustrated History.* London: Quartet, 1983.

469. O'Brien, M. *All the Girls.* London: Macmillan, 1982. Translated into Spanish, *Esses chicas.* Barcelona: Planeta, 1983.

470. O'Callaghan, S. *The White Slave Trade.* London: R. Hale, 1965.

A popular survey of the white slave trade.

471. O'Callaghan, S. *The Yellow Slave Trade: A Survey of the Traffic in Women and Children in the East.* London: A. Blond, 1968.

472. Orme, N. "The Reformation and the Red Light." *History Today* 37 (March 1987):36-41.

Examines the attempt to eliminate prostitution during the Reformation, in contrast to the medieval practice of toleration and regulation.

473. Osborne, R. *Las prostitutas.* Barcelona: Dopesa 2, 1978.

474. O'Toole, M. *Off the Beat.* London: Hodder & Stoughton, 1970.

475. Palmer, R. *Quando l'amore è mestiere; la prostituzione e i suoi vari aspetti.* Bologna: G. Malipiero, 1966.

476. Pinto, M.J. *O problema de prostituição.* Porto: Imprensa Social, 1962.

477. "Prostitution in Some Nineteenth Century European Cities." *Bulletin of the New York Academy of Medicine* 53(1) (January-February 1977):154-5.

Excerpt from William Acton's 1857 publication entitled *Prostitution, Considered in its Moral, Social & Sanitary Aspects, in London and Other Large Cities: with Proposals for the Mitigation and Prevention of its Attendant Evils.* (London: J. Churchill, 1857).

478. Rasp, R. *Chinchilla; Leitfaden zur praktischen Ausübung.* Reinbek bei Hamburg: Rowohlt, 1973.

479. Roskolenko, H. *Loose Women Throughout the World: The Story of What the World's Oldest Profession Is Doing Today.* New York: L. Stuart, 1964.

480. Sacotte, M. *La prostitución.* 3 ed. Barcelona: Editorial Fontanella, 1969.

There is also a French edition, Paris: Buchat-Chartel, 1971.

481. Sampaoli, A. *La prostituzione nel pensiero del settecento.* Rimini: Cosmi, 1973.

482. Sanger, W.W. *The History of Prostitution: Its Extent, Causes, and Effects Throughout the World, with Numerous Editorial Notes and an Appendix.* New Edition. New York: AMS, 1974.

This is a reprint of an 1858 publication. Sanger was an advocate of legalized, tolerated and inspected prostitution.

483.   Schreiber, H.   *The Oldest Profession: A History of Prostitution.*
        Translated from the German by J. Cleugh. London: Barker, 1967.

484.   Schulte, R.   *Sperrbezirke: Tugendhaftigkeit und Prostitution in der
        bürgerlichen Welt.* Frankfurt am Main: Syndikat, 1979.

485.   Scott, G.R. *A History of Prostitution from Antiquity to the Present Day.*
        New York: AMS, 1976.

        This is a reprint of the 1936 book.

486.   Scott, G.R. *Ladies of Vice: A History of Prostitution from Antiquity to the
        Present Day.* Completely Revised Edition. London: Tallis P., 1968.

        A revision of Scott's 1936 book.

487.   Servais, J.J.   *Histoire et dossier de la prostitution.*   Paris: Éditions
        Planète, 1965.

488.   Simons, G.L. *A Place for Pleasure: The History of the Brothel.* Lewes:
        Harwood-Smart, 1975. Illustrated.

489.   Skousen, W.C. "Perennial Problem of Prostitution." *Law and Order*
        22(4) (April 1974):8-12.

        Reviews superficially the spread of prostitution and consequent
        suppressive legislation. Discusses sexual practices and prostitution in
        ancient societies and in prewar Europe and America. Argues that the
        incidence of sex crimes and venereal disease in the United States has
        decreased due to American post-war repressive policies.

490.   Sohel, H. von. *El peor pecado.* Translated by E. Farinas. Barcelona:
        Producciones Editoriales, 1972.

491.   Symanski, R. *The Immoral Landscape: Female Prostitution in Western
        Societies.* Toronto: Butterworth, 1981.

492. United Nations. *International Agreement for the Suppression of White Slave Traffic, Signed at Paris on 18 May 1904, Amended by Protocol Signed at Lake Success, New York, 4 May 1949.* Malta: Department of Information, 1968.

493. United Nations. *International Convention for the Suppression of White Slave Traffic, Signed at Paris on 4 May 1910, Amended by Protocol Signed at Lake Success, New York, 4 May 1949. Presented to the House of Representatives by the Minister of Commonwealth Foreign Affairs, March 1968.* Malta: Department of Information, 1968.

494. Villa, R. "La prostituzione come problema storiografico." ("Prostitution as a Historiographic Problem.") *Studi Storici* 22(2) (1981):305-14.

Exemplifies the nineteenth-century study of prostitution as marginalization and deviance. Finds that this type of study depicts the prostitute as a stigmatized, segregated individual without autonomy or means of protection.

495. Wells, J. *A Herstory of Prostitution in Western Europe.* Berkeley: Shameless Hussy, 1982.

496. Wiesner, M.E. "Making Ends Meet: The Working Poor in Early Modern Europe." *Pietas et Societas: New Trends in Reformation Social History: Essays in Memory of Harold J. Grimm.* Edited by K.C. Sessions and P.N. Bebb. Kirksville, MO: Sixteenth Century Journal Publishers, 1985, pp. 79-88.

ANCIENT

497. Brown, J.P. "The Role of Women and the Treaty in the Ancient World." *Biblische Zeitschrift* 25(1) (1981):1-28.

Discusses the role and status of women through the evolution of the city-state. Argues that in the age before the city-state the status of women was that of concubine. During the age of the city-state, the woman is either housewife or harlot. With the advent of the Roman Empire, however, the autonomous male ruling class of the city-state disappeared and the status of women was improved.

498.   Collins, O.E.   "The Stem znh and Prostitution in the Hebrew Bible."
       (Thesis)   University Microfilms, Brandeis University, 1977.

499.   Fauth, W.   *Sakrale Prostitution im Vordered Orient und im
       Mittelmerraum.*   Münster   Westfalen: Aschendorffsche
       Verlagsbuchhandlung, 1988.

500.   Fisher, E.J.   "Cultic Prostitution in the Ancient Near East: A
       Reassessment."   *Biblical Theology Bulletin* (June-October 1976).

       Challenges the translation of "cultic prostitution" from the Hebrew bible.
       Discusses related terms and usages also thought to be references to cult
       prostitutes in the Ancient Near East. Argues that the view of cultic
       prostitution is a result of biased accounts and therefore invalid.

501.   Gibson, J.   "Tax Collectors and Prostitutes in First Century Palestine;
       Matthew 21:31."   *Journal of Theological Studies* (October 1981).

502.   Halperin, D.M.   "The Democratic Body--Prostitution and Citizenship in
       Classical Athens."   *South Atlantic Quarterly* 88(1) (1989):149-60.

503.   Huonker, T.   "Civilization and Prostitution."   *Du; Die Zeitschrift der
       Kulturi* (4) (1988):26-51.

504.   Lerner, G.   "The Origins of Prostitution in Ancient Mesopotamia."   *Signs*
       11(2) (1986):236-54.

       Believes that by the middle of the first millennium B.C. two kinds of
       prostitution were being carried out in or near the temples: religious
       prostitution and commercial prostitution.

505.   McGinn, T.   "The Taxation of Roman Prostitutes."   *Helios* 16(1)
       (1989):79-110.

506.   Pomeroy, S.   *Goddesses, Whores, Wives, and Slaves: Women in Classical*

Antiquity. New York: Schoken, 1975.

This book makes a turning point in classical studies of women and prostitution. Written from a feminist perspective.

507. Rossi, A. *Donne, prostituzione e immoralità nel mondo greco e romano.* Rome: L. Lucarini, 1979.

508. Saffrey, H.D. "Aphrodite à Corinthe: réflexions sur une idée réçue." *Repertoire Bibliographique* (July 1985).

Discusses the role of the prostitute in both private and official prayers to the goddess Aphrodite. Refutes the theory that the temple of the goddess was a center for sacred prostitution.

509. Salles, C. *Les bas-fonds de l'antiquité.* Paris: R. Laffont, 1982.

510. Vandertown, K. "Female Prostitution in Payment of Vows in Ancient-Israel." *Journal of Biblical Literature* 108(2) (1989):193-205.

511. Westbrook, R. "The Enforcement of Morals in Mesopotamian Law." *Journal of the American Oriental Society* 104(4) (October-December 1984):753-756.

512. Yamauchi, E.W. "Cultic Prostitution." *Orient and Occident: Essays Presented to Cyrus H. Gordon on the Occasion of his Sixty-fifth Birthday.* Edited by H.A. Hoffner. Kevelaer: Butzon & Bercker; Neukirchen Vluyn: Neurkirchen Verlag, 1973, pp. 213-222.

MEDIEVAL

513. Brundage, J.A. *Law, Sex and Christian Society in Medieval Europe.* Chicago: University of Chicago Press, 1987.

As a general survey of prostitution and other sexual behavior in the whole Middle Ages, useful but not exhaustive; as an analysis of canon law, placing prostitution in the context of other illicit and licit sexual behavior, thorough and indispensable. Argues that current Western attitudes towards sex can be traced back to medieval law. Amplifies his 1976 article (below). Prostitution is not discussed in a separate section of the book but rather in a section within each chapter.

514.   Brundage, J.A.   "Prostitution in Medieval Canon Law." *Signs* 1(4) (1976):825-45. (Reprinted in *Sexual Practices and the Medieval Church*. Edited by V.L. Bullough and James Brundage. Buffalo: Prometheus, 1982, pp. 149-60. And in *Sisters and Workers in the Middle Ages*. Edited by J.M. Bennett, E.A. Clark, J.F. O'Barr, et al. Chicago: University of Chicago Press, 1989, pp. 79-99.)

As its reprinting indicates, this is a seminal article. Although Brundage's book (above) amplifies the material, the reader concerned mainly with prostitution will want to read this article as well, because the development of canon law on this one topic may be more clearly seen here. It should be noted that it deals with canon law theorists and not with the enforcement of the law in practice.

515.   Brundage, J.A.   "Prostitution in Medieval Canon Law--Reply." (Letter) *Signs* 2(4) (1977):923-4.

Responds to J. Russ's criticism by pointing out that he was talking about the way medieval canonists described prostitution, not the way he thought it ought to be defined. Acknowledges that modern legislation, treating prostitution as a subcategory of promiscuity rather than as a form of patriarchial exploitation, does have its roots in medieval views.

516.   Brundage, J.A.   "Sumptuary Laws and Prostitution in Late Medieval Italy." *Journal of Medieval History* 13(4) (1987):343-55.

Discusses legislation in fifteen Italian towns concerning female apparel. Some tried to preserve decency; some tried to identify prostitutes, either by prescribing particular colors for them or by exempting them from restrictions placed on "respectable" women. Lucidly discusses sociological reasons for imposition of these laws. Much of this material is also found in Brundage's book but is pulled together here in a useful way.

517.   Bullough, V.L.   "The Prostitute in the Middle Ages." *Studies in Medieval Culture* 19 (1977):9-17. (Reprinted, slightly revised, as "The

Prostitute in the Early Middle Ages." *Sexual Practices and the Medieval Church.* Edited by V.L. Bullough and J.A. Brundage. Buffalo: Prometheus, 1982, pp. 34-42.)

Discusses classical attitudes towards prostitution, the patristic reaction, and the church's efforts to promote repentance. The best starting point for study of medieval prostitution.

518.   Bullough, V.L.   "Prostitution in the Later Middle Ages." *Sexual Practices and the Medieval Church.* Edited by V.L. Bullough and J.A. Brundage. Buffalo: Prometheus, 1982, pp. 176-86.

Discusses responses of secular authorities to the growing problem of prostitution: segregating prostitutes in a separate district and special clothing. Collectively, this and Bullough's other articles and books in this volume provide the most useful, although not exhaustive, summary of the history of medieval prostitution.

519.   Burford, E.J.   *Bawds and Lodgings: A History of the London Bankside Brothels c. 100-1675.* London: Peter Owen, 1976.

Uncritical and voyeuristic. A lot of research went into this book and many references to original sources may be usefully followed up, but the interpretation of any source is unreliable.

520.   Burford, E.J.   *The Orrible Synne: A Look at London Lechery from Roman to Cromwellian Times.* London: Calder & Boyars, 1973.

As with Burford's other work, can be used as a source of references but should not be used as a source of facts.

521.   Dillard, H.   *Daughters of the Reconquest.*   Cambridge: Cambridge University Press, 1984.

Prostitutes made up a large percentage of the earliest female colonists in the reconquered areas of southern Spain. Laymen were encouraged to marry and convert them. Harsh penalties including the hot-iron procedure and violence from any passer-by made prostitutes transient. The prostitute often followed bands of "swindlers and roughnecks" who offered her protection as well as livelihood.

522.   Dufresne, J.-L. "Les comportements amoureux d'après le registre de
        l'officialité de Cerisy." *Bulletin philologique et historique* (1973):131-53.

        Based on French episcopal court records, discusses sexual behavior in
        several localities. He finds that the accusations of prostitution decrease
        with time and by the end of the fifteenth century there are no more cases
        of sedentary prostitution (brothels), only wandering prostitutes. Useful
        tables show numbers of accusations of different offenses in different
        localities.

523.   Ennen, E. *The Medieval Woman.* Translated by E. Jephcott. Oxford:
        Basil Blackwell, 1989.

        A short section of this book discusses prostitution, mainly in Germany,
        focusing on the regulation of prostitutes in Cologne by the executioner.
        Ennen also discusses attempts to "convert" prostitutes.

524.   Ferris, S. "'His Barge Ycleped was the Maudelayne': Canterbury Tales
        A 410." *Names* 31 (1983):207-10.

        Discusses the significance of the name of the ship in Chaucer's Shipman's
        Tale. The author suggests that the common name referred to a connection
        between the prostitute-saint and the sea and ironically reflects as much
        "nautical piety" as "nautical bawdiness."

525.   Flandrin, J.-L. "Repression and Change in the Sexual Life of Young
        People in Medieval and Early Modern Times." *Journal of Family History*
        2 (1977):196-210. (Reprinted in *Family and Sexuality in French History.*
        Edited by R. Wheaton and T.K. Hareven. Philadelphia: University of
        Pennsylvania Press, 1980, pp. 22-48.)

        Includes a brief discussion of prostitution and rape in French cities during
        the later Middle Ages, which owes much to the work of J. Rossiaud.
        Prostitution was mainly an urban tradition: in France during the sixteenth
        century every large town had a municipal brothel.

526.   Gaillard, R. *Sex-bizz: essai sur l'amour gris: la prostitution sexuelle à
        Genève (Suisse) vers la fin du deuxième millénaire (après J.C.).* Genève:
        Grounauer, 1981.

527. Geremek, B. *The Margins of Society in Late Medieval Paris.* Translated from the French by J. Birrell. Cambridge: Cambridge University Press, 1987. The original was in Polish. French ed. Paris: Flammarion, 1976.

Chapter 7, "The World of Prostitution," gives a full account, based on original documents, of Parisian prostitution. It concentrates on social distinctions among the various sorts of prostitutes and discusses the extent to which they can really be considered marginal.

528. Goldberg, P.J.P. "Women in Fifteenth-Century Town Life." *Towns and Townspeople in the Fifteenth Century.* Edited by J.A.F. Thompson. Glouchester: Alan Sutton, 1988, pp. 107-28.

Considers prostitution in late medieval England in the context of women's economic activity, and the ambivalent attitudes of the authorities towards prostitutes.

529. Graus, F. "Randgruppen der stadtischen Gesellschaft im Spätmittelalter." *Zeitschrift für historische Forschung* 8 (1981):385-437.

Discusses prostitution as paradigmatic of marginal groups in late medieval urban society.

530. Grohmann, A. "I marginali nella Perugia tardo-medievale (The Marginal in Late Medieval Perugia)." *Annali della Facoltà di scienza politiche: Materiali si Storia (Italy)* 17(5 part 1) (1980-81):231-48.

Examines three marginal groups in late medieval Perugian society: the destitute, the Jews, and the prostitutes.

531. Irsigler, F., and A. Lassotta. *Bettler und Gaukler, Dirnen und Henker: Randgruppen und Aussenseiter in Köln 1300-1600.* Köln: Greven, 1984.

Extensive discussion of prostitutes in Cologne, considering them as one of several marginal groups. Discusses how authorities treated prostitution as a lesser of several evils at a time when only a small percentage of the population had the opportunity to marry. Cologne did not have an official brothel until the 1520s, the time when other towns were closing theirs, but prostitution was nevertheless extensive.

532.   Jacquart, D., and C. Thomasser. *Sexuality and Medicine in the Middle
       Ages.* Translated by M. Adamson. Princeton: Princeton University Press,
       1988.

       Some attention to the sexuality of prostitutes. They were thought to be
       infertile and uninfected carriers of leprosy.

533.   Karras, R.M.   "Holy Harlots: Prostitute Saints in Medieval Legend."
       Journal of the History of Sexuality 1 (1990):3-32.

       Discusses the development in the medieval West of the legends of Mary
       Magdalen, Mary of Egypt, Mary the niece of Abraham, Thais, Pelagia,
       and Afra, and what these have to say about medieval attitudes towards
       female sexuality.

534.   Karras, R.M.   "The Regulation of Brothels in Later Medieval England."
       Signs: Journal of Women in Culture and Society 14 (1989):399-433.
       (Reprinted in *Sisters and Workers in the Middle Ages.* Edited by J.M.
       Bennet, E.A. Clark, J.F. O'Barr, et al. Chicago: University of Chicago
       Press, 1989, pp. 100-34.)

       Discusses the officially sanctioned brothels of Southwark and Sandwich
       and the less official houses of prostitution elsewhere. Includes a modern
       English translation of the brothel regulations.

535.   Kowalski, M.   "Women's Work in a Market Town: Exeter in Late
       Fourteenth Century." *Women and Work in Preindustrial Europe.* Edited
       by B. Hanawait. Bloomington: Indiana University Press, 1986, pp. 145-
       164.

       Considers working women including brothelkeepers and prostitutes.

536.   Labarge, M.W.   *A Small Sound of the Trumpet: Women in Medieval Life.*
       Boston: Beacon, 1986.

       Chapter 9, "Women on the Fringe," deals with prostitutes, heretics and
       witches. Prostitution is discussed on pp. 195-204: a good summary of the
       situation of prostitutes in later medieval towns.

537. Lawner, L. *Lives of the Courtesans: Portraits of the Renaissance.* New York: Rizzoli, 1987.

Discusses courtesans in particular using evidence from art as well as literature. Courtesans were among the few women of the period to enjoy a degree of autonomy and economic freedom. The book focuses more on the image of them created by men than on their own correspondence.

538. Leclercq, J. *Monks on Marriage.* New York: Seabury, 1982.

Discusses monastic use of the prostitutes as a metaphor for humankind's faithlessness in the Old and New Testament and in the patristic literature. The prostitute was given symbolic value in order to draw men and women to repentance or conversion.

539. Le Goff, J. "Licit and Illicit Trades in the Medieval West." *Time, Work and Culture in the Middle Ages.* Translated by A. Goldhammer. Chicago: University of Chicago Press, 1980, pp. 58-70.

Discusses prostitution among other illicit trades (e.g. ursury) and the extent to which legal theorists attempted to justify and legitimize them.

540. Lorcin, M.-T. "La prostituée des fabliaux, est-elle integrée ou exclue?" *Exclus et systèmes d'exclusion dans la littérature et la civilisation médiévales.* Senefiance, 5. Aix-en-Provence: Centre universitaire d'études et de recherches médiévales, 1978, pp. 105-18.

Argues that the prostitute in the fabliaux, although an important and accepted figure in that community, is excluded permanently from the integrating institution of the family.

541. Malvern, M.M. *Venus in Sackcloth: The Magdalen's Origins and Metamorphoses.* Carbondale: S. Illinois University Press, 1975.

Discusses Mary Magdalen as a Christian version of a pagan goddess, representing the erotic element within religion.

542. McCall, A. *The Medieval Underworld.* London: Hamish Hamilton, 1979.

Briefly discusses the stews of Southwark and compares them to continental
brothels; he finds the English ones to be more sober and utilitarian. Not
particularly useful.

543. Moore, R.I.   *The Formation of a Persecuting Society: Power and
      Deviance in Western Europe, 950-1250.* New York: Basil Blackwell,
      1987.

      Argues that the increasing concern with prostitution in the Middle Ages,
      like that with the Jews, reflected a concern that money was in the process
      of dissolving traditional personal ties.

544. Otis, L.L.   "Prostitution and Repentance in Late Medieval Perpignan."
      Women of the Medieval World. Edited by J. Kirshner and S. Wemple.
      Oxford: Basil Blackwell, 1985, pp. 137-60.

      Describes the regulation and organization of prostitution in Perpignan and
      its relation to institutions of penance. Perpignan had an established and
      carefully fortified red-light district. Houses of Repentance were first
      established in the 1320s. These convents served as refuge for retired
      prostitutes and half-way houses for young prostitutes anxious to re-enter
      respectable society.

545. Otis, L.L.   *Prostitution in Medieval Society: The History of an Urban
      Institution in Languedoc.* An adaption of the author's thesis, Columbia
      University, 1980. Chicago: University of Chicago Press, 1985.

      A detailed and scholarly study of the regulation, institutionalization and
      finally closing of the brothels in the towns of the South of France.
      Suggests that municipal control arose out of concern for problems of
      public order, and that a general reaction to sexual laxity, not the
      Reformation in particular, led to the closure of the houses.

546. Otis, L.L.   "Nisi in Postribulo: Prostitution in Languedoc from the
      Twelfth to the Sixteenth Century." (Thesis) Columbia University, 1980.
      Also listed *DAI* 43(12) (1983):4064-A.

547. Pavan, E.   "Police des moeurs, societé et politique à Venise à la fin du
      Moyen Âge (Public Control of Morals, Society, and Politics in Venice at

the End of the Middle Ages)." *Revue Historique* (France) 264(2) (1980):241-88.

Discusses the public brothel opened in Venice in 1358, as an example of the concern with public order in the period. By the fifteenth- and sixteenth- centuries, prostitutes were diffused throughout the town, and there were relatively fluid boundaries between domestic service and prostitution. The second half of the article is devoted to homosexuality rather than prostitution.

548. Porteau-Bitker, A. "Criminalité et délinquance féminines dans le droit pénal des XIIIe et XIVe siècles." *Revue historique de droit français et étranger* 58 (1989):13-56.

Discusses which criminal offenses women committed and why. These tended to be crimes of passion, religious crimes, or moral offenses like prostitution or adultery. Prostitutes were not systematically prosecuted although there are some cases of banishment; usually they had a regular fee to pay, had to wear distinctive clothing, and could only live in certain parts of the towns. Draws on French custumals and court registers as evidence.

549. Post, J.B. "A Fifteenth-Century Customary of the Southwark Stews." *Journal of the Society of Archivists* (1977):418-28.

An edition of the regulations for the stews or brothels in the library of the Bishop of Winchester, Southwark. A modernized version based on Post's edition is found in Karras's article. See entry number 534.

550. Powers, J.F. "Frontier Municipal Baths and Social Interaction in Thirteenth Century Spain." *American Historical Review* 84 (1979):649-67.

Rape and other abuses of women, even verbal abuse became capital crimes within the walls of the bathhouses. Any woman present at the baths on days assigned to men, however, had her legal status reduced to that of a prostitute, who could be "abused with impunity" for men were subject to fines if they interfered in order to protect a prostitute.

551. Ratcliffe, M. "Adultresses, Mistresses and Prostitutes--Extramarital

Relationships in Medieval Castile." *Hispania--A Journal Devoted to the Teaching of Spanish and Portuguese* 67(3) (1984):346-50.

552. Roper, L. "Discipline and Respectability: Prostitution and the Reformation in Augsburg." *History Workshop* (1985):3-28.

Although the article's focus is on the effect of the Reformation on prostitutes, Roper describes in detail the situation in Augsburg (and other German towns) in the pre-Reformation period. Brothels were seen as meeting communal needs, but the understanding of who composed the "commune" was male defined.

553. Roper, L. *The Holy Household: Women and Morals in Reformation Augsburg.* Oxford: Clarendon, 1989.

Chapter 3 (pp. 89-131) deals with prostitution and basically combines material from Roper's two articles listed here.

554. Roper, L. "Mothers of Debauchery: Procuresses in Reformation Augsburg." *German History* 6 (1988):1-19. Originally appeared in *Memoria: Rivista di Storia delle Donne* 17(2) (1986):7-23.

Discusses the procuress or go-between in early modern Augsburg. As opposed to offical brothels which were run by men, the illicit trade was controlled by women. The system of procuresses became a way to blame women for the trade.

555. Rossiaud, J. *Medieval Prostitution.* Translated by L.G. Cochrane. Oxford: Basil Blackwell, 1988. (*La prostituzione nel medioevo.* Roma: Laterza, 1984.)

An expansion of the below articles. Focuses mainly on Dijon but includes material from elsewhere. Discusses marriage patterns and the role of young unmarried men in sexual violence; who became prostitutes and why; the influence of a general understanding of "nature" on attitudes towards prostitution; and the impact of preaching on its decline. Draws on a wealth of original documents, such as depositions, which give a real picture of what the life of a prostitute was like; some of them are translated as an appendix.

556. Rossiaud, J. "Prostitution, Sex and Society in French Towns in the Fifteenth Century." *Western Sexuality: Practice and Precept in Past and Present Times.* Edited by P. Aries and A. Bejin. Oxford: Blackwell, 1985, pp. 76-94.

Similar to the article mentioned in entry number 555.

557. Rossiaud, J. "Prostitution, Youth and Society in Towns of South Eastern France in the Fifteenth Century." *Annales, économies, sociétés, civilisations* 31(2) (1976):289-325. *Deviants and the Abandoned in French Society.* Edited by R. Forster and O. Ranum. Translated by E. Forster. Baltimore: Johns Hopkins University Press, 1978, pp. 1-46.

Places prostitution in the context not just of the moral order but also of the economy and demography of the towns of the Rhone valley. He places prostitution within the "sexual economy" of the town of Dijon, discussing in particular sexual violence.

558. Ruggiero, G. *The Boundaries of Eros: Sex Crimes and Sexuality in Renaissance Venice.* New York: Oxford University Press, 1985.

Argues that prostitution does not fit neatly within the definition of sex crimes as it both supported and undermined the dominant culture. It eased the customary postponing of marriage by providing a sexual outlet for young men that did not threaten wives and daughters of the city, yet this undermined traditional marriage-centered sexual morality. Ruggiero suggests that prostitution incorporated poor young women not eligible for marriage into greater social and economic life of the city.

559. Russ, J. "Comment on 'Prostitution in Medieval Canon Law' by James Brundage." (Letter) *Signs* 2(4) (1977):922-3.

Responds to Brundage's article. Criticizes Brundage for falling into the patriarchal view that prostitution is a subcategory of female promiscuity. Argues that, in a feminist view, even marriage is a form of prostitution, and that feminist analysis shows why patriarchal sexual morality distinguishes between the two (the promiscuous woman is not the property of the particular man).

560. Salisbury, J.E. *Medieval Sexuality: A Research Guide.* New York:

Garland, 1990.

Extremely useful annotated bibliography, more thorough for secondary than for primary sources. Works dealing mainly with prostitution are also found here, but a few additional ones that deal with it peripherally may be found in Salisbury's bibliography. Index is not complete; to be sure of finding everything, one must skim the whole bibliography (815 entries).

561.   Sargent, A.M.   "The Penitent Prostitute. The Tradition and Evolution of the Life of St. Mary the Egyptian."   University of Michigan, 1977.

A detailed study of the legend which does not focus particularly on the prostitute aspect.

562.   Scherer, R.   "Das System der chinesischen Prostitution: dargestellt am Beispiel Shanghais in der Zeit von 1840 bis 1949."   (Thesis) Frei Universität Berlin, 1983.

563.   Shahar, S.   *The Fourth Estate: A History of Women in the Middle Ages.* New York: Methuen, 1983.

Briefly discusses prostitutes on pp. 205-10. Unlike many other works which treat prostitution under the general theme of marginality, Shahar treats it under the general theme of townswomen and their occupations.

564.   Terroine, A.   "Le roi de ribauds de l'Hôtel du Roi: les prostituées parisiennes."   *Revue historique de droit* 56 (1978):253-67.

The King of the Ribalds was a royal official from 1214 to 1449 in charge of exercising control over the prostitutes of Paris. Other towns and noble households had similar officials. The article is accompanied by original documents.

565.   Trexler, R.   "La prostitution florentine au XVe siècle: patronages et clientèles."   *Annales E.S.C.* 36 (1981):983-1015.

Investigates who was employed at, and who patronized, the licensed Florentine brothels in the fifteenth century, and the functions the brothels served for the town: avoiding the greater evils of homosexuality and declining birthrate. Most of the prostitutes were foreigners; the customers were also mostly outsiders, petty tradespeople, and day laborers. By the sixteenth century public attitudes turned against the brothels.

566. Trexler, R. "Prostitution Networks in Quattrocento Florence." (French) *Annales* 36(6) (1981):931-1015.

Demonstrates that the Office of Decency did protect prostitutes from their clients and also settled suits between them. Places prostitutes within their larger setting of problems facing women at that time.

567. Ward, B. *Harlots of the Desert: A Study of Repentance in Early Monastic Sources*. Kalamazoo, MI: Cistercian, 1987.

568. Wildenberg-De Kroon, C.E.C.M. van den. *Das Weltleben und die Bekehrung der Maria Magdalena im deutschen religiösen Drama und in der bildenden Kunst des Mittelalters*. Amsterdam Publikationen zur Sprache und Literatur, 39. Amsterdam: Rodopi, 1979.

Discusses the life of Mary Magdalen before her conversion as it appeared in medieval drama and art; disagrees with Emile Male's thesis that the iconography derived from the drama. Includes consideration of how art and literature represented the Magdalen's sexual dissoluteness. English summary at the end of the book.

569. Wunderli, R.M. *London Church Courts and Society on the Eve of the Reformation*. Cambridge, MA: Medieval Academy of America, 1981.

Deals with the ecclesiastical legal system in late medieval London, based on extensive archival research in court records. Prostitution and procuring (pp. 92-101) were important among the sexual offences these courts dealt with; defamation, including accusations of prostitution (pp. 76-80), also formed an important part of their business.

HISTORY BY AREA FOR EARLY MODERN AND MODERN PERIOD

AFRICA

570.   Bujra, J.M.   "Women Entrepreneurs of Early Nairobi."   *Canadian Journal of African Studies* 9(2) (1975):213-34.

Interviews of 127 landlords, 72 of whom were women, found that most of them had been prostitutes. This enabled them to gain income enough to gain an unusual measure of equality with men.

571.   Hay, M.J.   "Queens, Prostitutes, and Peasants--Historical Perspectives on African Women, 1971-1986."   *Canadian Journal of African Studies-- Revue Canadienne des Études Africaines* 22(3) (1988):431-47.

572.   Entry omitted.

573.   Vanheyningen, E.B.   "The Social Evil in the Cape Colony 1868-1902: Prostitution and the Contagious Diseases Act."   *Journal of Southern African Studies* 10(2) (1984):170-197.

The enactment of the first contagious disease act in 1868 was ignored. Fear of a growing syphilis epidemic led to the enactment of a second act in 1885 which was enforced. The result was riot against the enforcement by the prostitutes. Continued growth of prostitution, enforced by appearance or growing number of foreign prostitutes, led to growth of social purity movement which won passage of anti-prostitution measures in the Morality Act of 1902.

574.   White, L.   *The Comforts of Home: Prostitution in Colonial Nairobi.* Chicago: University of Chicago Press, 1990.

575.   White, L.   "Prostitutes, Reformers, and Historians."   *Criminal Justice History* 6 (1985):201-27.

Discusses the functional origins of prostitution in Nairobi, Kenya, and the

United States. Questions the moralistic approach to the reform or study of prostitution. Emphasizes that important economic contributions by prostitutes to their families have been ignored. Treats prostitution as a solution to an economic problem as opposed to a creation of a social problem.

576.   White, L. "Prostitution, Identity, and Class Consciousness in Nairobi During World War II." *Signs* 11(2) (1986):255-73.

Describes prostitution in prewar Nairobi as a form of domestic labor. Discusses the evolution of prostitution from a means of survival to an occupation for profit during the changing conditions of the war.

577.   White, L. *Women's Domestic Labor in Colonial Kenya.* (Working Paper) Brookline, MA: African Studies Center, Boston University, 1980.

ASIA

China

578.   Gronewold, S. "Beautiful Merchandise: Prostitution in China: 1860-1936." *Women & History* 1 (Spring, 1982):1-114.

Offers a historical interpretation of prostitution in China. Outlines the decline of the industry from the mid-nineteenth- to twentieth-century, including the loss of status and the increase of disease and violence against prostitutes. Discusses the dichotomy between the desire for real reform and the desire for profit.

579.   Hershatter, G. "The Hierarchy of Shanghai Prostitution, 1870-1949." *Modern China* 15(4) (1989):463-98.

Examines prostitution in Shanghai in terms of its hierarchial structure, degree of control prostitutes had over their working conditions, and the efforts of prostitutes to move on to other work.

580.   Hirata, L.C. *Free, Enslaved, and Indentured Workers in Nineteenth Century America: the Case of Chinese Prostitution.* (Association paper)

UCLA: International Sociological Association, 1978.

Examines prostitution as an integral part in the development of capitalism. Discusses the economic and social function of the Chinese prostitute in both capitalist America and feudal China. Analyzes the exploitation of these prostitutes in nineteenth-century America.

581.   Jaschok, M. *Concubines and Bondservants: A Social History.* London; Atlantic Highlands, NJ: Zed, 1988.

History of prostitutes and concubinage in China.

582.   Kani, H. "Shinmatsu No 'Choka' Karamita Chugoku No Sakoku" (The Seclusion of China as Seen through Zhufa in the Late Qing Dynasty). *Shicho* (Japan) (15) (1984):46-64.

Discusses early emigration from China to French and British territories overseas. Due to social traditions, women were not allowed to leave China. This resulted in a low ratio of women to men in Chinese overseas settlements. As compensation, some Chinese women (zhufa) were sent over with no legal protection for immoral purposes.

India, Malaysia, and the Philippines

583.   Ballhatchet, K. *Race, Sex, and Class under the Raj: Imperial Attitudes and Policies and Their Critics, 1793-1905.* London: Weidenfeld and Nicolson, 1980.

The first half of the book is a detailed examination of the system of more or less state-regulated prostitution maintained by the British in their military catonments and to a lesser extent in the port cities. Also surveys attitudes to race, sex, and class as it pertains to the regulation of prostitution.

584.   Edwards, S.M. *Crime in British India: A Brief Review of the More Important Offences Included in the Annual Criminal Returns with Chapters on Prostitution and Miscellaneous Matter.* London; New York: Oxford University Press, 1924. Reprint. New Delhi: ABC Publishing, 1983.

Covers major criminal offences common in India in the early part of the twentieth century. The fourth chapter deals briefly with the historical and religious aspects of prostitution in India.

585. Grjebine, L., ed. *Reporting on Prostitution: The Media, Women, and Prostitution in India, Malaysia, and the Philippines.* Paris: UNESCO, 1987.

586. Joardar, B. *Prostitution in Nineteenth- and Early Twentieth-Century Calcutta.* New Delhi: Inter-India Publications, 1985.

587. Madras (State), Office of the Chief Inspector of Approved Schools and Vigilance Service. *Administration Report on the Working of the Suppression of Immoral Traffic in Women and Girls Act, 1956.* Madras, 1962.

588. Mathur, A.S., and B.L. Gupta. *Prostitutes and Prostitution.* Agra: Ram Prasad: 1965.

589. Pivar, D.J. "The Military, Prostitution, and Colonial Peoples: India and the Philippines, 1885-1917." *Journal of Sex Research* 17(3) (August 1981): 256-69.

Follows the transition during the period from 1885 to 1917 of British moral reform from antiprostitution agitation to a movement for social purification. After forcing the repeal of the Contagious Diseases Acts, which regulated prostitution in England, these reformers attempted the same reforms in the British colonies. Parallels this effort with the American effort in the Philippines. Discusses the role of antivice reforms in early "modernization" in India and in the Philippines.

Japan

590. De Becker, J.E. *The Nightless City; The History of the Yoshiwara.* Reprinted Rutland, VT: Tuttle, 1971.

This is reprint of a 1905 edition. Title varies with edition. It is an account of the brothel quarter of Tokyo which flourished from 1617 to 1958.

591.   Fitzpatrick, W. *Tokyo After Dark*. New York: Macfadden-Bartell, 1966.

Includes a chapter devoted to the history of the Yoshiwara district.

592.   Longstreet, S., and E. Longstreet. *Yoshiwara: The Pleasure Quarters of Old Tokyo*. Tokyo: Yen Books (Charles E. Tuttle), 1988. Originally published 1970.

A popular history.

593.   Wheat, L. *How the "Social Evil" Is Regulated in Japan*. (Microfilm) History of Women, no. 9873. New Haven, CT: Research Publications, Inc., 1977.

Comments on three types of prostitution in nineteenth-century Japan: the Jigoku (unlicensed women), the Shogi (licensed prostitutes), and the Geisha (professional singers and dancers). Includes excerpts from various narratives which describe prostitution in Japan during that time.

Singapore

594.   Lee, Y.K. "Prostitution and Venereal Disease in Early Singapore (1819-1889)--Part I." *Singapore Medical Journal* 21(5) (October 1980):720-31.

595.   Lee, Y.K. "Prostitution and Venereal Disease in Early Singapore (1819-1889)--Part II." *Singapore Medical Journal* 21(6) (December 1980):781-90.

Thailand

596.   Khin Thitsa. *Providence and Prostitution: Image and Reality for Women in Buddhist Thailand*. London: Change International Reports, 1980.

Includes a discussion of prostitution.

Vietnam

597.   Marnais, P. *Saigon After Dark*. (Microfilm) New York: MacFadden-

Bartell, 1967.

AUSTRALIA

598. Daniels, K., ed. *So Much Hard Work: Women and Prostitution in Australian History.* Sydney: Fontana: Collins, 1984.

599. McConville, C. "The Location of Melbourne's Prostitutes, 1870-1920." *Historical Studies* (Australia) 19(74) (1980):86-97.

Surveys prostitution in Melbourne. Finds that the center of activity was initially concentrated around Exhibition Street and Lonsdale Street. Slum clearance and increased policing forced the prostitutes to the suburbs of Carlton and FitzRoy. Discusses the relation of prostitution to crime, vice, and poverty as attributed during that time period.

600. Sissons, D.C.S. "Karayuki San: Japanese Prostitutes in Australia, 1887-1916." *Historical Studies* (Australia) 17(68) (1977):474-88.

Traces the origins, ages, immigration, importation, residences, and economic success of Japanese prostitutes in Australia. Suggests that Japanese prostitutes preceded traders and laborers, in contrast to the belief that pearlers and others were established first.

EUROPE

Austria

601. Oberzill, G.H. *Die bewussten Demoiselles: Glanz und Elend der leichten Mädchen in alter Zeit.* Vienna: Jugend und Volk, 1984.

History of prostitution in Austria.

Belgium

602. Schaepdrijver, S. de. "Regulated Prostitution in Brussels, 1844-1877: A

Policy and Its Implementation." *Historical Social Research* (37) (1986):89-108.

Profiles the city of Brussels as a classic example of nineteenth-century European regulation of commercial sex. Traces the history of the closed system of prostitution, describes daily reality, and the people involved. Concludes that the policy never lived up to its promise.

Denmark

603.   Jensen, J., et al. *Sociale Studier: Kriminalitet, Prostitution og Fattigdom i Århus ca. 1870-1906*. Århus: Universitetsforlaget, 1975.

604.   Matthiessen, H. *De kagstrøgne; et blad af prostitutionens historie i Danmark*. København: Gyldendal, 1964.

605.   Stevnsborg, H. "Aims and Methods of the Official Campaign Against Prostitution in Copenhagen, 1769-1780." *Scandinavian Journal of History* 6(3) (1981):207-227.

Describes the Danish government's attempts in the eighteenth-century to suppress prostitution through revisions of its policies. The revisions were influenced by the needs of the labor market, and the government attempted to force prostitutes into doing more productive work.

606.   Stevnsborg, H.   "Community Law and State Law: Laws and Their Enforcement in Copenhagen in Cases of Prostitution at the End of the 17th and the Beginning of the 18th Centuries." (Danish) *Historisk Tidsskrift* 82(1) (1982):1-26.

France

607.   Barbara. *La partagée*. Racontée à Christine de Coninck. Paris: Éditions de Minuit, 1977.

608.   Benabou, E. *La prostitution et la police des moeurs au XVIIIe siècle*. Paris: Librairie Académique Perrin, 1987.

Police and the control of prostitution in eighteenth-century France.

609. Bertaud, J.P. "The Sans-Culottes and the Prostitutes." (French) *Histoire* 48 (1982):88-9.

610. Boudard, A. *La fermeture: 13 avril 1946, la fin des maisons closes.* Paris: R. Laffont, 1986.

The closing of the tolerated houses of prostitution.

611. Briais, B. *Grandes courtisanes du second empire.* Paris: J. Tallandier, 1981.

612. Coffin, J. "Artisans of the Sidewalk." *Radical History Review* (26) (1982):88-101.

Reviews A. Corbin's *Les filles de noce: misère sexuelle et prostitution: 19e et 20e siècles* (1978), which notes the significant changes in prostitution in France as a business and as a form of sexuality between 1870 and 1914. Finds that Corbin overlooks the domination of men, the oppression of women, and the general sexual politics of prostitution.

613. Conner, S.P. "Politics, Prostitution, and the Pox in Revolutionary Paris, 1789-1799." *Journal of Social History* 22(4) (Summer 1989):713-34.

Explores various factors contributing to prostitution, including urban mobility, low wages, clientele availability, the official attack on begging, and the Estates-General's attempt to stamp out vices linked to the Ancien Regime. Discusses the emergence of a subculture of prostitutes with no other occupation as a consequence of worsening economic conditions and increasing repression.

614. Conner, S.P. "Prostitution and the Jacobin Agenda for Social Control (Revolutionary Paris during Year 2 for Poor Women)." *Eighteenth Century Life* 12(1) (1988):42-51.

615. Corbin, A. "Commercial Sexuality in Nineteenth Century France: A

System of Images and Regulations." *Representations* (14) (1986):209-19.

Discusses the complex system for the regulation of prostitutes in France during the nineteenth century. Describes this system as arising out of the social conventions of French society in addition to pragmatic health and safety concerns. See entry number 612.

616.   Corbin, A. *Les filles de noce: misère sexuelle et prostitution: 19e et 20e siècles.* Paris: Aubier Montaigne, 1978, and also Flammarion, 1982.

617.   Corbin, A. "Nineteenth Century Prostitutes and the 'Great Effort for Nothingness'." *Dénatalité: l'antériorité française (1800-1914).* Edited by Centre d'Études Transdisciplinaires, École des Hautes Études en Sciences Sociales. Paris: Seuil, 1986:259-75.

618.   Corbin, A. *Women for Hire: Prostitution and Sexuality in France after 1850.* Translated by A. Sheridan. Cambridge, MA: Harvard University Press, 1990.

619.   Davray, F. *Les maisons closes.* Paris: Pygmallion, 1980.

620.   Dawson, N.M. "The Filles-Du-Roy Sent to New France: Protestant, Prostitute, or Both." *Historical Reflections--Réflexions Historiques* 16(1) (1989):55-77.

621.   Grimmer, C. *La femme et le bâtard: amours illégitimes et secrètes dans l'ancienne France.* Paris: Presses de la Renaissance, 1983.

622.   Harsin, S.J. "Crime, Poverty and Prostitution in Paris, 1815-1848." (Ph.D. Dissertation) University of Iowa, 1981.

Examines the urban setting of the criminal poor by looking at prostitutes in Paris during the first half of the nineteenth-century. Studies the effects of government regulation on the lives of this group.

623.   Harsin, S.J.   *Policing   Prostitution   in   Nineteenth   Century   Paris.*

Princeton, NJ: Princeton University Press, 1985.

624. Jamet, F. *One Two Two (122 Rue de Provence)*. Paris: O. Orban, 1975. Translated into English as *Palace of Sweet Sin* by D. Coltman. London: W. H. Allen, 1977.

625. Jones, C. "Prostitution and the Ruling Class in Eighteenth Century Montpellier." *History Workshop Journal* 6 (1978):7-28.

Examines the records of the Bon Pasteur founded in 1698 to reform prostitutes. Its founders viewed prostitution as a social aberration and the institution emphasized vocational education in order to reintegrate prostitution into society.

626. Kunstle, M. *Notre Dame des esclandres*. Paris: Presses de la Cité, 1973.

627. Lefontenay, P. *Sex Slaves Underground*. Translated by M. Duprez. Los Angeles: Medco, 1967.

628. Matlock, J.A. "Scenes of Seduction: Prostitution, Hysteria, and Reading Difference in Nineteenth Century France." (Thesis) University of California, Berkeley, Comparative Literature, May 1988.

629. Parent-Duchâtelet, A.J.B. *La prostitution à Paris au XIXe siècle*. Paris: Seuil, 1981.

This a reprint of the classic studies of Parent-Duchâtelet.

630. Richard, G. *Histoire de l'amour en France: du Moyen Âge à la Belle Époque*. Paris: J.C. Lattes, 1985.

631. Richardson, J. *The Courtesans: The Demi-monde in Nineteenth Century France*. Cleveland: World Pub., 1967.

632. Riley, P.F. "Women and Police in Louis XIV's Paris." *Eighteenth-Century Life* 4(2) (1977):37-42.

Relates the difficulties encountered by Louis XIV and the Paris police in their attempt to rid Paris of prostitution between 1667 and 1715. By 1753, the police abandoned the policy of locking up prostitutes in workhouses and agreed to the establishment of regulated houses of prostitution.

633.   Rolland, M., ed. *La Rouquine*. Paris: Balland, 1976.

634.   Ronsin, F. "Les 'Prostitutées' de Rambervellers" (The 'Prostitutes' of Rambervillers). *Revue d'Histoire Moderne et Contemporaine* 34 (January-March 1987):138-53.

Attempts to explain the higher percentage of prostitutes in the population of Rambervillers. Finds no known causal factor for this concentration.

635.   Sonia. *Respectueusement votre*. Paris: Presses de la Cité, 1976.

636.   Termeau, J. "Nineteenth Century Brothel-Keepers in the French Provinces." *Annales de Bretagne et des pays de l'ouest* 94(2) (1987):199-222.

637.   Tricoire, J. *Libertinage et prostitution à Versailles dans le second moitié du XVIIIe siècle, 1747-1781*. Paris: [s.n.], 1973; (Microfiche) Paris: Hachette, 1976.

638.   Weston, E.A. "Prostitution in Paris in the Later Nineteenth Century: A Political and Social Ideology." (Thesis) State University of New York, Buffalo, 1979. *DAI* 40(4) (1979):2217-A.

Germany

639.   Bergmann, K., ed. *Schwarze Reportagen: aus dem Leben der untersten Schichten vor 1914: Huren, Vagabunden, Lumpen*. Hamburg: Rowohlt, 1984.

640.   Evans, R.J. "Prostitution, State, and Society in Imperial Germany." *Past and Present* (Great Britain) (70) (1976):106-129.

Discusses aspects of prostitution in Imperial Germany, including its control before 1871, government debates and public opinion, the social origins and characteristics of prostitutes, and the eventual decline after 1850, when prostitution was first considered widespead and endemic. Most prostitutes were daughters of factory workers or of artisans in declining trade and failed to get steady employment. Their plight mirrored the low demand and low pay for female workers.

641. Konieczka, V. *Prostitution im 19. Jahrhundert.* Frankfurt: R.G. Fischer, 1980.

642. Lockenstösser, M. *Die Erinnerungen der Maria Lockenstösser, von ihr aufgezeichnet.* Der Öffentlichkeit übergeben von Carl Borro Schwerla. München: K. Desch, 1972.

643. Neu, H. *Die ehemalige Arbeitsanstalt in Pützchen: ein Kapitel aus der Geschichte Beuels und der Bemühung um soziale Fürsorge um die Mitte des 19 Jahrhunderts.* Beuel: Stadtverwaltung, 1969.

Prostitution in Beuel in the nineteenth-century.

644. Seidler, F.W. *Prostitution, Homosexualität, Selbstverstümmelung. Probleme der deutschen Sanitätsführung 1939-1945.* Neckargemünd: Vowinkel, 1977.

645. Walser, K. "Prostitutionsverdacht und Geschlechterforschung: Das Beispiel der Dienstmadchen um 1900" (Prostitution Suspicion and Sex Research around 1900: The Example of the Serving Girl). *Geschichte und Gesellschaft* (West Germany) 11(1) (1985):99-111.

Shows that sex research at the turn of the century Germany asserted that serving girls tended to become prostitutes. Finds that this belief stemmed from the general conception of women who moved to the city to lead single independent lives during the industrialization and urbanization of Germany. These women were stigmatized as immoral and a threat to middle class family life.

646. Wiesner, M.E. "Paternalism in Practice: The Control of Servants and

Prostitutes in Early Modern German Cities." *The Process of Change in Early Modern Europe: Essays in Honor of Miriam Usher Chrisman.* Edited by P.N. Bebb and S. Marshal. Athens, OH: Ohio University Press, 1988, pp. 179-200.

Hungary

647. Dorin, R., P. Miroiu, and R. Popesco. "Une méthode à combattre la prostitution: la fresque des XVIIIe et XIXe siècles." *International Congress of the History of Medicine,* No. 24, Budapest, 1974. Budapest: 1976, pp. 917-23.

648. Renzo, V. Prostitution as a Problem of Historical Science. (Hungarian) *Vilagtortenet* 1(1982):119-30.

Argues that reliable historical information on the suppression of prostitution is scarce because police reports, medical sources, and contemporary literature are all highly colored by the prejudices of the observers.

Italy

649. Augias, C., M. Falzone del Barbaro, and M. Antonetto, eds. *Quelle Signorine.* Milano: Longanesi, 1980.

650. Carrà, E. *La prostituzione a Piacenza nell'età di Maria Luigia, 1814-1837.* S. Bonico, Piacenza: Tipolitografia Tip. Le. Co., 1982.

651. Cohen, S. "*The Convertite and the Malmaritate: Women's Institutions, Prostitution, and the Family in Counter-Reformation Florence.*" (Thesis) Princeton University, 1985.

652. Cutrera, A. *I ricottari: la mala vita di Palermo.* Palermo: Il vespro, 1979.

Concerns prostitution and crime in Palermo, Italy.

653. Gibson, M.S. *Prostitution and the State in Italy, 1860-1915.* New Bruswick, NJ: Rutgers University Press, 1986.

654. Gibson, M.S. *State and Prostitution: Prohibition, Regulation, or Decriminalization?* Rockville, MD: National Criminal Justice Reference Service Microfiche Program, 1979. Historical Approaches to Studying Crime, Workshop Papers, 1979.

Examines nature and implications of the policies of prohibition, regulation, and decriminalization of prostitution citing examples from nineteenth-century Italy.

655. Gibson, M.S. "Urban Prostitution in Italy, 1860-1915: An Experiment in Social Control." (Ph.D. Dissertation) Indiana University, 1979.

Using police and health official records, abolitionist tracts, and nineteenth century monographs, examines the conflict between the Italian government's policy of control of prostitution from 1860 through 1915 and the British and American "abolitionist" policy. The Italian policy included registration, biweekly health examinations, and hospital visits and was regarded by abolitionists as a policy sanctioning prostitution. Discusses the legal, administrative, and social aspects of the control policy and analyzes the relationship between Italian feminists and prostitutes.

656. Greco, G. *Lo scienziato e la prostituta: due secoli di studi sulla prostituzione.* Bari: Dedalo, 1987.

657. Larivaille, P. "How to Succeed in Prostitution . . . in Sixteenth Century Rome." (French) *Historia* 399 (1980):66-73.

658. Larivaille, P. *La vie quotidienne des courtisanes en Italie au temps de la Renaissance (Rome et Venise, XVe et XVIe siècles).* Paris: Hachette, 1975.

659. Salles, C. "The Prostitutes of Rome." (French) *Histoire* 90 (1986):6-13.

660. *Tariffa dell puttane di Venegia, accompagné d'un catalogue des*

principales courtisanes de Venise, tiré des archives vénitiennes (XVIe siècle) et traduit pour la première fois en français. Paris: Bibliothèque des curieux, 1911.

A schedule of Venetian prostitutes' fees in Italian text with French translation. Included here simply because it is one of the earliest surviving records.

661.   Villa, R. "The Process of Criminalization of Prostitution in the 19th Century." (Italian) *Movimento operaio e socialista* 4(3) (1981):269-285.

Netherlands

662.   Altink, S. *Huizen van illusies: bordelen en prostitutie van Middeleeuwen to heden.* Utrecht: Veen, 1983.

History of prostitution in the Netherlands.

663.   *'t Amsterdamsch hoerdom: behelzende de listen en streeken, daar zich de hoeren en hoere-waardinnen van dienen; benevens der zelver maniere van leeven, gebruik is.* Amsterdam: De Vries-Brouwers, 1976.

History of prostitution in Amsterdam.

664.   Huitzing, A.M.I. "Prostitutie in Leiden in de Tweede Helft Van de 19de Eeuw (Prostitution in Leiden in the Second Half of the Nineteenth Century)." *Spiegel Historiael* (Netherlands) 17(9) (1982):431-7.

Investigates the relationship between cultural milieu, personal history, the conditions and lifestyles of prostitutes in Leiden in the later nineteenth century. Follows the transition from prostitution as a means of eliminating economic hardship to prostitution stemming from a criminal underground.

665.   Stemvers, F.A. "Prostitutie, Prostituées en Geneeskunde in Nederland 1850-1900 (Prostitution, Prostitutes and Medicine in the Netherlands, 1850-1900)." *Spiegel Historiael* (Netherlands) 18(6) (1983):316-23.

Discusses social agitation over the issue of prostitution in the second half of the nineteenth century. Indicates causes of prostitution to be poverty and great economic inequities. Finds prostitutes to have a greater immunity to epidemic diseases and life expectancy equal to that of the general population.

666. Stemvers, F.A. "Geschachtsziektenbestrijding 1850-80" (Struggle Against Venereal Diseases, 1850-80). (Dutch) *Tijdschrift voor de Geschiendenis der Geneeskunde* 4(l) (1981):1-24.

Struggle against venereal disease in the nineteenth century focused on attempts to control prostitution including medical inspection. Legislation, however, was left to municipal authorities. Problem with legislation was that the definition of who was a prostitute was ambiguous, many prostitutes went underground, medical science was not yet able to diagnose VD beyond doubt, vigorous enforcement was costly, potential for corruption was rampant, and there was considerable resistance to enforcement by many segments of the population.

667. Vandenbroeke, C. "De Prijs Van Betaalds Liefde" (The Price of Purchased Love). *Spiegel Historiael* (Netherlands) 18(2) (1983):90-4.

Estimates the price of a prostitute in the period since 1327 to be close to the average daily wage of a worker.

Poland

668. Karpinski, A. "Prostitution in Major Polish Cities (Cracow, Lublin, Poznan, Warsaw) During the Sixteenth and Seventeenth Centuries." (French) *Acta Poloniae Historica* (59) (1989):5-40.

Portugal

669. Cruz, F.I. dos S. *Da prostituição na cidade de Lisboa.* Reprinted, Lisboa: Publicaç˜oes Dom Quixote, 1984.

Cruz died in 1859.

670. Pais, J.M. *A prostituição e a Lisboa boémia do séc. XIX aos inícios do séc. XX.* Lisbon: Querco, 1985.

671.   Pessoa, A.A.   *Os bons velhos tempos da prostituição em Portugal: antologia de histórias e documentos colhidos na historia da prostituiç̃ao em Portugal.* Lisboa: Editoria Arcádia, 1976.

Russia/Soviet Union

672.   Bordyugov, G.A.   "Social Parasitism or Social Anomalies (The History of the Battle Against Alcoholism, Begging, Prostitution and Vagrancy in the USSR in the 1920s and 1930s."   (Russian) *Istoriya SSSR* (1) (1989):60-73.

673.   Engel, B.A.   "Saint Petersburg Prostitutes in the Late Nineteenth Century: A Personal and Social Profile."   *Russian Review* 48(1) (January 1989):21-44.

Explores socio-economic background and personal characteristics to determine a profile for the turn-of-the-century Russian prostitute. Compares this profile with that of the English and French prostitute for the same period. Concludes that all three were similar.

674.   Entry omitted.

675.   Englestein, L.   "Gender and the Juridical Subject: Prostitution and Rape in Nineteenth-Century Russian Criminal Codes."   *Journal of Modern History* 60(3) (September 1988):458-495.

Examines the influence of gender on the treatment of females in the nineteenth-century Russian criminal code for sexual crimes, particularly rape and prostitution.

676.   Meliksetyan, A.S.   "Prostitution in the Twenties."   (Russian) *Sotsiologicheskie Issledovaniya* (3) (1989):71-4.

677.   Stites, R.   "Prostitute and Society in Pre-Revolutionary Russia."   (English) *Jahrbucher für Geschichte Osteuropas* 31(3) (1983):348-64.

Spain

678. Artz, R. *Las citas sexuales: las "Call Girls"*. Barcelona: Editorial Vergi, 1976.

679. Cañas, J.M. *La prostitución después de la guerra civil*. Barcelona: Producciones Editoriales, 1977.

680. Carandell, J.M. *Taxi-sexo: las mercenarias del amor*. Barcelona: Editorial Bruguera, 1976.

681. De Dieu, J.P. "The Inquisition and Popular Culture in New Castile (and Judicial Procedure of the Holy Office)." *Inquisition and Society in Early Modern Europe*. Edited by S. Haliczer. Totowa, NJ: Barnes & Noble, 1987, pp. 129-146.

682. Harrison, N. "Nuns and Prostitutes in Enlightenment Spain." *British Journal for Eighteenth Century Studies* 9(1) (1986):53ff.

683. Nash, M. *Mujer, familia y trabajo en España (1875-1936)*. Barcelona: Anthropos, 1983.

684. Perry, M.E. "Deviant Insiders: Legalized Prostitutes and a Consciousness of Women in Early Modern Seville." *Comparative Studies in Society and History* 27(1) (January 1985):138-58.

Proposes that legalized prostitution existed in Seville in the sixteenth and seventeenth centuries. Suggests this is an expression of a general perception of all women, as well as a response to socio-economic conditions. Provides insight into the rationalization and treatment of prostitution and its relation to power, gender, deviance, and sexual ideology in early modern Seville, and today.

685. Perry, M.E. "'Lost Women' in Early Modern Seville: The Politics of Prostitution." *Feminist Studies* 4(1) (February 1978):195-214.

Determines whether prostitutes in early modern Seville represented social pathology or social adaption. Finds that prostitution was promoted by socio-economic and political factors, which are discussed in detail.

Sweden

686. Frykmen, J. *Horan i bondesamhälleh (Whores in Peasant Society).* Lund: Liber Läromedel, 1977.

Unmarried mothers and prostitution in rural society.

687. Lundquist, T.K.O. "Den disciplinerade dubbelmoralen: studier i den reglementerade prostitutionem historika i Sverige 1859-1918." Göteborg: Historiska Institutionen, 1982. English translation: "The Disciplined Double Standard: Studies in the History of Regulated Prostitution in Sweden, 1859-1918." (Swedish) (Ph.D. Dissertation) Göteborg University (Sweden), 1982.

There is a summary in English.

Switzerland

688. Cairoli, A. *Le déclin des maisons closes: la prostitution à Genève à la fin du XIXe siècle.* Carouge-Genève: Zoé, 1987.

689. Herz, L.G. *Venere in provincia: uno studio su prostituzione e società, Lugano 1800-1914.* Comano (Switzerland): Edizioni Alice, 1987.

690. Javet, D. "Medical Treatises on Prostitution in Late Nineteenth Century Lausanne." *Schweizerische Zeitschrift für Geschichte* 34(3) (1984):410-19.

691. Javet, D. *La prostitution à Lausanne au XIXe siècle.* Lausanne: Université de Lausanne, 1984.

692. Javet, D. "La prostituée et le discourse médical. L'exemple Lausannois à la fin du XIXe siècle." *Schweizerische Zeitschrift für Geschichte* 34(3) (1984):410-19.

Even though there was a decline in the incidence of venereal diseases in Lausanne at the end of the nineteenth century, demands for control of prostitution grew ever more insistent, in large part because of medical agitation. The physicians, in effect, became the major forces of repression of prostitution, and went far beyond the medical knowledge of the day.

693. Ulrich, A. *Bordelle, Strassendirnen und burgerliche Sittlichkeit in der Belle Epoque: eine sozialgeschichtliche Studie der Prostitution am Beispiel der Stadt Zürich.* Zürich: Druckerei Schultheiss, 1985.

694. Ulrich, A. "Marie Trottoir--The Social Status of Prostitutes in Zurich During the Belle-Epoque." (German) *Schweizerische Zeitschrift für Geschichte* 34(3) (1984):420-30.

Finds that Niederdorf and the Langestrasse were the centers of prostitution in Zurich prior to World War I. Establishes a pattern of the personal characteristics and background of prostitutes and examines conditions which encouraged the prostitutes to dissociate themselves from the profession.

United Kingdom

695. Bauer, C., and L. Ritt. "'A Husband Is a Beating Animal': Frances Power Cobbe Confronts the Wife Abuse Problem in Victorian England." *International Journal of Women's Studies* 6(2) (March-April 1983):99-118.

Documents the abuse women, especially working-class wives, were subjected to in nineteenth-century England. Outlines Cobbs' goal of precipitating a change in the social attitude that accepted wife beating. Discusses the role of prostitution in promoting this attitude.

696. Bristow, E.J. *Vice and Vigilance: Purity Movements in Britain Since 1700.* Totowa, NJ: Rowman and Littlefield, 1977.

697. Bullough, V.L. "Prostitution and Reform in Eighteenth Century England." *Eighteenth Century Life, Williamsburg, VA* 9(3) (May 1985):61-74.

Summarizes attempts to deal with prostitution which were usually stymied because they could see no alternative work for prostitutes except as potential wives, laundresses, or servants.

698.   Byrd, M.   "The Madhouse, the Whorehouse, and the Convent . . ."
       Partisan Review 44(2) (1977):268-78.

       Finds three types of houses to be symbolic prisons where irrational
       energy, read sexuality, was locked away. Using various types of English
       literature, but particularly the novel, finds the three houses were but one.

699.   Chesney, K.   *The Anti-Society: An Account of the Victorian Underworld.*
       London: Gambet, 1970.

700.   Chester, L., D. Leitch, and C. Simpson.   *The Cleveland Street Affair.*
       London: Weidenfeld and Nicolson, 1977.

       Examines the nineteenth-century case known as the Cleveland Street
       scandal which involved male prostitution.

701.   Cox, G.S., ed.   *The Night Walker, or, Evening Rambles in Search after
       Lewd Women. An Anonymous Seventeenth Century Pamphlet.*   Mount
       Durand, St. Peter Port, Guernsey: Toucan, 1970.

702.   Dunton, J.   *The Night-Walker, or, Evening Rambles in Search After Lewd
       Women.*   Reprinted New York: Garland, 1985.

       Original pamphlet published in 1696. See Cox above for another one.

703.   Engel, A.J.   "Immoral Intentions: The University of Oxford and the
       Problem of Prostitution, 1827-1914."   *Victorian Studies* 23(1) (1979):79-
       107.

       Authorities of Oxford University exercised special powers to curtail
       prostitution throughout the nineteenth century. During this period, the
       town had an average of 300 to 500 prostitutes, many of them former
       servant girls. Undergraduates usually escaped punishment for infractions
       of rules because authorities believed the fault lay with the women.
       Prostitution ceased to be a problem with the arrival of more lower-income
       undergraduates and changing social mores.

704. Finnegan, F. *Poverty and Prostitution: A Study of Victorian Prostitutes in York.* New York: Cambridge University Press, 1979.

705. Frattini, R. "Prostituzione e prostitute nell età vittoriana" (Prostitution and Prostitutes in the Victorian Era). *Movimento operaio e socialista* (Italy) 7(3) (1984):395-403.

Discusses contemporary work on prostitution in the Victorian era, including J.R. Walkowitz's *Prostitution and Victorian Society* (1980), F. Finnegan's *Poverty and Prostitution: A Study of Victorian Prostitutes in York* (1979), and others. Shows that there was an almost pathological dependence on prostitutes at this time in spite of morals, standards, and beliefs imposed by Victorian society.

706. Great Britain, Committee on Homosexual Offences and Prostitution. *Report.* London: H.M. Stationery Office, 1957, reprinted 1968.

This is the famed Wolfenden report, which has been reprinted several times.

707. Great Britain, Parliament, House of Commons, Select Committee on Contagious Diseases Acts. "Report, together with the proceedings of the committee, minutes of the evidence, and appendix." Ordered, by the House of Commons, to be printed, 30 July 1879. [London, 1879]. Irish University Press series of British parliamentary papers. *Health: Infectious Diseases* 6 (1970):9-229.

708. Great Britain, Parliament, House of Commons, Select Committee on Contagious Diseases Acts. "Report, together with the proceedings of the committee, minutes of the evidence, and appendix." Ordered, by the House of Commons, to be printed, 10 March 1880. [London, 1880]. Irish University Press series of British parliamentary papers. *Health: Infectious Diseases* 6 (1970):231-308.

709. Great Britain, Parliament, House of Commons, Select Committee on Contagious Diseases Acts. "Report, together with the proceedings of the committee, minutes of the evidence, and appendix." Ordered, by the House of Commons, to be printed, 26 July 1880. [London, 1880]. Irish University Press series of British parliamentary papers. *Health: Infectious*

Diseases 6 (1970):309-14.

710.   Great Britain, Parliament, House of Commons, Select Committee on
       Contagious Diseases Acts. "Report, together with the proceedings of the
       committee, minutes of the evidence, and appendix." Ordered, by the
       House of Commons, to be printed, 28 July 1881. [London, 1881]. Irish
       University Press series of British parliamentary papers. *Health: Infectious
       Diseases* 6 (1970):315-914.

711.   Great Britain, Parliament, Select Committee on the Contagious Diseases
       Bill. "Special Report; with the proceedings of the committee." Ordered,
       by the House of Commons, to be printed, 20 April 1866. [London, 1866].
       Irish University Press series of British parliamentary papers. *Health:
       Infectious Diseases* 4 (1970):9-16.

712.   Hamilton, M. "Opposition to the Contagious Diseases Act, 1864-1886."
       Albion 10(1) (1978): 14-27.

       The four Contagious Disease Acts of 1864-69 called for the arrest and
       forced medical treatment of suspected prostitutes in certain military areas.
       Acts that initially passed without much public reaction became a basis of
       political campaign for abolition of regulated prostitution and ultimately
       even of prostitution.

713.   Harrison, F. *The Dark Angel: Aspects of Victorian Sexuality.* New York:
       Universe Books, 1977.

714.   Harrison, M. *Fanfare of Strumpets.* London: W.H. Allen, 1971.

715.   Holton, S.S. "State Pandering, Medical Policing and Prostitution: The
       Controversy within the Medical Profession Concerning Contagious
       Diseases Legislation 1864-1886." *Research in Law, Deviance and Social
       Control* 9 (1988):149-70.

       Suggests that during the controversy over the Contagious Disease Acts of
       the 1860s in Great Britain, a more sophisticated social science was
       becoming incorporated into the understanding of sexually transmitted
       diseases within the medical community. Instead of enforced medical

supervision of prostitutes, a more liberal policy of education and free medical treatment for prostitutes and clients was adopted.

716. Hude, H.M. *The Cleveland Street Scandal.* London: W.H. Allen, 1976.

Another view of the Cleveland Street affair. See Chester above.

717. L'Esperance, J.L. "Woman's Mission to Woman: Explorations in the Operation of the Double Standard and Female Solidarity in Nineteenth-Century England." *Social History* 12(24) (1979):316-38.

Argues that in nineteenth-century England, women were divided into two classes, the pure and the impure and that women themselves attempted to overcome the separation through charitable work with prostitutes. Women made connections between their economic and social disabilities and the prevalence of prostitution.

718. Lewis, B.R. "Hummums and Whore Houses." *British Heritage* 3(3) (1982):20-5.

Describes the deterioration of Covent Garden to a "red-light district" after 1682. Focuses on crime and prostitution.

719. *The London-bawd, with Her Character and Life.* New York: Garland, 1985. Reprint of the 4th ed.: London: J. Gwillim, 1711.

720. Mahood, L. *The Magdalenes: Prostitution in the Nineteenth Century.* London; New York: Routledge, 1990.

721. Mawby, R.I. "Social Action and Criminological Theory: The Case of Josephine Butler." *Howard Journal of Penology and Crime Prevention* 14(2) (1975):30-42.

Examines the writings of Josephine Butler, a nineteenth-century social activist who was a leader in the fight to abolish the Contagious Diseases Act in England. Many of her writings focus on the effect of laws on deviant behavior.

722.   Mayhew, H. *London's Underworld; Being Selections From "Those That Will Not Work,"* the Fourth Volume of "London Labour and the London Poor."* Edited by Peter Quennell. London: Spring Books, 1965.

Comments on social conditions in London during the Victorian era. Chapter 1 is devoted to prostitution in London, and includes topics such as the prostitutes of the Haymarket, dependants of prostitutes, clandestine prostitutes, and trafficking in foreign women.

723.   McHugh, P. *Prostitution and Victorian Social Reform.* London: Croom Helm, 1980; New York: St. Martin's, 1980.

724.   Mennell, J.E.   "The Politics of Frustration: 'The Maiden Tribute of Modern Babylon' and the Morality Movement of 1885." *North Dakota Quarterly* 49(1) 1981:68-80.

Discusses the morality movement against prostitution in England. Traces the crusade from the first articles in Pall Mall Gazette to the downfall of two prominent politicians.

725.   Nash, S.D.   "Prostitution and Charity: The Magdalen Hospital: A Case Study." *Journal of Social History* 17(4) (Summer 1984):617-28.

Founded in 1758 to carry out a program of reform and rehabilitation of prostitutes, the voluntary hospital shared many of the characteristics of the prison. It also anticipated the kind of human engineering common in later generations. Regards it as an enlightened alternative to earlier treatment of social deviants.

726.   Nash, S.D.   "Social Attitudes Towards Prostitution in London from 1752 to 1829." (Thesis) *DAI* 41(6) (1980):2728-A.

727.   Nelson. T.G.A.   "Women of Pleasure." *Eighteenth Century Life* 11(1) (1987):181-98.

Explores the differing perceptions of prostitution in eighteenth-century English texts. Describes both the mythologization and the condemnation of prostitution.

728. Pearsall, R. *The Worm in the Bud.* London: Weidenfeld and Nicholson, 1969.

Includes a discussion of prostitution.

729. Pearson, M. *The Age of Consent: Victorian Prostitution and Its Enemies.* Newton Abbot: David and Charles, 1972.

730. Pearson, M. *The Five Pound Virgins.* New York: Saturday Review, 1972.

The campaign against abolition and the involvement of Stead and the *Pall Mall Gazette.*

731. Petrie, G. *A Singular Iniquity: The Campaigns of Josephine Butler.* New York: Viking, 1971.

Another view of the efforts of Josephine Butler.

732. Post, J.B. "A Foreign Office Survey of Venereal Disease and Prostitution Control." *Medical History* 22(3) (1978):327-34.

In response to possible extension of the Contagious Diseases Acts, the Privy Council and Foreign Office collaborated on a questionnaire to obtain information on venereal disease in 22 foreign cities. Returns were never put to official use but information gives insights into prostitution and venereal disease control in various European cities. Also discusses why the reports were never used.

733. *Prostitution in the Victorian Age: Debates on the Issue from Nineteenth Century Critical Journals.* Introduction by Keith Nield. Farnborough: Gregg, 1973.

Selections of important sources.

734. Royal Commission on Contagious Diseases. "Report of the Royal Commission upon the Administration and Operation of the Contagious Disease Acts." (London: H.M. Stationery Office, 1871.) Irish University

Press Series of British parliamentary papers. *Health: Infectious Diseases* 5 (1971).

735.   Selby, D.E.   "Cardinal Manning, Campaigner for Children's Rights." *Journal of Ecclesiastical History* (1976).

       Also discusses prostitution.

736.   Society for the Rescue of Young Women and Children. *The Greatest Moral Hypocrisy of the Day.* London: The Society, 1873. Microform: New Haven, CT: Research Publications, 1977, 1 microform, 35 mm.

737.   Stafford, A., pseud.   *The Age of Consent.*   London: Hodder and Stoughton, 1964.

738.   Storch, R.D.   "Police Control of Street Prostitution in Victorian London: A Study in the Context of Police Action"   *Police and Society.* D.H. Bayley.   Newbury Park, CA: Sage Publications, 1977, pp. 49-72.

       Studies police policies and treatment of prostitutes in nineteenth-century London, specifically examining the impact of societal influences on these policies and practices.

739.   *Vigilance Committee and Their Works: Containing the New Law for the Protection of Girls with Suggestions as to Its Enforcement.* By the Chief Director of the Secret Commission.   London, n.d. *History of Women.* New Haven, CT: Research Publications, Inc., 1977.   Microfilm.

       Pamphlet explaining the Criminal Law Amendment Act of 1885, a British law dealing with the export of English women and girls abroad for immoral purposes.

740.   Walkowitz, J.R.   "Notes on the History of Victorian Prostitution: Review Article." *Feminist Studies* 1(1) (1972):105-14.

       Looks at two nineteenth-century studies of prostitution by William Acton (1857) and Henry Mayhew (1861) and compares them with two recent studies by Pearsall and Chesney.

741. Walkowitz, J.R. *Prostitution and Victorian Society: Women, Class, and the State.* Cambridge, England; New York: Cambridge University Press, 1980.

742. *The Wandering Whore: Numbers 1-5, 1660-1661.* Published in London by John Garfield (assumed also to be the author). (Reprint) Exeter: The Rota at the University of Exeter, 1977. Also reprinted (parts 1-6) in New York: Garland, 1986.

743. Wooten, N.A. "Temporary Favors: Women, Prostitution, and Choice in Eighteenth Century London." (Ph.D.Dissertation) University of Delaware, 1987. *DAI* 48(6) (1987):1521-A.

744. Wyke, T.J. "The Manchester and Salford Lock Hospital, 1818-1917." *Medical History* 19(1) (1975):73-86.

The nineteenth century saw the growth in specialist hospitals including those devoted to venereal diseases, i.e.,"lock" hospitals. In Manchester the lock hospitals operated from 1819 to World War I. Purpose was not only to treat or cure venereal diseases but to reform the female. This is a history of one such hospital.

Yugoslavia

745. Cuirn, J. "The History of Prostitution in Celje at the End of the Nineteenth Century." (Slovene) *Kronika* 33(2-3) (1985):142-7.

Though prostitution was controlled in the Austrian-Hungarian Empire, instructions were vague and it was not until 1896 that the first legal brothel was established in Celje. Irregular prostitutes continued to operate.

LATIN AMERICA AND THE CARIBBEAN

746. Arcourt, L. d' *Las elegantes prostituídas.* México: Posada, 1973.

747. Bremser, B. *Troia: Mexican Memoirs.* New York: Croton, 1969.

748. Court, G. "The Socioeconomic Context of Prostitution in Contemporary Latin America." (Thesis) UCLA, 1982.

749. Fonseca, G. *História da prostituição em São Paolo*. São Paolo: Editora Resenha Universitária, 1982.

750. Glickman, N. *La trata de blancas: estudio critico*. Buenos Aires: Editorial Pardes, 1984.

History of prostitution in Argentina as well as in the writings of Leib Malaj.

751. Goldar, E. *La "mala vida."* Buenos Aires: Centro Editor de América Latina, 1971.

History of prostitution in Argentina.

752. Guy, D.J. "White Slavery, Public Health, and the Socialist Position on Legalized Prostitution in Argentina, 1913-1936." *Latin American Research Review* 23(3) (1988):60-80.

753. Honore, N.F. *Brief aperçu sur l'évolution de la prostitution en Haïti*. Port-au-Prince: Imp. Haïti Presse, 1981.

754. Jesus, C.M. de. *Beyond All Pity*. Translated from the Portuguese by D. St. Clair. London: Panther, 1970.

Prostitution in Brazil.

755. McCreery, D. "This Life of Misery and Shame: Female Prostitution in Guatemala City, 1880-1920." *Journal of Latin American Studies* 18(2) (1986):333-353. (Also published in Spanish in *Mesoamérica* 7(11) (1986):35-59.)

Recounts the Guatemalan system of controlled prostitution during the late nineteenth century which reinforced prevailing national patterns of class, race, and gender domination.

756. Muriel, J. *Los recogimientos de mujeres: respuesta a una problemática social novohispana.* México: Universidad Nacional Autónoma, 1974. History of prostitution in Mexico.

757. Saavedra, A.M. "Prostitution in Mexico--The Problem as Observed over a Century Ago." (Spanish) *Medicine* 41 (supplement 1961):145-50.

758. Soares, L.C. *Prostitution in Nineteenth Century Rio de Janeiro.* (Occasional Paper) London: University of London, Institute of Latin American Studies, 1988.

MIDDLE EAST

759. Khalaf, S. *Prostitution in a Changing Society; a Sociological Survey of Legal Prostitution in Beirut.* Beirut: Khayats, 1965.

An excellent survey of prostitution in Beirut up to the 1960s.

NORTH AMERICA

Canada

760. Backhouse, C.B. "Nineteenth-Century Canadian Prostitution Law: Reflection of a Discriminating Society." *Social History* 18(36) (1985):387-423.

Describes approaches to prostitution of nineteenth-century Canadian legislators and social reformers. Asserts that each approach involved class, racial, ethnic, or sexual discrimination.

761. Bedford, J. "Prostitution in Calgary 1905-1914." *Alberta History* 29(2) (1981):1-11.

Relates the history of prostitution in Calgary from 1905 to 1914. Contends that until 1904 prostitution was tolerated, but in 1905 a smallpox epidemic in the red light district prompted a crackdown on prostitution which then became regarded as a major crime.

762. Gray, J.H. *Red Lights on the Prairies.* New York: New American Library, 1973. (First published Toronto: Macmillan of Canada, 1971.)

763. Horrall, S.W. "The (Royal) North-West Mounted Police and Prostitution on the Canadian Prairies." *Prairie Forum* 10(1) (1985):105-127.

Describes methods of dealing with prostitution during the initial settlement period of the Canadian prairies.

764. Levesque, A. "Le bordel: milieu de travail controlé." *Labour* 20 (1987):13-31.

Examines brothels in Montreal and the agents of control associated with them: police, social reformers, clergy, medical professionals, pimps, madames, and housekeepers. Notes changes taking place in interwar period.

765. Levesque, A. *La norme et les deviantes: des femmes au Québec pendant l'entre deux guerres.* Montréal: Éditions du Remue Ménage, 1989.

766. Levesque, A. "Turning Off the Red Light--Reformers and Prostitution in Montreal, 1865-1925." (French) *Urban History Review--Revue d'Histoire Urbaine* 17(3) (1989):191-201.

767. Nouvelle-France, Conseil souverain. *Condamnation de bannissement à Catherine Gichelin, épouse de Nicholas Buteau, Catherine Basset, épouse de Pierre Bourgouin dit LeBourguignon, convaincues de prostitutions à Québec en 1675.* Vanier, Ontario: Éditions Quesnel de Fomblanche, 1977.

This and the following two publications offer historical case studies.

768. Nouvelle-France, Conseil souverain. *Procès d'Anne Bauge, épouse de Guillaume Corruble, accusée de mener une vie scandaleuse à Québec en*

1676. Vanier, Ontario: Éditions Quesnel de Fomblanche, 1978.

769. Nouvelle-France, Conseil souverain. *Procès de Marguerite Leboeuf, épouse de Gabriel Lemieux, accusée d'adultère et de réputation de fire de femmes et de filles le crime d'impudicité, à Québec le 1er avril 1667.* Édité par A. Quesnel. Vanier, Ontario: Éditions Quesnel de Fomblanche, 1985.

United States

770. Adler, F. "Oldest and Newest Profession." *Criminology of Deviant Women.* F. Adler and R.J. Simon. Boston: Houghton Mifflin, 1979. And *Sisters in Crime: The Rise of the New Female Criminal.* F. Adler, and H.M. Adler. New York: McGraw-Hill, 1975, pp. 55-83.

Documents the changes in the character of prostitution and its marketing in America. Analyzes various motivations for becoming a prostitute. Discusses the contemporary prostitute: the working conditions, the lifestyle, and emotional and economic factors.

771. Aiken, K.G. "The National Florence Crittenton Mission, 1883-1925: A Case Study in Progressive Reform." (Thesis) Washington State University, 1980.

772. American Bureau of Moral Education. *A Statement of Purpose.* Chicago: American Bureau of Moral Education, n.d. A pamphlet on microfilm: New Haven, CT.: Research Publications, 1977.

773. Anderson, E. "Prostitution and Social Justice: Chicago, 1910-15." *Social Service Review* 48(2) (1974):203-228.

Discusses government policy towards prostitution in the Progressive Era. Traces the transformation of the national attitude from toleration to suppression. Draws attention to the campaign against prostitution, the ideology of vice reform, and the link of these concepts to progressivism.

774. Anderson, R.L. *The Diggs-Caminette Case, 1913-1917: For Any Other Immoral Purpose.* Lewiston, NY: Mellen, 1990.

775. Bancroft, C. *Six Racy Madams of Colorado*. Boulder, CO: Johnson, 1965.

Gives accounts of Jennie Rogers, Mattie Silks, Laura Evans, Lillian Powers, Pearl de Vere, and Cock-Eyed Liz.

776. Barnhart, J.B. "The Fair but Frail: Prostitution in San Francisco, 1849-1900." (Based on thesis, University of California, Santa Cruz, 1976; Photo copy University Microfilms International, Ann Arbor, 1984). Reno: University of Nevada Press, 1986.

Examines how prostitutes were viewed by the people of San Francisco from 1849 through to the end of the century. Citizens first admired the women as entrepreneurs but with the arrival of respectable wives and daughters to enforce Victorian moral values, prostitutes experienced ostracism. French prostitutes were preferred over Chinese or Latin American prostitutes.

777. Baxter, A.K., and B. Walter. *Inwood House: One Hundred and Fifty Years of Service to Women*. New York: Inwood House, 1980.

Had an affiliation with the Magdalen Society and among its many missions was rehabilitating prostitutes.

778. Benjamin, H., and R.E.L. Masters. *Prostitution and Morality: a Definitive Report on the Prostitute in Contemporary Society and an Analysis of the Causes and Effects of the Suppression of Prostitution*. New York: Julian, 1964. English edition entitled *Prostitution and Society*. London: Mayflower, 1966.

Includes information on legislation, institutions, and varieties of prostitution. Argues for the removal of government sanctions. Contains considerable amounts of historical data.

779. Bernstein, R.A. "Boarding House Keepers and Brothel Keepers in New York City, 1880-1910." (Thesis) Rutgers University, 1984.

780. Best, J. "Careers in Brothel Prostitution: St. Paul, 1865-1883." *Journal of Interdisciplinary History* 12(4) (1982):597-619.

Traces the routes of young girls into prostitution, examines the management and operation of brothels, and concludes that geographical mobility was common among St. Paul prostitutes but social mobility was not since routes out of prostitution were limited.

781. Blackburn, G.M., and S.L. Ricards. "The Prostitutes and Gamblers of Virginia City, Nevada: 1870." *Pacific Historical Review* 48(2) (1979):239-58.

Finds that while gambling was legal and prostitution illegal, both were considered socially acceptable in Virginia City, Nevada, in 1870. Notes that both gamblers and prostitutes were seeking monetary gain but few ever attained economic success.

782. Blair, K.R. *Ladies of the Lamplight*. Colorado Springs, CO: Little London, 1971.

783. Block, A. "Aw! Your Mother's in the Mafia-Women Criminals in Progressive New York." *Contemporary Crises* 1(1) (January 1977):5-22.

Most women classified as criminals in the Jewish underworld were prostitutes.

784. Bowman, I.A. "Prostitution and the Medical Profession in the Nineteenth Century." *Bookman* 9(1) (January 1982):3-9.

785. Brenzel, B. "Better Protestant than Prostitute: A Social Portrait of a Nineteenth Century Reform School for Girls." *Interchange* 6(2) (1975):11-22.

Describes the functioning of a model juvenile training school established for poor and deviant girls in the nineteenth century.

786. Bullough, V.L. "The American Brothel." *Medical Aspects of Human Sexuality* 7(4) (April 1973):198-211.

Describes brothels operated by Everlieght sisters in Chicago, Nell Kimball and Kate Townsend in New Orleans, and others. States that the last two decades of the nineteenth and first decade of the twentieth century were the golden age of brothels. Commentary following the article includes some details on brothels in New York.

787. *Bureau of Social Hygiene Project and Research Files (1913-1940); a collection of the Rockefeller Archive Center of the Rockefeller University.* Wilmington, DE: Scholarly Resources, 1980. This is also available at the Rockerfeller Archive Center.

788. Burnham, J.C. "Medical Inspection of Prostitutes in America in the Nineteenth Century: the St. Louis Experiment and Its Sequel." *Bulletin of the History of Medicine* 45 (May-June 1971):203-18.

St. Louis had first system of government inspection in U.S.. Explains why it failed.

789. Butler, A.M. "The Tarnished Frontier: Prostitution in the Trans-Mississippi West, 1865-1890." (Thesis) University of Maryland, 1979. Microfilm, Ann Arbor, MI: University Microfilms International, 1980; also Doctoral Dissertations in History 4(2) (1979):22.

790. Butler, A.M., G.J. Barker-Benfield, G. Riley, et al. *Daughters of Joy, Sisters of Misery: Prostitutes in the American West, 1865-1890.* Urbana: University of Illinois Press, 1985.

Based on primary research in depositories in 12 western states, authors describe the role played by prostitutes as workers in the development of the West's institutions.

791. Carlisle, M.R. "Disorderly City, Disorderly Women: Prostitution in Antebellum Philadelphia." *Pennsylvania Magazine of History and Biography* 110(4) (1986):549-68.

Describes prostitution in antebellum Philadelphia before major attempts to eliminate it. Discusses the factors that lured women into prostitution as well as the working climate attributed to the early nineteenth-century policy of toleration. Based on Ph.D. dissertation.

792. Carlisle, M.R. "Prostitutes and Their Reformers in Nineteenth-Century Philadelphia." (Thesis) Rutgers University, 1982.

793. Chambliss, W. *In Wilma.* Crystal Bay, NV: Crystal, 1980.

794. Chicago Vice Commission. *The Social Evil in Chicago.* New York: Arno, 1970.

A reprint of an earlier report.

795. Chicago Society of Social Hygiene. *For the Protection of Wives and Children From Venereal Contamination.* Chicago: [s.n.], n.d.; Microfilm: New Haven, CT: Research Publications, 1977.

796. Connelly, M.T. "Fear, Anxiety, and Hope: The Response to Prostitution in the United States, 1900-1920." (Ph.D. Dissertation) Rutgers University, 1977.

Studies the response to prostitution in the United States from 1900 to 1920 as expressed in laws, themes, and styles. Contends that prostitution was a "master symbol" for social and moral changes, such as immigration, rural decline and urban corruption, shifts in sexual values, and in the status of women. Asserts that this master symbol threatened strict moral codes which had prevailed from the Civil War until World War I.

797. Connelly, M.T. *The Response to Prostitution in the Progressive Era.* Chapel Hill: University of North Carolina Press, 1980.

Discusses the Chicago Vice Commission Report, the White Slavery scare, and the World War I purity campaign as responses to regulation and suppression of prostitution.

798. Cordasco, F. *The White Slave Trade and the Immigrants: A Chapter in American Social History.* Detroit, MI: Blaine Ethridge, 1981.

799. Couch, J.G. *Those Golden Girls of Market Street: Denver's Infamous Redlight District: An Historical Glimpse.* Fort Collins, CO: Old Army, 1974.

800.   Daly, K.   "Social Control of Sexuality: A Case Study of the Criminalization of Prostitution in the Progressive Era." *Research in Law, Deviance and Social Control* 9 (1988):171-206.

Examines social and political factors involved in the antiprostitution campaign in New York City between 1900 and 1920. Compares it to the current campaign to control commercialized sex and warns against the resulting criminalization of women.

801.   Del Castillo, M.   *The Ladies of the Night, or, A Short History of Prostitution in Nevada County, California.*   Grass Valley, CA: M. Janicot, 1986.

802.   De Young, M.   "Help, I'm Being Held Captive: The White Slave Fairy Tale of the Progressive Era."   *Journal of American Culture* 6(1) (1983):96-9.

Explores the white slavery myth and its role in the Progressive Era. Finds that few cases were ever brought to the courts, in spite of attempts made by groups such as the American Vigilance Society and the Immigrants' Protective League.

803.   Feitz, L.   *Myers Avenue; A Quick History of Cripple Creek's Red-Light District.*   Colorado Springs: Dentan-Berkeland, 1967.

804.   Feldman, E.   "Prostitution, the Alien Woman and the Progressive Imagination, 1910-15."   *American Quarterly* 19 (1967):192-206.

805.   Fishbein, L.   "Harlot or Heroine: Changing Views of Prostitution, 1870-1920."   *Historian* 43(1) (1980):23-35.

Describes the nineteenth-century reformers' campaign against prostitution through the utilization of republican institutions and the creation of economic opportunity. Suggests that this group was torn between reforming prostitution and eradicating it. Discusses the misrepresentation of prostitution by the abolitionists.

806.   Frost, H.G., and W. Clayton.   *The Gentleman's Club: The Story of*

Prostitution in El Paso. El Paso, TX: Mangan, 1983.

A chronicle of prostitution from 1848-1977 in El Paso, Texas, based on records and interviews.

807. Gardner, J.F. "Microbes and Morality; the Social Hygiene Crusade in New York City, 1892-1917." (Thesis) Indiana University, 1974. Ann Arbor, MI: University Microfilms International, 1974.

808. Gentry, C. *The Madams of San Francisco: An Irreverent History of the City of the Golden Gate.* Garden City, NY: Doubleday, 1964.

809. Gilfoyle, T.J. "City of Eros: New York City, Prostitution and the Commercialization of Sex, 1790-1920." (Thesis) Columbia University, 1987.

Traces the evolution of prostitution in New York City from 1790 to 1920, distinguishing three periods: establishment (1790-1839), halcyon years of commercial sex (1840-1870), and Victorian (1871-1920). During the halcyon years, leisure institutions such as the theater, concert hall, masked ball, and saloon used prostitutes to attract patrons. After this period prostitution receded.

810. Gilfoyle, T.J. "Strumpets and Misogynists--Brothel Riots and the Transformation of Prostitution in Antebellum New York City." *New York History* 68(1) (1987):45ff.

Based on the Ph.D. dissertation.

811. Gilfoyle, T.J. "The Urban Geography of Commercial Sex: Prostitution in New York City, 1790-1860." *Journal of Urban History* 13(4) (1987):371-93.

Outlines the three stages in the geography of prostitution in nineteenth-century New York City: segregation, integration, and finally the emergence of the first large-scale red-light district.

812. Goldman, M.S. "Communication: Prostitutes and Gamblers of Virginia

City, Nevada, 1870." *Pacific Historical Review* 49(1) (1980):169-70.

813.   Goldman, M.S.   "Prostitution and Virtue in Nevada." *Society* 10(1) (1972):32-8.

814.   Goldman, M.S.   "Sexual Commerce on the Comstock Lode." *Nevada Historical Society Quarterly* 21(2) (1978):98-129.

Describes the influx of prostitutes to Nevada's Comstock Lode and the creation of three vice districts at Gold Hill and Virginia City. Discusses the political support for economic reasons of this sexual commerce.

815.   Goldman, M.S., and A.M. Butler. *Gold Diggers and Silver Miners: Prostitution and Social Life on the Comstock Lode.* Ann Arbor, MI: University of Michigan Press, 1981.

This is based on the author's Ph.D. dissertation, University of Chicago, 1977.

816.   Greer, R.A.   "Collarbone and the Social Evil." *Hawaiian Journal of History* 7 (1973):3-17.

Follows the laws and social attitudes toward prostitution in the Iwilei district of Honolulu through much of the nineteenth century. Called "Collarbone," Iwilei was the prostitution district that was finally closed in 1917.

817.   Hapke, L. *Conventions of Denial: Prostitution in Late Nineteenth Century American Anti-Vice Narrative.* (Michigan occasional papers in women's studies.) Ann Arbor, MI: Women's Studies Program, University of Michigan, 1982.

818.   Hapke, L.   "The Late Nineteenth Century American Streetwalker: Images and Realities." *Mid-America* 65(3) (1983):155-62.

Presents the stereotype of prostitutes in Victorian America. These women were generally believed to have been seduced, abandoned, and thus transformed into predators. As such they were viewed as physically and morally corrupted by their sins.

819. *Hell's Belles of Tombstone.* Tombstone, AZ: Red Marie's Bookstore, 1984.

820. Hewitt, J.D. "Patterns of Female Criminality in Middletown: 1900-1920." *Indiana Social Studies Quarterly* 38(2) (Autumn 1985):49-59.

Addresses the nature of female criminality and its control from 1900 to 1920. Uses historical data to make provide a context for understanding female criminality on a national scale.

821. Hewitt, J.D. "Prostitution during the Progressive Era: the Middletown Experience." *The Wisconsin Sociologist* 24(2-3) (Spring-Summer 1987):99-111.

Focuses on prostitution during the Progressive Era in a medium-sized midwestern town with a small but growing industrial economy. Indicates that sexual sevices were increasingly available during the period studied, a finding that is in direct correlation to what was occurring in large metropolitan areas.

822. Hirata, L.C., C.R. Berkin, M.B. Norton, et al. "Chinese Immigrant Women in Nineteenth Century California." *Women of America: A History.* Edited by C.R. Berkin and M.B. Norton. Boston: Houghton Mifflin, 1979, pp. 223-44.

Describes the role of the Chinese immigrant woman in nineteenth-century Californian society. As a result of the high ratio between men and women, these women often became prostitutes and were frequently economically successful.

823. Hobson, B.M. *Uneasy Virtue: the Politics of Prostitution and the American Reform Tradition.* Chicago: University of Chicago Press, 1990. (Reprint, with new preface. Originally published, New York: Basic Books, 1987.)

Focuses on three periods of reform: the evangelical religious movement of 1840s, the Progressive Era, and the 1970s. Examines social constituencies of each and their failures.

824.   Holmes, K.A.   "Reflections by Gaslight: Prostitution in Another Age."
       Issues in Criminology 7(1) (Winter 1972):83-101.

       Examines the enforcement of anti-prostitution laws in late nineteenth- and
       early twentieth-century America. Details the goals and composition of the
       different humanitarian groups. Finds that little has changed in the
       American attitude toward prostitution.

825.   Hori, J.   "Japanese Prostitution in Hawaii during the Immigration Period."
       Hawaiian Journal of History 15 (1980):113-24.

       Explores the Japanese prostitution industry in Hawaii from 1870 to 1915.
       Discusses the role of the male who profited and that of the woman who
       was exploited. In spite of campaigns and protests this industry continued
       almost unaffected until 1914.

826.   Hughs, M.E.   "Red-Lights at the 'Green Light': Prostitution and Port
       Townsend at the Turn of the Century."   (Thesis) Western Washington
       University, 1987.

827.   Humphrey, D.C.   "Prostitution and Public Policy in Austin, Texas, 1870-
       1915."   *Southwestern Historical Quarterly* 86(4) (1983):473-516.

       Describes the unsuccessful attempts made by city officials in Austin,
       Texas, to eliminate prostitution during the late nineteenth century.

828.   Ichioka, Y.   "Ameyuki San: Japanese Prostitutes in Nineteenth Century
       America."   *Amerasia Journal* 4(1) (1977):1-21.

       Observes that the first significant immigration of Japanese women to
       America were prostitutes in the late 1880s. Discusses the ways in which
       these women were brought to the United States and exploited. Describes
       the early twentieth-century exclusion movement.

829.   Johnson, H.A.   "The Other Flexner Report: How Abraham Flexner was
       Diverted from Medical Schools to Brothels."   *Pharos* 49(2) (1986):9-12.

Description of Abraham Flexner's visits to Europe in 1911 and 1913 which resulted in the book *Prostitution in Europe.*

830. Jones, Jr, J.J. "A Tale of Two Cities: The Hidden Battle Against Venereal Disease in Civil War Nashville and Memphis." *Civil War History* 31(3) (1985):270-76.

When the Union Army occupied Nashville, authorities attempted to expel white prostitutes in an effort to control venereal disease. When this proved unsuccessful, the army instituted a system of legalized prostitution based on licenses and regular medical inspection. This was copied by Memphis in 1864.

831. Joseph, J.L.V. "The Nafkeh and the Lady: Jews, Prostitutes, and Progressives in New York City, 1900-1930." (Ph.D. Dissertation) SUNY at Stony Brook, 1986. Photocopy. Ann Arbor, MI: U.M.I. Dissertation Information Service, 1987.

Examines the reaction of established Jewish-Americans to appearance of prostitutes from first and second generation of East European Jews. Also focuses on the Progressive Movement in New York City from 1900 to 1930.

832. Kasindorf, J., and G.L. Cunningham. *The Nye County Brothel Wars: a Tale of the New West.* New York: Simon & Schuster, 1985.

Prostitutes, the Mafia, and judicial corruption in Nye County, Nevada.

833. Kneeland, G. J. *Commercialized Prostitution in New York City.* Reprinted Montclair, NJ: Patterson Smith, 1969.

The original appeared in 1917 and was one of the Rockfeller-Bureau of Social Hygiene sponsored studies.

834. Leonard, C. "Prostitution and Changing Social Norms in America." (Ph.D. Dissertation) Syracuse University, 1979; *DAI* 40(5) (1979):2930-31A.

835.   Leonard, C., and I. Wallimann. "Prostitution and Changing Morality in
       the Frontier Cattle Towns of Kansas." *Kansas History* 2(1) (1979):34-53.

       Despite the fact that prostitution was illegal in Kansas, no effort was made
       to suppress it. Instead, prostitutes were arrested and fined on schedule to
       raise funds for the local government. Based on newspapers, police court
       records, and city council records.

836.   Lewin, H., ed. *A Community of Clowns: Testimonies of People in Urban
       Rural Mission.* Geneva: W.C.C., 1987.

837.   Lilly, P.R. "What Happened in Hinton (A West Virginia Town's
       Rebellion Against Bootlegging and Prostitution)." *American Heritage*
       39(5) (1988):86.

838.   Mackey, T.C. "Red-Light Law: An Aspect of the Study of Prostitution."
       E. C. Barksdale Student Lectures (8) 1983-84:31-52.

       Discusses aspects of prostitution in nineteenth-century America, including
       prostitution law and municipally-sanctioned vice districts.

839.   Mackey, T.C. "Red Lights Out: A Legal History of Prostitution,
       Disorderly Houses, and Vice Districts, 1870-1917." (Ph.D. Dissertation)
       Rice University, 1984; also published by New York: Garland, 1987.

       Examines the legal changes and continuities in law applied to prostitutes
       and bawdy houses in the nineteenth and early twentieth century.
       Describes municipalities' use of state police power to district their
       disorderly houses and women, especially in St. Louis and New Orleans.

840.   MacDonald, N. "The Diggs-Caminetti Case of 1913 and Subsequent
       Interpretation of the White Slave Trade Act." *Pacific Historian* 29(1)
       (1985):30-39.

       Describes the federal government's prosecution and conviction of Drew
       Caminetti and Maury Diggs under the Mann Act which was enacted in
       1910. Examines the meaning and intent of this act.

841. MacPhail, E.C. "When the Lights Went out in San Diego: The Little Known Story of San Diego's 'Restricted' District." *Journal of San Diego History* 20(2) (1975):1-28.

Describes the Stingaree and Red-light Districts of San Diego from the 1870s to 1917; and the efforts of the city health inspector, Walter Bellon, to clean them up.

842. Marchant, J. *The Master Problem.* Reprinted New York: Garland, 1979. Originally published in 1917; deals with prostitution in United States.

843. Mark, N., and L. Weinberg. *Mayors, Madams, and Madmen.* Chicago: *Chicago Rev.*, 1979.

844. Martin, C., and E. West. *Whiskey and Wild Women: An Amusing Account of the Saloons and Bawds of the Old West.* New York: Hart, 1974.

845. Mazzulla, F., and J. Mazzulla. *Brass Checks and Red Lights; Being a Pictorial Pot Pourri of Historical Prostitutes, Parlor Houses, Professors, Procuresses and Pimps.* Denver: [s.n.], 1966.

Includes photos of brass checks.

846. McCormick, J.S. "Red Lights in Zion: Salt Lake City's Stockade, 1908-11." *Utah Historical Quarterly* 50(2) 1982:168-81.

847. McGovern, J.R. "'Sporting Life on the Line': Prostitution in Progressive Era Pensacola." *Florida Historical Quarterly* 54(2) (1975):131-44.

Lists the advantages of a confinement policy toward prostitution. Uses Progressive Era Pensacola as an example.

848. McKanna, Jr., C.V. "Hold Back the Tide: Vice Control in San Diego, 1870-1930." *Pacific History* 28(3) (1984):54-64.

Traces attempts to control prostitution in San Diego during the late nineteenth and early twentieth century. Asserts that the objective was often to confine prostitution to one district of the city.

849. Mensch, J.U. "Social Pathology in Urban America: Desertion, Prostitution, Gambling, Drugs and Crime Among Eastern European Jews in New York City Between 1881 and World War I." (Ph.D. Dissertation) Columbia University, New York, 1983.

Highlights the poverty of Eastern European Jews who entered the United States between 1881 and 1920 by examining deviant behavior such as desertion and prostitution.

850. Michelson, H. *Sportin' Ladies . . . : Confessions of the Bimbos.* Radnor, PA: Chilton, 1975.

851. Miller, R.D. *Shady Ladies of the West.* Los Angeles: Westernlore, 1964.

852. Murphy, M. "The Private Lives of Public Women: Prostitution in Butte, Montana, 1878-1917." *Frontiers* 7(3) (1984):30-5.

Describes the exclusive lifestyle that results from prostitution. Holds that the public nature of the activity provided little opportunity for a private life.

853. Naske, C.M. "The Red Lights of Fairbanks: Prostitution in Alaska in 1909." *Alaska Journal* 14(2) (1984):27-32.

Reports on the employment of alien immigrants as prostitutes in Fairbanks, Alaska in 1909. The reporting officer, the Alaska chief of the Immigration Service, found that the general population of Fairbanks was sympathetic toward both the prostitutes and their pimps and was unwilling to participate in any effort to control their activities.

854. Newcomb, J.M. "Captain Newcomb and the Frail Sisterhood." (A documentary account from 1863.) *American Heritage* 33(4) (1982):98-9.

855. Newman, F., E. Cohen, P. Tobin, and G. MacPherson. "Historical

Perspectives on the Study of Female Prostitution." *International Journal of Women's Studies* 8(1) (1985):80-86.

Summarizes literature on the twentieth-century evolution of female prostitution, and describes four schools of interpretation: (1) Victorian moralistic and biological determinism; (2) progressive reform; (3) academic sociology from the 1930s, and (4) psychoanalysis from the 1940s.

856. Olson, G. "Prostitutes and Other Perplexities." *Social Studies Review* 15(1) (Fall 1975):20-2.

Emphasizes the importance of studying California state history in order to understand the phenomenon of prostitution.

857. Pascoe, P. "Gender Systems in Conflict: The Marriages of Mission-Educated Chinese American Women, 1874-1939." *Journal of Social History* 22(4) (Summer 1989):631-52.

Contrasts the Chinese and Victorian gender systems. Discusses the contribution of American missionaries to the development of a Chinese-American culture, by rescuing Chinese immigrant women from exploitation by prostitution and attempting to integrate them into the Victorian gender system. Acknowledges the racism and ethnocentrism of the missionaries as well as their positive attributes.

858. Peffer, G.A. "Forbidden Families: Emigration Experiences of Chinese Women Under the Page Law, 1875-1882." *Journal of American Ethnic History* 6(1) (1986):28-46.

Recounts the manner in which American officials in China interpreted the Page Law's prohibition against the immigration of prostitutes to apply to almost all women of marriageable age. Argues that this policy was responsible for the very small number of Chinese families in the United States.

859. Petrik, P.E. "The Bonanza Town: Women and Family on the Rocky Mountain Mining Frontier, Helena, Montana, 1865-1900." (Thesis) State University of New York at Binghamton, 1981.

860. Petrik, P.E. "Strange Bedfellows: Prostitution, Politicians, and Moral
      Reform in Helena, 1885-1887." *Montana* 35(3) (1985):2-13.

      Discusses the controversy over prostitution in Helena following the
      completion of the Northern Pacific Railroad in 1883. Merchant pioneers
      were in favor of continued toleration. New businessmen arriving in the
      area advocated eradication and moral reform. A compromise was
      implemented in the adoption of a policy aimed at controlling prostitution.

861. Pillors, B.E. "The Criminalization of Prostitution in the United States:
      The Case of San Francisco, 1854-1919." (Ph.D. Dissertation) University
      of California, Berkeley, 1982.

      Traces the process of criminalizing prostitution in San Francisco over 60
      years. Discusses problems inherent in the criminal law's regulation of any
      private morality issue.

862. Pivar, D.J. *Purity Crusade: Sexual Morality and Social Control, 1868-
      1900.* Westport, CT: Greenwood, 1973.

      A pioneering work that focuses on the efforts of Progressives dealing with
      prostitution.

863. Pivar, D.J. "The Transformation of Abolitionist Morality: 1868-1921."
      Festschrift in Honor of Dr. Morton C. Fierman. Edited by J. Kalir.
      Fullerton, CA: Dept. of Religious Studies, California State University,
      1982.

864. Pivar, D.J. "Sisterhood Lost/Sisterhood Regained." *Reviews in American
      History* 11(2) (1983):243-7.

      Reviews Ruth Rosen's *The Lost Sisterhood: Prostitution in America, 1900-
      1918.*

865. *The Prostitute and the Social Reformer: Commercial Vice in the
      Progressive Era.* New York: Arno, 1974.

866. *Prostitution in America: Three Investigations, 1902-1914.* New York:

Arno, 1975.

Part of Arno series *Social Problems and Social Policy: The American Experience.* Outlines the perception of prostitution of the American public in the early twentieth century. Finds that prostitution was generally considered a major social problem and a threat to the health and well-being of the entire nation. Also shows prevailing attitudes toward sex roles and prostitution. Reprints investigations of special committees in New York City, Boston, and Syracuse.

867. Quayle, P.B. *Tales of Old Skid Row.* Murphys, CA: Philter, 1984.

868. Rapp, M.S. "Harlot's Progress: Prostitution and Contemporary Culture." (Ph.D. Dissertation) University of Chicago, 1986.

869. Riegel, R.E. "Changing American Attitudes Towards Prostitution: 1800-1920." *Journal of the History of Ideas* 29:(1968):439-52.

A pioneering attempt to explore the topic.

870. Roby, P.A. "Politics and Prostitution: A Case Study of the Formulation, Enforcement and Judicial Administration of the New York State Penal Laws on Prostitution, 1870-1970." (Ph.D. Dissertation) New York University, 1971.

Traces the formulation, enforcement, and judicial administration of N.Y. State's penal laws pertaining to prostitution between 1870-1970. Argues that laws on victimless crimes may reflect the sentiments of only a small but active segment of the community and may develop out of political struggles having little to do with the prostitution itself.

871. Rose, A., J.J. Jackson, and T.C. Reeves. *Storyville, New Orleans, Being an Authentic, Illustrated Account of the Notorious Red-Light District.* Birmingham: University of Alabama Press, 1974.

Based on interviews the author conducted with surviving madams, prostitutes, musicians and customers of Storyville, the area in New Orleans where prostitution thrived between 1898 and 1917 (and afterwards as well).

872.   Rosen, R. "Go West Young Woman? Prostitution on the Frontier."
        Reviews in American History 14(1) (1986):91-6.

        Reviews A. Butler's *Daughters of Joy, Sisters of Misery: Prostitutes in the
        American West, 1865-90.* (Urbana: University of Illinois Press,1985).
        Concludes that Butler misrepresents evidence in support of her argument
        that prostitutes experienced rejection, were poor parents, and expressed
        hostility toward each other.

873.   Rosen, R. *The Lost Sisterhood: Prostitution in America, 1900-1918.*
        Baltimore: Johns Hopkins University Press, 1982.

        Focuses on prostitution as a symbol, social structure, and subculture.
        Examines attitudes and actions of Progressives toward prostitution as a
        microcosm through which to study American values.

874.   Rothman, D.J., and S.M. Rothman. *Low Wages and Great Sins: Two
        Antebellum American Views on Prostitution and the Working Girl.* New
        York: Garland, 1987.

        Reprints C.H. Dall's *Woman's Right to Labor*, and J.Tuckerman's *An
        Essay on Wages Paid to Females for Their Labor.* Includes a discussion
        of prostitution.

875.   Ruggles, S. "Fallen Women: The Inmates of the Magdalen Society
        Asylum in Philadelphia: 1836-1908." *Journal of Social History* 16(4)
        (1983):65-82.

        Examines the Magdalen Society of Philadelphia and the case records of its
        2000 inmates. Inmate age shifted downward between 1878 and 1890 and
        failure rates declined. There was a growing acceptance of prostitution as
        inevitable.

876.   Ryan, J.C. *The Lumberjack Queens.* Duluth, MN: St. Louis County
        Historical Society, 1988.

        Loggers and prostitutes in the Duluth, Minnesota area.

877.   Saxon, G.D., and J.R. Summerville. "The Chicken Ranch: A Home on

the Range." *Red River Valley Historical Review* 7(1) (1982):33-44.

Presents the history of The Chicken Ranch, a notorious brothel near LaGrange, Texas. Describes the brothel, its supporters, and the campaign against it led by the Channel 13 news team and Marvin Zindler. As a result of this campaign, The Chicken Ranch was closed in 1973.

878. Shumsky, N. L. "The Municipal Clinic of San Francisco: A Study in Medical Structure." *Bulletin of the History of Medicine* 52 (1978):542-49.

Surveys records of the Municipal Clinic in San Francisco which opened in 1911 as an effort to decrease the incidence of venereal disease. Between its opening and December 1912, clinic doctors examined 60,736 prostitutes, an average of 116 per day. (Many had more than one exam.)

879. Shumsky, N.L. "Tacit Acceptance--Respectable Americans and Segregated Prostitution, 1870-1910." *Journal of Social History* 19(4) (1986):665-79.

880. Shumsky, N.L. "Vice Responds to Reform: San Francisco, 1910-1914." *Journal of Urban History* 7(1) (1980):31-47.

Describes criminal elements in San Francisco who tried to subvert control of prostitution in order to protect their own interests. Finds that reformers supporting regimentation were bankrolled and organized petition drives were arranged through front organizations.

881. Shumsky, N.L., and L.M. Springer. "San Francisco's Zone of Prostitution, 1880-1934." *Journal of Historical Geography* 7(1) (1981):71-89.

Analyzes the causal factors for spacial changes in San Francisco's red-light district. Includes discussions on the selective law enforcement, social attitudes, and commercial expansion which were all forces in providing stimuli for this change.

882. Siegel, A. "Brothels, Bets and Bars: Popular Literature as a Guidebook to the Urban Underground, 1840-70." *North Dakota Quarterly* 44 (1976):6-22.

883.   Silbert, F.   "American Ladies of the Night (Prostitutes and Past Attitudes to Prostitution in the U.S.)."   (French) *Histoire* 71 (1984):81-2.

884.   Szopa, A.   "Images of Women in Muncie Newspapers: 1895-1915." (Ph.D. Dissertation) Ball State University, Muncie, Indiana, 1986.

Includes a descriptive account of images of women labeled as prostitutes and their changing image at ten year intervals: (1) In 1895, prostitutes were presented as stigmatized but integral members of the community; (2) in 1905, the prostitute had become a symbol of individual and communal decay; (3) by 1915, the prostitute had become a victim of the socio-economic processes.

885.   Tandberg, G.D.   "Sinning for Silk: Dress-for-Success Fashions of the New Orleans Storyville Prostitute." *Women's Studies International Forum* 13(3) (1990):229-248.

Fashions adopted by prostitutes emulated those worn by upper class society. Argues that clothing itself seduced many women into prostitution.

886.   Terrell, K.A.   "Exposure of Prostitution in Western Massachusetts: 1911." *Historical Journal of Massachusetts* 8(2) (1980):3-11.

Describes the crusade launched by the *Chicopee News* to expose prostitution in Westfield, Massachusetts. The publication of articles on this issue resulted in the arrest of newspaper employees and the end of the crusade.

887.   Vogliotti, G.R.   *The Girls of Nevada.* Greenwich, CT: Fawcett, 1975.

888.   Wagner, R.R.   "Virtue against Vice: A Study of Moral Reformers and Prostitution in the Progressive Era." (Thesis) University of Wisconsin, Madison, 1971.

889.   Waterman, W.C.   *Prostitution and its Repression in New York City, 1900-1931.* New York: AMS, 1968.

890. West, E. "Scarlet West: The Oldest Profession in the Trans-Mississippi West." *Montana* 31(2) (1981):16-27.

Refutes histories of prostitution in the nineteenth-century trans-Mississippi West. Argues that they are biased by social attitudes about sex and an eastern Victorian perspective. Contends that Western prostitution was a common and more accepted social phenomenon. Concludes that finding a profile for a "typical" prostitute is impossible.

891. Whiteaker, L. "Moral Reform and Prostitution in New York City, 1830-1860." (Thesis) Princeton University, 1977. Photocopy, Ann Arbor, MI: University Microfilms International, 1987.

892. Williams, G. *The Redlight Ladies of Virginia City, Nevada.* Riverside, CA: Tree by the River Pub., 1984.

893. Williams, G. *Rosa May. The Search for a Mining Camp Legend.* Riverside, CA: Tree by the River Pub., 1980.

894. Wilson, S.P. *Chicago by Gaslight.* Chicago: [s.n.], 1910. Reissued on microfilm: New Haven, CT: Research Publications, 1976.

Prostitution in Chicago.

895. Winick, C., and P.M. Kinsie. *The Lively Commerce: Prostitution in the United States.* Chicago: Quandrangle Books, 1971.

Offers a comprehensive and authoritative study of prostitution. Contains information from the files of the American Social Health Association and over two thousand interviews with prostitutes, pimps, clients, and law enforcement officials.

896. Woodiwiss, M. *Crime, Crusades and Corruption: Prohibitions in the United States, 1900-1987.* Totowa, NJ: Barnes & Noble, 1988.

Discusses attempts by law enforcement agencies to enforce laws prohibiting drinking, drug use, gambling, and prostitution. Argues that the laws promote a level of crime and corruption much greater than that found in more tolerant societies, and that these laws were selectively enforced.

897. Worthington, G.E., and R. Topping. *Specialized Courts Dealing With Sex Delinquency: A Study of the Procedure in Chicago, Boston, Philadelphia, and New York.* Montclair, NJ: Patterson Smith, 1969.

Study jointly sponsored by the American Social Hygiene Association and the Bureau of Social Hygiene. Reprint of the 1925 edition.

898. Wunsch, J.L. "Prostitution and Public Policy: From Regulation to Suppression, 1858-1920." (Ph.D. Dissertation) University of Chicago, 1976.

Focuses on St. Louis and New York City during the last quarter of the nineteenth century, where brothels were licensed in order to confine prostitution and prevent the spread of venereal disease. Finds that attitudes changed after 1900, and during the Progressive era legal and judicial efforts targeted the suppression of vice districts in American cities.

899. Wunsch, J.L. "The Social Evil Ordinance." *American Heritage* 33(2) (1982):50-55.

Outlines implementation of the "social evil law" by the St. Louis City Council in 1870, in an attempt to license and regulate brothels. After ten years, St. Louis joined most other American cities in prohibiting brothels.

ART

900. Alcalá Flecha, R. *Matrimonio y prostitución en el arte de Goya.* Cáceres, Spain: Servicio de Publicaciones de la Universidad de Extremadura, 1984.

Discusses prostitution and marriage in the art of Francisco Goya (1746-1828).

901. Andersson, C. *Ausgewählte Zeichnungen von Urs Graf.* Basel: GS-Verlag, 1978.

Examines prostitutes, soldiers, fools and jesters in the art of Urs Graf (ca. 1485-ca. 1527).

902. Atwood, J.E. *Nachtlicher Alltag: meine Begegnung mit Prostituierten in Paris: eine fotografische Studie.* München: Mahnert-Lueg Verlag, 1980.

A photographic study of a prostitute's entrance to the profession in Paris.

903. Barzaghi, A. *Donne o cortigiane?: la prostituzione a Venezia: Documenti di costume dal XVI al XVIII secolo.* Verona: Bertani, 1980.

Discusses the costumes of sixteenth- to eighteenth-century Venetian prostitutes and their history.

904. Bazal, J. *Marseille galante; Photographic Illustration under the Direction of Marcel Baudelaire.* Marseille: P. Tacussel, 1980.

Examines prostitution in Marseille.

905. Bellocq, E.J. *Storyville Portraits.* Edited by John Szarkowski. New York: Museum of Modern Art, 1970.

Photographs from the New Orleans red-light district, ca. 1912. Reproduced from prints made by Lee Friedlander.

906. Bernheimer, C. *Figures of Ill Repute: Representing Prostitution in Nineteenth-Century France.* Cambridge: Harvard University Press, 1989.

Examines prostitution of nineteenth-century France through art and literature; most subject matter is criminal in essence.

907. Bertholon, G. *Vivent les putes!* Paris: P. J. Oswald, 1973.

Caricatures and Cartoons.

908. Bodurtha, J. "Magdalen Hospital Engraved by George Quinton, 1797, after a painting by T.S. Duche." *Journal of the History of Medicine and Allied Sciences* 34(3) (1979):353.

909. Bradley, D.S., J. Boles, and C. Jones. "From Mistress to Hooker: 40 Years of Cartoon Humor in Men's Magazines." *Qualitative Sociology* 2(2) (September 1979):42-62.

Analyzes mass media humor and changing male sexual mores regarding prostitution through content analysis of 405 cartoons published in *Esquire* or *Playboy* from 1934 to 1974. Shows the change in the image of the prostitute, which reflects subtle changes in sexual mores.

910. Brown, M.R. "The Harem Dehistoricized: Ingres' Turkish Bath." *Arts Magazine* LXI(10) (Summer 1987):58-68.

Reevaluates Ingres's image of the harem in his painting, "Turkish Bath" (Paris, Louvre), in light of recent revisionism in the study of Orientalism, the Turkish harem in Ingres's day, and the ideology of the work, including its relation to contemporary Parisian prostitution.

911. Clark, T.J. *The Painting of Modern Life: Paris in the Art of Manet and His Followers.* New York: Knopf, 1985.

Discusses popular culture and prostitution in French Impressionist painting.

912. Clayson, [S.] H. "Prostitution and the Art of Later Nineteenth-Century France: On Some Differences Between the Work of Degas and Duez." *Arts Magazine* LX(4) (December 1985):40-5.

Compares the treatment of the prostitute in the works of Hilaire Germain Edgar Manet, painter and sculptor (1834-1917); and Ernest Ange Duez, painter (1843-1896).

913. Clayson, [S.] H. "Representations of Prostitution in Early Third Republic France." (Ph.D. Dissertation) University of California at Los Angeles, 1984; also published in Ann Arbor, MI: University Microfilms International, 1985.

Presents evidence of the marked interest in prostitution among artists and writers during the early years of France's Third Republic. Argues that artists were attracted to the subject because of the ways in which prostitutes embody the notion of modernity.

914. Deutsche, R. "Alienation in Berlin: Kirchner's Street Scenes." *Art in America* LXXI(1) (January 1983):64-72.

Offers a political interpretation of Kirschner's images and discusses representation of dehumanization, sexuality, and the significance of Kirschner's prostitutes.

915. Eliel, C.S. "Louis-Leopold Boilly's The Galleries of the Palais-Royal." *Burlington Magazine* 974 (May 1984):275-9.

Shows a contrast between Boilly's Galleries of the Palais-Royal, 1809 (Musée Carnavalet, Paris), and works of his contemporaries. His painting suggests that prostitutes are victims of society's imperfections rather than a cause of them, while his contemporaries concentrate on the high society of palace gardens and galleries and treat the subject with an air of levity.

916. *Filles de Joie: The Book of Courtesans, Sporting Girls, Ladies of the Evening, Madams, a Few Occasional and Some Royal Favorites.* Secaucus, NJ: Castle Books, 1967. Illustrated.

An interesting collection of photographs.

917.   Gill, S.   "Theophile Steinlen; a Study of his Graphic Art, 1881-1900."
        (Ph.D. Dissertation) City University of New York, 1982.

        Discusses Steinlen's work for four major periodicals. Shows he was a
        proselytizer for the poor, the oppressed, and the working class, and
        created a series of stereotypes and allegorical figures that operated as left-
        wing propaganda. Examines his influence on Pablo Picasso, Edward
        Penfield, and John Sloan.

918.   Gilman, S.L.   "Black Bodies, White Bodies: Toward an Iconography of
        Female Sexuality in Late Nineteenth-Century Art, Medicine, and
        Literature."   *Critical Inquiry* 12(1) (Autumn 1985):204-42.

        Examines the work of Emile Zola, including *Nana*, in order to illustrate
        icons of prostitutes and black women in the nineteenth century.

919.   Gilman, S.L.   "Hottentots and the Prostitute: Toward an Iconography of
        Female Sexuality."   *Clio Medica, Netherlands* 19(1-2) (1984):111-35.

        Examines the late eighteenth-century view that Khoisan (Hottentot) women
        were physically abnormal, with large genitals and buttocks and the ensuing
        belief that Khoisan women had excessive and primitive sexual urges.
        Describes how these attitudes were applied to black women and prostitutes
        and shows their bases in European men's insecurity about their own
        sexuality and fear of losing authority over women.

920.   Gronberg, T.A.   "Femmes de brasserie."   *Art History* VII(3) (September
        1984):329-44.

        Investigates the imagery depicting women employees and customers in
        Parisian brasseries, the chief sites of clandestine prostitution of the late
        nineteenth-century. Examines the complex relationship between women's
        work and sexuality and suggests that Impressionist iconography frequently
        alludes to women engaged in clandestine prostitution.

921.   Hall, M.   "Manet's Ball at the Opera: A Matter of Response."   *Rutgers
        Art Review* V (Spring 1984):28-45.

Analyzes the moral, social, and political implications of Manet's "Ball at the Opera" (National Gallery of Art, Washington, DC). The painting depicts bourgeois gentlemen openly associating with prostitutes in a public place.

922. "The Happiest Hookers: Cartoons from *Playboy*." Chicago: Playboy, 1974.

Illustrates caricatures and cartoons, and American male sexual humor from *Playboy* magazine.

923. Hennig, J-L. *Grisélidis, courtisane*. Paris: A. Michel, 1981. Illustrated. Prostitutes in Geneva, Switzerland.

924. Hobhouse, J. "The World, the Flesh, and Modigliani." *Connoisseur* 215(8821) (1985):42-49.

925. Hofmann, W. *Nana, Mythos und Wirklichkeit*. Köln: DuMont, 1973.

Examines works of Edouard Manet, Emile Zola, and Joachim Heusinger von Waldegg.

926. Kinser, S.L. "Prostitutes in the Art of John Sloan." *Prospects (U.K.)* 9 (1984):231-54.

Examines the paintings and etchings depicting American prostitutes produced by John Sloan during the years 1907-13. Posits that Sloan catered neither to those academicians who found the subject disgusting nor to the reformers who viewed prostitutes as hapless victims and that Sloan used this subject as an example of one more result of the new urbanization.

927. Kunzle, D., V. Tufte, and B. Myerhoff. *William Hogarth: The Ravaged Child in the Corrupt City*. New Haven: Yale University Press, 1979.

Examines Hogarth's presentation of the child as an essentially parentless creature, exposed to cruelty and neglect. Examines his recordings of the characteristic evils of eighteenth-century London and his vision of reform through private philanthropy. Discusses these ideas in the context of his series *Harlot's Progress, Rake's Progress and Cruelty*, and their influence on Dickens.

928. Legrand, F-C. "Rops et Baudelaire." *Gazette des Beaux-Arts* CVIII (December 1986):191-200.

Examines the friendship between the two Symbolistes, Rops and Baudelaire. Both were fascinated with women of easy virtue and with Satan and death.

929. Leja, M. "'Le vieux marcheur' and 'Les deux risques': Picasso, Prostitution, Venereal Disease, and Maternity, 1899-1907." *Art History* VIII(1) (March 1985):66-81.

Examines a number of Picasso's paintings, including images of prostitutes, mothers, and children in Paris within the context of the contemporary controversy between rightist abolitionists and leftist new-regulationists over the issue of prostitution.

930. Liebmann, M.J. "Ein 'Ungleiches Paar' Cranach." (An 'Odd-Couple' by Cranach). *Acta historiae artium* XXIV(1-4) (1978):233-6.

Discusses the relationship of a lithograph by J.B. Mauzaisse of a farmer and prostitute to a painting of the same subject (private collection, Moscow) attributed by the author to Cranach's workshop.

931. Mathews, P. "The Minotaur of London." *Apollo* CXXIII(291) (May 1986):338-41.

Analyzes G.F. Watt's moral crusades, puritanical writings, and art and supports the view that his painting 'The Minotaur' (Tate Gallery, London) was created in direct response to an 1885 exposé of child prostitution in London.

932. Mathieu, L., et al. *Lautrec: 'elles'*. Albi: Société des Amis du Musée d'Albi, 1976.

Catalogue and text of an exhibition dealing with prostitution and Lautrec.

933.   Nead, L. "A Definition of Deviancy: Prostitution in High Art in England
       c. 1860." *Block* 11 (Winter 1985-1986):40-7.

       Explores contradictions involved in the representation of prostitution in
       mid-Victorian painting. The belief that the effects of vice and immorality
       must show themselves in the prostitute's outward appearance was difficult
       to reconcile with the ideal of woman as an object of aesthetic pleasure and
       moral admiration.

934.   Nead, L. "Seduction, Prostitution, Suicide: On the Brink by Alfred
       Elmore." *Art History* V(3) (September 1982):310-22.

       Interprets the painting (Fitzwilliam Museum, Cambridge) exhibited at the
       Royal Academy, London, in 1865, as the moment of choice between good
       and evil after losing at the gambling table, and discusses contemporary
       reviews in the context of Victorian attitudes toward female sexuality and
       seduction.

935.   Nead, L. "The Magdalen in Modern Times: The Mythology of the Fallen
       Woman in Pre-Raphaelite Painting."   *Oxford Art Journal* VII(1)
       (1984):26-37.

       Examines visual and verbal images of ideal womanhood (the madonna) in
       contrast to those of fallen womanhood (the magdalen), and proposes that
       such images not only reflected but participated in the Victorians'
       definitions of sexual respectability and deviancy.

936.   Paul, D.L. "Willumsen and Gaugin in the 1890s." *Apollo* CXI(215)
       (January 1980):36-45.

       Discusses Gaugin's influence on Willumsen after their meeting in Brittany,
       including the depiction of women and prostitutes.

937.   Shesgreen, S.   "A Harlot's Progress and the Question of Hogarth's
       Didacticisms." *Eighteenth Century Life* II(2) (December 1975):22-8.

       Shows that "A Harlot's Progress" is not merely a condemnation of the
       protagonist of Hogarth's most popular series, as has often been imagined,
       but is a keen attack on the economically motivated urban culture of which
       Moll Hackabout is a part, a culture which played a considerable part in
       her fate.

938. Snell, J.W. *Painted Ladies of the Cowtown Frontier*. Kansas City: Kansas City Posse of the Westerners, 1965.

Examines prostitution in the American West with illustrations.

939. *Specchio de la puttana.(The Whore's Mirror)*. Venice?: s.n., 165-?.

Lacks title page or equivalent source of information. Twelve prints or adaptations of prints by Federico Agnelli with engraved verse.

940. Van Tilborgh, L. "Freudian Motifs in the Oeuvre of Pyke Koch." *Simiolus* (Netherlands) 15(2) (1985):131-50.

Discusses the work of Dutch magic realist painter Pyke Koch (b. 1901), and focuses on illustrations of the theories of Freud, and Freudian interpretations of his themes in his paintings of prostitutes. Discusses links made between Freudian theories and other individual paintings where symbols of impotence are juxtaposed with images of women.

941. Vargas, A. "La Casa de Cita: Mexican Photographs from the Belle Epoque." London: Quartet Books, 1986.

Collection of photographs of Mexican women, nudes, and prostitutes.

942. Welsh-Ovcharov, B. *Emile Bernard, 1868-1941: The Theme of Bordellos and Prostitutes in Turn-of-the-Century French Art*. Organized by P.D. Cate. Catalogue by B. Welsh-Ovcharov. Exhibit held at Jane Voorhees Zimmerli Art Museum, Rutgers, the State University of New York, April 3-May 31, 1988.

THEATER AND OPERA

943. Campbell, C. *The French Procuress: Her Character in Renaissance Comedies*. New York: P. Lang, 1985.

Discusses procuresses and prostitution in French drama and literature of the sixteenth and seventeenth centuries.

944. Davis, T.C. "Actresses and Prostitutes in Victorian London." *Theatre Research International* 13(3) (Autumn 1988):221-34.

945. Feindel, J. "Developing a Particular Class of Women." *Canadian Theatre Review* 59 (Summer 1989):38-41.

Discusses the play *A Particular Class of Women*; illustrates its aspects of female sexuality and the creative process.

946. Gallagher, C. "Who Was That Masked Woman? The Prostitute and the Playwright in the Comedies of Aphra Behn." *Women's Studies: An Interdisciplinary Journal* 15(1-3) (1988):23-42.

947. Gier, A. "Rodrigo Cota und Fernando de Rojas: Comedia de Calisto y Melibea (Celestina)." *Das Spanische Theater: Vom Mittelalter bis zur Gegenwart*. Düsseldorf: Schwann-Bagel, 1988, pp. 23-35.

Examines the didacticism of the Spanish medieval fictional work, *La Celestina*.

948. Haselkorn, A.M. *Prostitution in Elizabethan and Jacobean Comedy*. Troy, NY: Whitson, 1983.

949. Ingram, A.J.C. *In the Posture of a Whore: Changing Attitudes to 'Bad' Women in Elizabethan and Jacobean Drama*. Salzburg: Institut fur Anglistik und Amerikanistik, Universitat Salzburg, 1984.

950. Jackson, L. "Labor Relations: An Interview with Lizzie Borden." *Cineaste: America's Leading Magazine on the Art and Politics of the Cinema* 40(3) (1987):4-9.

Deals with the prostitution of Lizzie Borden.

951. Johnson, C.D. "That Guilty Third Tier: Prostitution in Nineteenth-Century American Theaters." *American Quarterly* 27(5) (1975):575-84.

Discusses the problems in theaters resulting from assignment of prostitutes to the third tier and traces the subsequent acceptance of theater in American life through its disassociation from prostitution.

952.   Millstone, A.H.   "French Feminist Theater and the Subject of Prostitution, 1870-1914." *The Image of the Prostitute in Modern Literature.* Edited by P.L. Horn and M.B. Pringle. New York: Ungar, 1984, pp. 19-27.

Discusses feminism and prostitution in French theater and drama, using the works of Jeanne Marie Francoise Marni and Eugene Brieux.

953.   Ratcliffe, M.   "Prostitute I May Be But Common I'm Not." *Drama* 142 (1981):43.

954.   Sun, C.   *Courtisanes chinoises à la fin des Tang, entre circa 789 et le 8 janvier 881, Pei-litche (anecdotes du quartier du Nord), par Souen Ki.* Paris: Presses Universitaires de France, 1968.

Discusses prostitution, courtesans, and theater in China from 789 to 881.

955.   Toledo, M.   *El drama de la prostitución: las que nacieron para perder: Coleccion Testimonos.* México, D.F.: Editores Mexicanos Unidos, 1981.

MUSIC

956.   Grawe, K.D.   "L'uno e gli altri. Osservazioni sulla drammaturgia verdiana di conflitto interumano e della sua soluzione." *Atti del IIIo congresso internazional di studi verdiani* (RILM76 171):27-33.

Shows Verdi's heroines as representative of minorities on the fringe of a homogeneous society, yet successful in achieving positions of prominence; but when these roles are exceeded, there begins a conflict between individual and society that can be resolved only by death.

957.   Henry, E.O.   "Record Reviews: Indian Music." *Ethnomusicology*, California State University at San Diego 24(2) (May 1980):328-30.

Discusses the following recordings: 1) Middle caste religious music from India: musicians, dancers, prostitutes, and actors (Lyrichord LLST 7323), and 2) Lower-caste religious music from India: monks, transvestites, midwives, and folksingers (Lyrichord LLST 7324), both recorded by R. Schenkler.

958.   Johannesson, K. "Bellman som musikalisk diktare." In: *Lyrik i tid och otid; lyrikanalytiska studier tilläganade Gunnar Tideström*. Edited by Gunilla and Staffan Bergsten. Lund: Gleerup, 1971.

Analyzes the combination of musical and verbal elements used by the Swedish poet Bellman. Shows that Bellman used aristocratic minuet tunes or sorrowful opera arias to describe a world of drunkards and prostitutes and created a tension between the different styles and social worlds of his time.

959.   Longstreet, F. *Sportin' House: A History of the New Orleans Sinners and the Birth of Jazz*. Los Angeles: Sherbourne, 1965.

Gives a history of jazz music, jazz musicians, and prostitutes in New Orleans.

960.   Mead, J.H. "Sea Shanties and Fo'c'sle Songs, 1768-1906." (Ph.D. Dissertation) University of Kentucky, 1973.

Examines fo'c'sle (forecastle) songs, which were sung by sailors in their off-duty hours at the sea shanties. Shows that sailors preferred songs about their loves ashore, and about home, family, and friends and that songs of death at sea, drinking and prostitution were less frequent.

961.   Mendes Barcellos, L.R. "Die musiktherapeutische Behandlung von Amusie bei einer Patientin mit musikalischer Vorbildung." *Therapeutische Umschau* IV (1983):205-12.

Describes the treatment of prostitution with music therapy; gives a case study of a patient with musical training.

962.   Samovar, M., and F. Sanders. "Language Patterns of the Prostitute-Some Insights into a Deviant Subculture." California State University at San

Diego, Department of Speech Communications 35(1) (1978):30-6.

963.   Schneider, U.   "Die Londoner Music Hall und ihre Songs."   Tübingen,
        Germany: Neimeyer, 1984.

        Examines the London music halls from 1850 to 1920 in terms of society,
        politics, prostitution, and the roles which blacks played in music hall
        society.

LITERATURE

964.   Accad, E. H.   "The Prostitute in Arab and North African Fiction."   *The
        Image of the Prostitute in Modern Literature*. Edited by P.L. Horn and
        M.B. Pringle. New York: Ungar, 1984, pp. 63-75.

        Discusses North African, West Asian, and Arabic literature, including *La
        Statue de Sel* (The Pillar of Salt) and *Hunters in a Narrow Street*.

965.   Aldaraca, B.A.   "The Ideology of Domesticity: Galdos and the Spanish
        Tradition."   *Dissertation Abstracts International* 48(12) (June 1982).

        Examines the work of Benito Perez Galdos, and discusses such themes as
        money, marriage, motherhood, adultery, and prostitution.

966.   "All Through the Night: Stories of the World's Oldest Profession."
        Chicago: Playboy Press, 1975.

967.   Baker, S.R.   "Théodore, vierge et martyre (1645): A Case of
        Prostitution."   *Degré Second: Studies in French Literature* 10 (September
        1986):1-15.

968.   Bernheimer, C.   "Female Sexuality and Narrative Closure: Barbey's 'La
        vengeance d'une femme' and 'A un dîner d'athées'".   *Romanic Review*
        74(3) (May 1983):330-41.

969.   Bernheimer, C.   "Prostitution and Narrative: Balzac's 'Splendeurs et

miseres des courtisanes'." *L'Esprit Créateur* 25(2) (Summer 1985):22-31.

970. Best, J. "Looking Evil in the Face, Being an Examination of Vice and Respectability in St. Paul as Seen in the City's Press, 1865-83." *Minnesota History* 50(6) (1987):241-51.

Surveys how the four daily newspapers covered prostitution when the city of St. Paul regulated it through monthly "fines." The interface between "deviant" behavior and respectability involved the roles of the general public as customer, observer, landlord, regulator, and hostile opponent.

971. Billingsley, B.A. "Take Her Up Tenderly: A Study of the Fallen Woman in the Nineteenth-Century English Novel." (Ph.D. dissertation) University of Texas, 1962.

Discusses social problems and moral conditions of prostitutes in nineteenth-century English literature.

972. Bose, J.H. *Had de mensch met een vrou niet connen leven: prostitutie in de literatuur van de zeventiende eeuw.* Zutphen: Walburg Pers, 1985.

Examines the prostitute in seventeenth-century Dutch literature.

973. Braendlin, B.H. "The Prostitute As Scapegoat: Mildred Rogers in Somerset Maugham's 'Of Human Bondage'." *The Image of the Prostitute in Modern Literature.* Edited by P.L. Horn and M.B. Pringle. New York: Ungar, 1984, pp. pp. 9-18.

Discusses the role of Mildred Rogers as prostitute and scapegoat.

974. Brooks, P. "The Mark of the Beast-Prostitution, Melodrama, and Narrative." *New York Literary Forum* 7 (1980):125-40.

975. Butler, J.E.G. *The Josephine Butler Letter Collection: 12 March 1816 - October 1906.* (Microform) Zug, Switzerland: Inter Documentation, 1983.

Illustrates, by her personal letters, the social and moral conditions of women and prostitutes in Butler's time (1828-1906).

976. Carstens, B.H. "Prostitution in the Works of Odon von Horvath."
(Dissertation) University of North Carolina, Chapel Hill, 1980; *DAI* 42(2)
(August 1981). Published as a book under the above title, Stuttgart:
Akademischer Verlag Hans-Dieter Heinz, 1982.

977. Christophe, M.A. "Sex, Racism, and Philosophy in Sartre, Jean-Paul,
'The Respectful Prostitute'." *College Language Association Journal* 24(1)
(1980):76-86.

978. *Colección el arco de Eros: Prostibulario 2.* Buenos Aires: Editorial
Merlin, 1969.

A collection of stories about prostitution.

979. Collins, W.J. "Taking on the Champion: Alice as Liar in 'The Light of
the World'." *Studies in American Fiction* 14(2) (Autumn 1986):225-32.

Discusses the prostitute in Ernest Hemingway's short story.

980. Crampton, E.J. *Letters to Emma Jane.* London: Eyre Methuen, 1977.

A collection of letters to a British prostitute.

981. Cruz, A.J., and S. Fisher. "Sexual Enclosure, Textual Escape: The
Picara as Prostitute in the Spanish Female Picaresque Novel." *Seeking the
Woman in Late Medieval and Renaissance Writings: Essays in Feminist
Contextual Criticism.* Edited by J.E. Halley. Knoxville: University of
Tennessee Press, 1989, pp. 135-59.

982. Czyba, L. "Paris et la lorette." *Paris au XIXe siècle: Aspects d'un mythe
littéraire.* Lyon: La Presse Universitaire du Lyon, 1984, pp. 107-22.

983. Donaldson-Evans, M. "The Decline and Fall of Elisabeth Rousset: Text
and Context in Maupassant's 'Boule de suif'." *Australian Journal of
French Studies* 18(1) (January - April 1981):16-34.

Examines the symbolism of prostitution of Maupassant's work in relation to the Franco-Prussian War.

984. Du Sorbier, F. "Le corps venal ou la prostituée et sa représentation dans le recit au début du dix-huitième siècle." *Échanges: Actes du Congrès de Strasbourg*. Paris: Didier, 1982, pp. 203-15.

Discusses the works of Alexander Smith, Bernard Mandeville, and Daniel Defoe and their handling of prostitution.

985. Eckley, G. "Beef to the Heel: Harlotry with Josephine Butler, William T. Stead, and James Joyce." *Studies in the Novel* 20(1) (Spring 1988):64-77.

986. Evans, J. "Mother Africa and the Heroic Whore: Female Images in 'Petals of Blood'." *Contemporary African Literature*. Washington, DC: Three Continents & African Literature Association, 1983, pp. 57-65.

987. *Examen subi par Mademoiselle Flora à l'effet d'obtenir son diplôme de putain et d'être admise au bordel de Mme. Lebrun 68 bis, rue de Richelieu*. S.l.: s.n.

Prostitution and poetry.

988. Fernández de Moratín, N. *Arte de las putas*. Madrid: Ediciones Siro, 1977.

Prostitution and poetry.

989. Ferran, P. *Vocabulaire des filles de joie*. Catalog by Pierre Ferran, Mane: R. Morel, 1970.

Prostitute slang.

990. Fishbein, L. "Prostitution, Morality, and Paradox: Moral Relativism in Edith Wharton's 'Old New York: New Year's Day (The 'Seventies)'." *Studies in Short Fiction* 24(4) (Fall 1987):399-406.

Discusses prostitution, adultery, and moral relativism in the work of Edith Wharton.

991.   Foster, D.W.   "Cela and Spanish Marginal Culture."   *The Review of Contemporary Fiction* 4(3) (Fall 1984):55-9.

Examines prostitution, marginality, and censorship in Spanish literature.

992.   Fricke, D.G.   "Swift, Hogarth, and the Sister Arts."   *Eighteenth-Century Life* 2(2) (1975):29-33.

Compares the satire of William Hogarth and Jonathan Swift using the "sister arts" and Zeitgeist approaches. They draw similar character portraits of prostitutes and satirize the corruption of the times.

993.   Gallagher, C.   "George Eliot and Daniel Deronda: The Prostitute and the Jewish Question."   *Sex, Politics, and Science in the Nineteenth-Century Novel.* Edited by Ruth Bernard Yeazell. Baltimore: Johns Hopkins University Press, 1986, pp. 39-62.

Discusses works of George Eliot in reference to prostitution.

994.   Garfield, J.   "The Wandering Whore", vol. 1-5, 1660-1661.   Exeter: Rota, 1977.
Seventeenth-century erotic literature, reprinted.

995.   Glickman, N.   "The Jewish White Slave Trade in Latin American Writings."   *American Jewish Archives* 34(2) (1982):178-89.

Outlines the literary treatment of the Jewish white slave trade to Argentina prevalent in the late nineteenth and early twentieth century. Mid-twentieth-century Argentine writers portrayed the polacas (European Jewish women imported for the purpose of prostitution) as evil and unredeemable.

996.   Goldgar, B.A.   "Fielding and the Whores of London."   *Philological Quarterly* 64(2) (1985):265-73.

Discusses the English prostitute and her treatment in eighteenth-century literature by Henry Fielding.

997.   Greenwald, H., and A. Krich.   *The Prostitute in Literature.*   New York:

Ballantine, 1960.

998. Groves, D. "James Hogg's Confessions and Three Perils of Woman and the Edinburgh Prostitution Scandal of 1823." *The Wordsworth Circle* 18(3) (Summer 1987):127-31.

Discusses the Scottish literature of James Hogg, particularly "The Three Perils of Woman" and "Confessions of a Justified Sinner," and also work by Mary McKinnon.

999. Guidi, L. "Prostitute e carcerate a Napoli: Alcune indagini tra fine '800 e inizio '900." *Memoria: Rivista di Storia delle Donne* 4 (1982):116-24.

Surveys a number of works by social scientists and literary figures that provide eyewitness accounts of the conditions of "marginal" women in Naples, among them orphans, migrants, prostitutes, and criminals. Describes the environment inside and outside prisons, and prostitutes' circumstances and motivations.

1000. Guilfoyle, C. "Ower Swete Sokor: The Role of Ophelia in Hamlet." *Drama in the Renaissance: Comparative and Critical Essays. AMS Studies in Renaissance* VIII(12) (1986):163-77.

Discusses the issues of innocence and prostitution in regards to Ophelia in William Shakespeare's *Hamlet*.

1001. Gun, W.H. *La courtisane romantique et son rôle dans La comédie humaine de Balzac.* Assen: Van Gorcum, 1963.

1002. Hapke, L. *Girls Who Went Wrong: Prostitutes in American Fiction, 1885-1917.* Bowling Green: Popular Culture, 1989.

1003. Hapke, L. "Maggie's Sisters: Nineteenth Century Literary Images of the American Streetwalker." *Journal of American Culture* 5(2) (Summer 1982):29-35.

Reviews the depiction of prostitution in nineteenth-century American literature, and focuses on the emergence of the naturalist perspective and on awareness of prostitution as a social phenomenon.

1004. Hapke, L. "Those That Will Not Work: Nineteenth Century American Literature and the Woman of the Streets." *The Nassau Review: The Journal of Nassau Community College Devoted to Arts, Letters, and Sciences* 4(5) (1984):71-82.

1005. Harris, D.A. "D.G. Rosetti's 'Jenny': Sex, Money, and the Interior Monologue." *Victorian Poetry* 22(2) (Summer 1984):197-215.

1006. Harskamp, J.T. *Hoeren en heren: in de 19de-eeuwse literatuur.* Utrecht: HES, 1988.

Examines prostitution in nineteenth-century literature.

1007. Hayward, C. *Dictionary of Courtesans; An Anthology, Sometimes Gay, Sometimes Tragic, of the Celebrated Courtesans of History from Antiquity to the Present Day.* New edition, introduction by V.L. Bullough. New Hyde Park, NY: University Books, 1962.

Famous prostitutes in history and literature.

1008. Hillsman, D.F. "Crane's 'Maggie' and Huysmans' 'Marthe': Two Naturalist Prostitute Novels." *Dissertation Abstracts International* 48(3) (September 1987).

1009. Horn, P.L., and M.B. Pringle. *The Image of the Prostitute in Modern Literature.* New York: Ungar, 1984.

1010. Howard, J.A. *Dietrich von Bern (1597).* Würzburg: Königshausen & Neumann, 1986.

Prostitution and German literature of the sixteenth-century.

1011. Hughes, J.M. "The Uncommon Prostitute: The Contemporary Image in an American Age of Pornography." *The Image of the Prostitute in*

Modern Literature. Edited by P.L. Horn and M.B. Pringle. New York: Ungar, 1984, pp. 101-18.

1012. Ibieta, G. "El personaje de la prostituta segun Manuel Galvez: Aproximaciones a Dostoievski." *Revista de Estudios Hispanicos* 21(3) (October 1987):11-9.

Compares the persona of Galvez's prostitutes to characters of Dostoyevsky.

1013. Ibitokun, B.N. "Prostitution or Neurosis (A Note on Ekwensi, Cyprian 'Jagua Nana')." *Nsukka Studies in African Literature* 3 (1980):81-7.

1014. Johnson, A. "Arthur Symons's 'The Life and Adventures of Lucy Newcome': Preface and Text." *English Literature in Transition (1880-1920)* 28(4) (1985):332-45.

1015. Johnson, R.D. "Folklore and Women: A Social Interactional Analysis of the Folklore of a Texas Madam." *Journal of American Folklore* 86(341) (1973):211-24.

Examines the role of a brothel madam as a social controller.

1016. Johnston, D. "Pieces on Prostitution." *Meanjini* 40(2) (1981):139-46.

1017. Jordan, C. "The Harlot in Yeats' 'The Death of Cuchulain'." *English Language Notes* 24(4) (June 1987):61-5.

1018. Jourdan, P. "Les manifestations du naturalisme en Espagne: deux romans de Lopez Bago: El periodista et La prostituta." *Iris* 1 (1988):69-105.

1019. Kiminsky, A.K. "Women Writing About Prostitutes: Amalia Jamilis and Luisa Valenzuela." *The Image of the Prostitute in Modern Literature.* Edited by P.L. Horn and M.B. Pringle. New York: Ungar, 1984, pp. 119-31.

1020. Kishtainy, K. *The Prostitute in Progressive Literature.* London: Allison & Busby, 1982.

1021. Langbauer, L. "Dickens's Streetwalkers: Women and the Form of Romance." *ELH* 53(2) (Summer 1986):411-31.

1022. Lecarme-Tabone, E., J. Lecarme, and B. Vercier. "Enigme et prostitution." *Maupassant, miroir de la nouvelle.* Paris: Presse Universitaire de Vincennes, 1988, pp. 111-23.

1023. "Le pornographe; état de la prostitution chez les anciens." Paris: Editeurs d'Aujourd'hui, 1983.

A reprint of Restif de la Bretonne.

1024. Lifshin, L. "Wanted Poet-Prostitute." *Event* 11(1) (1982):65.

1025. Marco, V. *O império da cortesã: Lucíola, um perfil de Alencar.* São Paulo: Martins Fontes, 1986.

1026. McCarthy, P.A. "The Jeweleyed Harlots of His Imagination: Prostitution and Artistic Vision in Joyce." *Eire-Ireland: A Journal of Irish Studies* 17(4) (Winter 1982):91-109.

Discusses the treatment of women, prostitution, and sexuality in the fictional works of James Joyce.

1027. McCombs, N. *Earth Spirit, Victim or Whore? The Prostitute in German Literature, 1880-1925.* New York: Peter Lang, 1986.

1028. McHaney, T.L., M. Gresset, and P. Samway. "The Development of Faulkner's Idealism: Hands, Horses, Whores." *Faulkner and Idealism: Perspectives from Paris.* Edited by M. Gresset. Jackson: University Press of Mississippi, 1983, pp. 71-85.

1029. McKay, H.B., and D.J. Dolff. *Impact of Pornography--A Decade of Literature.* Ottawa: Canada Department of Justice, 1984.

Reviews sociological, criminal justice, and psychological literature to examine the impact of pornography and prostitution on society, with respect to views supporting and against these institutions.

1030. Mendez, J.L. "La dialécto del amo y el esclavo en La cándida Erendira de Gabriel García Marquez." *La Torre: Revista de la Universidad de Puerto Rico* 1(1) (January - March 1987):59-68.

1031. Moore, R.D. *Personification of the Seduction of Evil: "The Wiles of the Wicked Woman."* R. Qui, 1981.

Analyzes the historical poem not as a polemical tract in which the harlot symbolized an enemy of the Qumran community, but rather as a poem with a broader theological message, the personification of the seduction of evil.

1032. Murray, H.M. "Literary Revolution as Bordello Romance: The Ideology of Gender and the Gender of Ideology in the Dawn of German Modernism." *DAI* 47(3) (September 1986):920A-921A.

1033. Myer, V.G. "Jane Austen and the Soul of a Prostitute." *Notes and Queries* 35(3) (1988):305.

1034. Nadeau, Y. "Death, The Drunkard, and the Prostitute (Horace, 'Carmina' 1, 35)." *Maia-Rivista di Letterature Classiche* 38(3) (1986):223-9.

1035. Nathan, M. "Les derniers scandales de Paris par Dubut de Laforest: des maisons closes au phalanstère." *Romantisme: Revue du Dix-Neuvième Siècle* 16(53) (1986):97-105.

1036. Nelson, T.G.A. "Women of Pleasure." *Eighteenth-Century Life* 11(1) (February 1987):181-98.

1037. Nwachukwu, J.O.J. "Society Challenged: A Prostitute's Bravado in Okot p'Bitek's 'Song of Malaya'." *Kola: A Black Literary Magazine* 2(1) (Spring 1988):29-36.

Examines the Ugandan poem dealing with the subject of prostitution.

1038. Ofuani, O.A. "The Image of the Prostitute: A Re-Consideration of Okot p'Bitek's Malaya." *Kunapipi* 8(3) (1986):100-14.

Re-examines the Ugandan poem dealing with the subject of prostitution.

1039. Perrot, M. "Les filles de noce." *Histoire* (9) (1979):83-5.

Review article of Alain Corbin's *Les filles de noce: misère sexuelle et prostitution aux XIXe et XXe siècles* (Paris: Aubier-Montaigne, 1978), which traces the history of prostitution.

1040. Peter, B.S. "Prostitutes and Prostitution in the Short Stories of Maupassant, Guy, de." *Du--Die Zeitschrift der Kultur* (4) (1988):52-7.

1041. Radner, J.B. "The Youthful Harlot's Curse: The Prostitute as Symbol of the City in 18th Century English Literature." *Eighteenth-Century Life* 2(3)(1976):59-64.

1042. Radtke, E. *Sonderwortschatz und Sprachschichtung: Materialien zur sprachlichen Verarbeitung des Sexuellen in der Romania.* Tubingen: G. Narr, 1981.

Prostitution and slang in Romania.

1043. Reed, A. "Coleridge, the Sot, and the Prostitute--A Reading of 'The Friend.'" *Studies in Romanticism* 19(1) (1980), pp. 109-28.

1044. Richard, C. "Scarlet Pornography (Woman as a Form of Prostitute in 'The Scarlet Letter')." *Revue Française d'Études Américaines* 20 (1984):185-94.

1045. Rossella, D. S. "Aspetti della prostituzione indiana: La 'basavi' e la 'putrika'." *Acme: Annali della Facoltà di lettere e filosofia* 35(2-3) (May-December 1982):517-29.

Discusses folk rituals, sexual and wedding rites, and prostitution of the Madras Indians.

1046. Salten, F. *Meine Tochter Peperl, Josephine Mutzenbacher.* München: Heyne Verlag, 1980.

1047. Schneider, L.M. "La iglesia de Onetti: El prostibulo." *Texto Crítico* 6(18-19) (July-December 1980):87-9.

Prostitution in Uruguayan literature.

1048. Schofield, M.A. "Descending Angels: Salubrious Sluts and Pretty Prostitutes in Haywood's Fiction." *Fetter'd or Free? British Women Novelists, 1670-1815.* Edited by M.A. Schofield and C. Macheski. Athens: Ohio University Press, 1986, pp. 186-200.

1049. Sebald, W.G. "Die Mädchen aus der Feenwelt: Bemerkungen zu Liebe und Prostitution mit Bezügen zu Raimund, Schnitzler und Horvath." *Neophilologus* 67(1) (January 1983):109-17.

1050. Seymour-Smith, M. *Fallen Women: A Sceptical Inquiry into the Treatment of Prostitutes, Their Clients and Their Pimps, in Literature.* London: Nelson, 1969.

Part of a series on the natural history of society.

1051. Shugg, W. "Chekhov's Use of Irony in 'A Nervous Breakdown'." *Studies in Short Fiction* 21(4) (Fall 1984):395-8.

Discusses the use of irony, sentimentality, and prostitution in Anton Chekhov's story.

1052. Sicker, P. "The Belladonna: Eliot's Female Archetype in 'The Waste

Land'." *Twentieth Century Literature: A Scholarly and Critical Journal* 30(4) (Winter 1984):420-31.

1053. Siegel, C.F. "Hands Off the Hothouses: Shakespeare's Advice to the King." *Journal of Popular Culture* 20(1) (1986):81-8.

Shakespeare advised the new monarch, James I, in *Measure for Measure*, that he should ignore the ongoing outcries of Puritan clergy for restrictive legislation and allow the hothouses or "stews" (brothels) along the Thames to continue to operate in "benign neglect."

1054. Simpson, D. "What Bothered Charles Lamb About Poor Susan?" *Studies in English Literature, 1500-1900* 26(4) (Autumn 1986):589-612.

1055. Slater, M. "The Bachelor's Pocket Book for 1851." *Tennessee Studies in Literature* 27 (1984):128-40.

1056. Smith, E.M. "Nana, Santa, et Nacha Regules: trois courtisanes modernes." (Thesis) University of Georgia, 1974. Photocopy of typescript, Ann Arbor, MI: University Microfilms International, 1977.

1057. Speck, P.K. "Underworld: Sexual Satire in Three Latin American Novelists." *New Scholar: An Americanist Review* 8(1-2) (1982):235-44. Includes discussion of prostitution.

1058. Stummer, P.O. "Prostitution als narrative Chiffre im afrikanischen Roman." *Matatu: Zeitschrift fur afrikanische Kultur und Gesellschaft* 1(1) (1987):1-18.

1059. Sun, J., and Y. Xiong. "Self-Destruction and the Courtesan--What Links the Fates of Du Shiniang and Marguerite Gautier?" *Cowrie: A Chinese Journal of Comparative Literature* 1(1) (1983):63-80.

Discusses Chinese literature of the Ch'ing dynasty period.

1060. Swatos, W.H., and J.A. Kline. "The Lady Is Not a Whore: Labeling the

Promiscuous Woman." *International Journal of Women's Studies* 1(2) (Mar-Apr. 1978):159-166.

Challenges the notion that the words "whore" and "prostitute" are synonymous. Reports results of a study in which subjects were asked the meaning of the two terms.

1061. *Taschenbuch für Grabennymphen auf das Jahr 1787.* Vienna: Rosenheim, 1982.

A photoreproduction of the first edition of 1787 which is in the collection of the Osterreichischen Nationalbibliothek, Wien.

1062. Thompson, R. "The London Jilt." *Harvard Library Bulletin* 23(3) (1975):289-94.

Describes the content and style of this anonymous 1683 story of prostitution of the rogue tale genre. Presents background to explain its popularity and details the provenance of the surviving copy in Houghton Library.

1063. Vinas, D. *Antología preparada por Roberto Ruiz Rojas.* Bogotá: Latina, 1977.

1064. Warren, J. "Zola's View of Prostitution in *Nana.*" *The Image of the Prostitute in Modern Literature.* Edited by P.L. Horn and M.B. Pringle. New York: Ungar, 1984, pp. 29-41.

1065. Watt, G. *The Fallen Woman in the Nineteenth-Century English Novel.* London: Croom Helm, 1984.

1066. Weir, A.L. "Courtesans and Prostitutes in South Asian Literature." *The Image of the Prostitute in Modern Literature.* Edited by P.L. Horn and M.B. Pringle. New York: Ungar, 1984, pp. 77-89.

1067. Whissen, T. "The Magic Circle: The Role of the Prostitute in Isak

Dinesen's *Gothic Tales." The Image of the Prostitute in Modern Literature.* Edited by P.L. Horn and M.B. Pringle. New York: Ungar, 1984, pp. 43-51.

1068. Woestelandt, E. "Le corps venal: Rosanette dans *L'éducation sentimentale.*" *Nineteenth-Century French Studies* 16(1-2) (Fall-Winter 1987-88):120-31.

PHOTOGRAPHY AND FILM

1069. Bassan, R. "Moi, Christiane F., 13 ans drougée, prostituée" par Edel, U. *Revue de Cinéma* 364 (1981):58-9.

1070. Bassan, R. "La prostituée " par Garnett, T. *Revue de Cinéma* 383 (1983):36.

1071. Bendtsen, T. "Prostitueret " par Garnett, T. *Kosmorama* 27(153) (1981):125.

1072. Branco, R. "The Women of Maciel (Photographs of Brazilian Prostitutes)." *Aperture* 92 (1983):48-65.

1073. Jaehne, K. "Hooker (Recent Spate of Films With Prostitution as the Theme)." *Film Comment* 23(3) (1987):25-32.

1074. Johnson, E. "The Business of Sex: Prostitution and Capitalism in Four Recent American Films." *Journal of Popular Film and Television* 12(4) (Winter 1984-85):148-55.

Analyzes the relationships between prostitutes, the middle-class,and male protagonists who become pimps in four comedy films during 1982-83. Concludes that the most important message conveyed by these films is that American capitalism condones prostitution on the basis of its success at making money.

1075. Kroll, E. *Sex Objects: An American Photodocumentary.* Danbury, NH: Addison House, 1977.

Discusses sex customs, sex oriented business, and prostitution in the U.S..

1076. Lovelace, L. *Ordeal.* New York: Bell, 1983.

Linda Lovelace was a porno star who achieved fame as the star of *"Deep Throat."* She later regretted her role and has told her story in this book and in *Out of Bondage.*

1077. Lovelace, L. *Out of Bondage.* New York: Berkeley Books, 1987.

1078. McDonald, K. "Thematic Conflict and Mode of Representation in Mizoguchi's Street of Shame." *Holding the Vision: Essays on Film.* Edited by D. Radcliff-Umstead. Kent, Ohio: International Film Society, Kent State University, 1983, pp. 16-20.

1079. Mora, C.J. "Feminine Images in Mexican Cinema--The Family Melodrama, Garcia, Sara, the Mother of Mexico, and the Prostitute." *Studies in Latin American Popular Culture* 4 (1985):228-35.

1080. Rausch, A. "The Trauerspiel of the Prostituted Body, or Woman as Allegory of Modernity." *Cultural Critique, University of Minnesota* 10 (1988):77-88.

1081. "We're Here Now: Prostitution." Filmmaker's Library, 1983.

Film about seven former prostitutes who have left "the life" and are struggling to return to the mainstream of society.

1082. Able-Peterson, T. *Children of the Evening*. New York: Putnam, 1981.

1083. Ahart, G.J. "Sexual Exploitation of Children: A Problem of Unknown Magnitude." *Report to the Chairman, Subcommittee on Select Education, House Committee on Education and Labor*. Division of Human Resources. Washington, DC: General Accounting Office, 1982.

An extensive literature search by the General Accounting Office (GAO) on teenage prostitution and child pornography, and the federal, state and local efforts to deal with the problem. Includes results of a survey of police departments and mayors' offices of the 22 largest U.S. cities and all 50 states.

1084. Allegri, D., et al. *Signes particuliers, aucun : regard sur la prostitution des mineurs à Genève*. Annales du Centre de Recherche sociale, no. 12. Genève: Institut d'études sociales, Centre de Recherche sociale, 1981.

1085. Allen, E.E., R.J. Pregliasco, and J.B. Rabun, Jr. "Prepared Statement." Exploitation of Children (Hearing), 63-86, 1981. Rockville, MD: National Institute of Justice, National Criminal Justice Reference Service Microfiche Program, 1982.

Describes the work of the Jefferson County Task Force on Child Prostitution and Pornography and makes recommendations for action at the federal level for dealing with the sexual exploitation of children.

1086. Allsebrook, A., and A. Swift. *Broken Promise*. London: Headway, 1989.

1087. American Bar Association National Legal Resource Center for Child Advocacy and Protection. "Child Sexual Exploitation Background and Legal Analysis." *Exploitation of Children*. Washington, DC: American Bar Association National Legal Resource Center for Child Advocacy and

174

Protection, 1982.

Analyzes the problems of child pornography and prostitution and discusses the state and federal laws passed to counter them. Recommends improvements in legislation.

1088. Arrick, F. *Steffie Can't Come Out to Play.* Scarsdale, NY: Bradbury, 1978.

1089. Backe, L. *Liderlige Lolita: om børnepornografi og -prostitution: om krop, kon og sexualitet som vare.* København: Borgen, 1980.

1090. Bagley, C. "Child Sexual Abuse and Juvenile Prostitution--A Commentary on the Badgley Report on Sexual Offences Against Children and Youth." *Canadian Journal of Public Health (Revue Canadienne de Santé Publique)* 76(1) (1985):65.

1091. Bagley, C., and L. Young. "Juvenile Prostitution and Child Sexual Abuse: A Controlled Study." *Canadian Journal of Community Mental Health* 6(1) (Spring 1987):5-26.

Constructs a model linking family disruption and violence to entry into prostitution, specifically, the correlation of sexual abuse in childhood with poor mental health and low self-esteem in the adult who then turns to prostitution.

1092. Baizerman, M., and J. Thompson, eds. *Adolescent Female Prostitution.* New York: Haworth, 1988.

1093. Baizerman, M., J. Thompson, and K. Stafford-White. "Adolescent Prostitution." *Children Today* 8(5) (September-October 1979):20-24.

Examines adolescent prostitution with respect to its history, nature, and potential control based on the analysis of two years of the case histories of over 300 prostitutes in the Minneapolis-St.Paul area.

1094. Baizerman, M., and J. Thompson, eds. *Understanding Adolescent Female*

Prostitution. New York: Haworth, 1986.

Provides a look at adolescent female prostitution. Suggests approaches to understanding and working with them. Describes and examines the patterns by which these youth become prostitutes focusing on family dynamics.

1095. Baker, C.D. "Preying on Playgrounds: The Sexploitation of Children in Pornography and Prostitution." *Pepperdine Law Review* 5(3) (1978):809-846.

Establishes the close relationship between the industry of child pornography and the practice of child prostitution. Discusses proposed legislation and judicial decisions affecting the industry.

1096. Balanon, L.G. "Street Children: Strategies for Action." *Child Welfare* 68(2) (March-April 1989):159-166.

Documents the plight of Filipino children who are forced to support themselves and their families in the face of economic crisis and inadequate services.

1097. Barclay, K. "Family of Prostitute." *Corrective Psychiatry and Journal of Social Therapy* 18(4) (1972):10-16.

1098. Beatty, J.W., and H.M. Carlson. "Street Kids: Children in Danger." Paper presented at the 93rd Annual Convention of the American Psychological Association, Los Angeles, August 23-27, 1985.

Analyzes the successes of Project LUCK (Linking Up the Community for Kids), an administrative organization designed to coordinate and combine the efforts of 34 youth-serving agencies. The goals of Project LUCK are public education with an emphasis on juvenile prostitution as a form of child abuse and direct service for the street youths in the form of counseling centers, shelters, vocational training and employment placement, support groups for teenage mothers, and outreach programs.

1099. Bell, M. *Streetwise.* (Videocassette) New York: Angelika Films, 1985.

Portrays the lives and relationships of nine runaway children between the ages of thirteen and nineteen in the streets of Seattle, Washington.

1100. Bour, D.S., J.P. Young, and R. Henningsen. "Comparison of Delinquent Prostitutes and Delinquent Non-Prostitutes on Self-Concept." Paper presented at the annual meeting of the Academy of Criminal Justice Sciences, San Antonio, March 22-26, 1983. *Gender Issues, Sex Offenses, and Criminal Justice: Current Trends.* Edited by S. Chaneles. New York: Haworth, 1984.

Studies the similarities and differences of delinquent prostitutes and delinquent non-prostitutes focusing on self-concept. Recommends that programs dealing with juvenile prostitution include strict legal discipline and provision for education, vocational training, guidance, and healthy homes.

1101. Bour, D.S., J.P. Young, and R. Henningsen. "A Comparison of Delinquent Prostitutes and Delinquent Non-Prostitutes On Self-Concept." *Journal of Offender Counseling, Services and Rehabilitation* 9(1-2) (Fall-Winter 1984):89-101.

Compares sociodemographic statistics of 25 female juvenile delinquent prostitutes with 25 age-matched juvenile delinquent nonprostitutes to ascertain differences in self-concept. Utilizes self report questionnaire, in addition to the Tennessee Self-Concept Scale (TSCS). Self-Concept scales indicate that the groups differ significantly only on the Physical Self subscale of the TSCS.

1102. Boyer, D., and J. James. "Easy Money: Adolescent Involvement in Prostitution." *Justice for Young Women: Close-Up On Critical Issues.* Edited by S. Davidson. Tucson: New Directions for Young Women, 1982.

Analyzes the etiology of female prostitution specifically in regard to the early loss of self esteem. Includes a discussion of the historical and cultural forces which fosters the objectified female role in society.

1103. Boyer, D., and J. James. "Juvenile Prostitution." *Female Offender.* Edited by C.T. Griffiths, and M. Nance. Burnaby, BC: Simon Fraser University Criminology Research Centre, 1980.

Discusses the causes and motivations for entrance into prostitution by female adolescents. Outlines a four-stage pattern of progression into prostitution consisting of adaptation, acculturation, assimilation, and commitment.

1104. Boyer, D., G. Robinson, and R.W. Deisher. "Entrance Into Adolescent Prostitution (Male and Female)." (Meeting Abstract) *Journal of Adolescent Health Care* 3(2) (1982):144.

1105. Boyer, D., and J. James. "Prostitutes as Victims." *Deviants: Victims or Victimizers?* Edited by D.E.J. MacNamara and A. Karmen. Beverly Hills, CA: Sage, 1983, pp. 109-84.

Examines hazards of the prostitute's trade for both males and females.

1106. Bracey, D.H. *Baby-Pros: Preliminary Profiles of Juvenile Prostitutes.* Criminal Justice Center Monograph, no. 12. New York: Criminal Justice Center, John Jay College of Criminal Justice, 1979.

1107. Bracey, D.H. "Concurrent and Consecutive Abuse: The Juvenile Prostitute." *Criminal Justice System and Women.* Edited by B.R. Price, and N.J. Sokoloff. New York: Clark Boardman, 1982.

Describes the cycle of abuse and victimization that results in the entrance into a pattern of sexual or occupational deviance. Assesses and analyzes the level to which abuse is maintained once the juvenile is established in the profession of prostitution.

1108. Bracey, D.H. "The Juvenile Prostitute: Victim and Offender." Proceedings of the Second International Institute On Victimology: Victimology: International Perspectives, Bellagio, Italy, 1982; also *Victimology* 8(3-4):151-160.

1109. Bracey, D.H., F. Marden, and K. Jefferson. *Juvenile Prostitution in Midtown Manhattan (NY).* New York: John Jay College of Criminal Justice, 1977.

Supplies facts about youthful prostitutes and evaluates the data.

Recommends development of specific programs to discourage prostitution.

1110. Brock, D.R., and G. Kinsman. "Patriarchal Relations Ignored: An Analysis and Critique of the Badgley Report on Sexual Offenses Against Children and Youths." *Regulating Sex*. Edited by J. Lowman. Stoneham, MA: Butterworths, 1986.

Critiques the report of Canada's Committee on Sexual Offenses Against Children and Youths (Badgley Report) for its failure to address the dominant patriarchal cultural influences. Argues that those influences foster abusive incestuous relations between parents and children. Recommends a redirection of efforts from a law centered protectionist approach of childhood sexuality to a reconstruction of cultural norms, institutions, and practices.

1111. Brown, F.E. "Juvenile Prostitution: A Nursing Perspective." *Journal of Psychiatric Nursing* 18(12) (December 1980):32-34.

1112. Brown, M.E. "Teenage Prostitution." *Adolescence* 14(56) (Winter 1979):665-680.

Outlines the precipitating social conditions which may predispose a juvenile to prostitution and the motivations for entering into sexual and occupational deviant behavior. Criticizes the existing juvenile justice system for overprosecution and excessive moralization. Recommends rehabilitation and treatment of juvenile prostitutes.

1113. Burgess, A.W., and H.J. Birnbaum. "Youth Prostitution." *American Journal of Nursing* 82(5) (May 1982):832-834.

1114. California Legislature. Senate. Select Committee on Children and Youth. *Runaway Youth and Resulting Prostitution and Drugs*. Senate Hearing, April 13, 1984. Sacramento: Joint Publications Office, 1984.

1115. Campagna, D.S., and D.L. Poffenberger. *The Sexual Trafficking in Children: An Investigation of the Child Sex Trade*. Dover, MA: Auburn House, 1988.

1116. Canada. Ministry of National Health and Welfare. Ministry of Justice. Solicitor General. *Report of the Committee on Sexual Offences Against Children and Youths and the Report of the Special Committee on Pornography and Prostitution.* Text in English and French. (Discussion Paper) Ottawa: Government of Canada, 1985.

Questions various recommendations suggested by two reports on sexual offenses against minors: the Bagdley Committee Report and the Fraser Committee Report. Discusses the topics of dealing with child sexual abuse, pornography, and prostitution as well as the responsibility of the Canadian government, the private sector, and individual citizens in formulating a plan for action and reform.

1117. Canada. *Guide to the Federal Government's Response to the Reports on Sexual Abuse of Children, Pornography and Prostitution.* Text in English and French. Ottawa: Government of Canada, 1986.

1118. Canadian Committee on Sexual Offences Against Children and Youth. *Sexual Offences Against Children.* 2 vols. Hull, Quebec: Canadian Government Publishing Centre Supply and Services Canada, 1984.

Considers the prevalence of sexual offenses against minors, including the extent and nature of juvenile prostitution and child pornography. Provides definitions and analyses. Discusses the existing legislation central to these issues and makes recommendations for improvement.

1119. Cangemi, J.P. "Some Observations of Marriage and Family Practices in Eastern Venezuela." *Psychology* 13(4) (November 1976):49-52.

Studies the Venezuelan practice of marital and familial customs in the Guayana region for the purpose of comparative social analysis and focuses on such socially acceptable phenomena as prostitution and concubinage among lower socioeconomic groups.

1120. Caplan, G.M. "The Facts of Life about Teenage Prostitution." *Crime and Delinquency* 30(1) (January 1984):69-74.

Argues that teenagers turned to prostitution specifically as a means of acquiring a pimp, merging their own identities with his. They do not become attached to pimps because of the protective services offered or fear of the consequences of leaving them. Rather the pimp meets deeply felt needs. Suggests that rehabilitative programs for teenage prostitutes are likely to fail unless they are treated as their adult counterparts.

1121. Carmichael, B.J. "Youth Crime in Urban Communities: A Descriptive Analysis of Street Hustlers and Their Crimes." *Crime and Delinquency* 21(2) (April 1975):139-148.

1122. Cave, C., and E. Goldberg. "A Health Profile of Teen-Age Prostitutes." (Meeting Abstract) *Clinical and Investigative Medicine (Médecine Clinique et Expérimentale)* 9(3) (1986):138.

1123. Celier, P., et al. *La prostitution des jeunes: entre le drame et la banalité.* Montréal: Éditions Convergence, 1984.

1124. Chaplin, B. "Heartbreak Kids." *Washington Post Magazine* (November 12, 1978):10-13,15-16.

Describes the state of juvenile prostitution in Washington, D.C., with attention to existing and proposed approaches for dealing with the issue. Argues for the decriminalization of prostitution.

1125. Cohen, M.I. "Effective Law Enforcement Strategies for Handling Juvenile Prostitution." *The National Sheriff* 39(4) (August-September 1988):49-52.

Outlines a step-by-step guide to aid elected officials, law enforcement personnel, and social service providers in local communities to deal with the problem of juvenile prostitution based on the examples of successful programs established by cities and counties across the United States.

1126. Cohen, M.I. *Identifying and Combating Juvenile Prostitution: A Manual for Action.* Washington, DC: National Association of Counties Research. Tulsa, OK: National Resource Center for Youth Services, University of Oklahoma, 1987.

1127. Crowley, M.B. "Female Runaway Behavior and Its Relationship to

Prostitution." (Master's thesis) Sam Houston State University, Institute of Contemporary Corrections and the Behavioral Sciences, 1977.

Examines selected variables related to runaway behavior in order to determine if these variables are significantly related to prostitution.

1128. Csapo, M. "Juvenile Prostitution." *Canadian Journal of Special Education* 2(2) (1986):145-170.

Reviews recent research and Canadian government committee reports concerning juvenile prostitution. Describes existing programs for dealing with the problem and proposes reform in legislative and social policy.

1129. Davidson, H.A., and G.A. Loken. *Child Pornography and Prostitution: Background and Legal Analysis.* Washington, DC: National Center for Missing and Exploited Children: National Obscenity Enforcement Unit, U.S. Department of Justice, 1987.

Surveys and analyzes federal and state laws and court decisions relevant to the sexual exploitation of minors, specifically in the areas of child pornography and juvenile prostitution.

1130. Davidson, H.A. "Sexual Exploitation of Children: An Overview of Its Scope, Impact, and Legal Ramifications." *FBI Law Enforcement Bulletin* 53(2) (February 1984):26-31. (First published in *The Prosecutor, the Journal of the National District Attorney's Association* 16(5) (Summer 1982):6-11.)

Explores the scope of child sexual exploitation and profiles both offender and victim. Argues for effective prosecution under child pornography laws and child prostitution laws with emphasis on the legal protection of the victimized child.

1131. Davidson, S. "Young Women and the Justice System." *New Designs for Youth Development* 2(3) (May-June 1981):3-7.

1132. Deisher, R.W., G. Robinson, and D. Boyer. "The Adolescent Female and Male Prostitute." *Pediatric Annals* 11(10) (October 1982):819-825.

Compares perspectives on male and female prostitution.

1133. Densen-Gerber, J., and S.F. Hutchinson. *Medical-Legal and Societal Problems Involving Children, Child Prostitution, Child Pornography and Drug-Related Abuse: Recommended Legislation.* Baltimore: University Park Press, 1978.

Describes the exploitative abuse and neglect of children including child prostitution and pornography. Presents case histories of intrafamial sexual abuse. Concludes that all child protective systems should operate on the assumption that there exists a causative relationship between a parent or guardian who is a substance abuser and the likelihood that the parent or guardian will be a child abuser. Argues that the victim's needs must become a priority concern of the government at the Cabinet level.

1134. Densen-Gerber, J., and S.F. Hutchinson. "Sexual and Commercial Exploitation of Children: Legislative Responses and Treatment Challenges." *Child Abuse and Neglect* 3(1) (1979):61-66.

Portrays the scope of the sexual exploitation of minors in the United States. Recommends legislative and treatment strategies to counter the growing problem.

1135. Dorais, M., and D. Menard. *Les enfants de la prostitution.* Montréal: VLB, 1987.

1136. Enablers, Inc. *Juvenile Prostitution in Minnesota: The Report of a Research Project.* Minneapolis: Enablers, 1978.

1137. Ennew, J. *The Sexual Exploitation of Children.* New York: St. Martin's, 1986.

1138. Fahmi, K., et al. *La prostitution des mineurs: construction d'un problème social.* Montréal: s.n., 1987.

1139. Feschet, J. *À seize ans au trottoir: piègées par le système.* Paris: Éditions ouvrières, 1975.

1140. Finkel, K.C. "Child Sexual Abuse and Juvenile Prostitution." *Canadian Journal of Public Health (Revue Canadienne de Santé Publique)* 76(6) (1985):419.

1141. Finstad, L., L. Fougner, and V.L. Holter. *Oslo-prosjektet: erfaringer fra to års forsøksvirksomhet blant barne- og ungdomsprostituerte i Oslo 1979-1981.* Oslo: Barnevernskontoret, 1981.

1142. Fisher, B., and D.K. Weisberg. *Juvenile Prostitution.* Lexington, MA: Lexington Books, D.C. Heath, 1983.

Profiles adolescent males involved in prostitution. Provides new information regarding the relationship between adolescent prostitution and other sexually exploitative activities and outlines programmatic approaches and community efforts for working with juvenile prostitutes.

1143. Fletcher, C.W. "Early Sexual Experience and Female Prostitution." (Ph.D. Dissertation) California School of Professional Psychology, Los Angeles, 1982.

1144. Foste, W. *Verkaufte Träume: Kinderarbeit und Kinder-prostitution in Thailand.* Thailand Correspondenz, no. 9. Politische Bilderbücher zum Fernen Osten. Thailand. München: Simon and Magiera, 1982.

1145. Friend, S.A. "Sexual Exploitation of Children and Youth: Human Resources Series." *State Legislative Reports* 8(6) (October 1983).

Explores the problem of child pornography and juvenile prostitution. Examines some of the strategies federal, state and local governments employ to address these problems and recommends various means of strengthening and clarifying laws.

1146. Gibson, A.I., D.I. Templer, R. Brown, et al. "Adolescent Female Prostitutes." *Archives of Sexual Behavior* 17(5) (October 1988):431-438.

Compares the characteristics and functioning of adolescent females prostitutes with nonprostitute delinquents and female adolescents in general. Concludes that prostitutes display greater psychopathology, are more likely to have been in special education classes, and have more negative attitudes towards men than subjects in the other two groups.

1147. Goldman, R.L., and V.R. Wheeler. *Silent Shame: The Sexual Abuse of Children and Youth.* Danville, IL: Interstate, 1986.

1148. González Jara, M.A. *El delito de promoción o facilitación de corrupción o prostitución de menores: análisis dogmático y crítico del artículo 367 del Código penal.* Santiago: Editorial Jurídica de Chile, 1986.

1149. Gray, D. "Teenage Prostitution." *Crime in Society.* Edited by L.D. Savitz and N. Johnston. New York: Wiley, 1978. Reprinted from "Turning Out: A Study of Teenage Prostitution." *Urban Life and Culture* 1 (January 1973):401-425.

Presents a model of the process by which a juvenile female becomes a prostitute based on the study of the subject's social background and family situation. Analyzes the entrance into prostitution and the relationship to pimps, customers, and other prostitutes.

1150. Gray, D. "Turning-Out: A Study of Teenage Prostitution." *Urban Life and Culture* 1(4) (January 1973):401-425.

Describes the social development patterns common in juvenile female prostitutes and traces the means by which prostitution is upheld as a viable occupation in minds of these adolescents.

1151. "Hearings on Child Pornography Measure Held in the House." *Juvenile Justice Digest* 5(10) (May 27, 1977):6-7.

1152. Herrmann, K.J. "Children Sexually Exploited for Profit: A Plea for a New Social Work Priority." *Social Work* 32(6) (November/December 1987):523-5.

Draws attention to the sexual exploitation of children in the form of child prostitution and child pornography and describes the magnitude to which these practices have become a multi-billion dollar industry. Argues that this should be considered a major issue for social work practice and policy.

1153. Hersch, P. "Coming of Age on City Streets." *Psychology Today* 22(1) (January 1988):28-37.

Profiles runaways and their high risk for contacting AIDS through the exposure to multiple sex partners in prostitution and through the use of intravenous drugs.

1154. Hogg, J.A. "Female Adolescent Prostitution: A Humanistic Model for Intervention and Therapy." (Master's thesis) University of Oregon, 1979.

Outlines the motivations of female adolescents for entering into prostitution and the areas in which intervention and treatment may prove effective.

1155. Hoshino, K. "Crime, Victimization, Suicide and Accidental Death As Results of Running Away From Home." *Reports of the National Research Institute of Police Science* 14(2) (December 1973):145-154.

Reports on runaways who become victims of illegal employment agencies and are forced into prostitution.

1156. Hutchinson, S.F. "Juvenile Prostitution." *Sixth National Conference on Juvenile Justice.* (Audiocassette) University of Nevada at Reno: National Council of Juvenile and Family Court Judges, 1979; Chicago: Teach 'Em Inc., 1979.

Surveys the scope of juvenile prostitution and suggests crime-specific countermeasures.

1157. Inciardi, J.A. "Little Girls and Sex: A Glimpse at the World of the 'Baby Pro'." *Deviant Behavior* 5(1-4) (1984):71-78.

Discusses the issue of child prostitution, and the vector for entrance by girls between the ages of eight and twelve years of age. Documents their drug use and reaction to early experience with sex.

1158. Ivers, K.J., and H.M. Carlson. *Needs Assessment of Female Street Kids: Children in Danger.* (Conference Paper) Paper presented at the 95th Annual Convention of the American Psychological Association, New York, August 28-September 1, 1987.

Assesses the situation of homeless girls with an emphasis on juvenile prostitution. Recommends breaking the cycle of victimization of juvenile prostitutes at three points of intervention in an overall comprehensive program for treatment.

1159. James, J., and J. Meyerding. "Early Sexual Experience and Prostitution." *American Journal of Psychiatry* 134(12) (December 1977):1381-1385.

1160. James, J., and J. Meyerding. "Early Sexual Experience as a Factor in Prostitution." *Archives of Sexual Behavior* 7(1) (1978):31-42.

Studies the sexual histories of prostitutes versus that of nonprostitutes concluding that early sexual abuse is likely to lower a girl's concept of self worth, thereby rendering her more vulnerable to prostitution and other deviant behaviors.

1161. James, J. *Entrance into Juvenile Prostitution: Final Report.* Seattle: University of Washington Department of Psychiatry and Behavioral Sciences, 1980.

Provides basic statistical and descriptive data on female juvenile prostitution in King County, Seattle, Washington to evidence the increase in and changing pattern of prostitution. Includes counseling and referral information, a training session format, and a project evaluation. Reports on family dynamics and income, religious upbringing, parental occupation, arrest record, and criminal involvement.

1162. Janus, M.D., B. Scanlon, and V.A. Price. "Youth Prostitution." *Child Pornography and Sex Rings.* Edited by A.W. Burgess and M.L. Clark. Lexington, MA: Lexington Books, D.C. Heath, 1984.

Examines teenage prostitution in Metropolitan Boston and profiles its participants. Focuses on hustling, male prostitution, and the vehicle for entry into occupational and sexual deviant behavior.

1163. *Juvenile Prostitution.* (Audiocassette) Washington, DC: National Public Radio, 1982.

1164. Kagan, H. "Prostitution and Sexual Promiscuity Among Adolescent Female Offenders." (Dissertation) University of Arizona, 1969.

Questions whether prostitution and sexual promiscuity can be better treated as a symptom of existing social conditions or as a symbolic manifestation of emotions.

1165. Kanter, M. "Prohibit or Regulate? The Fraser Report and New Approaches to Pornography and Prostitution." *Osgoode Hall Law Journal* 23(1) (Spring 1985):171-194.

Reviews the political and social context of Canada's Fraser Report on pornography and prostitution. Presents and analyzes the report's content and proposes a more extensive and detailed framework for addressing the abusive character of pornography and prostitution, including the equalization of power relations between the sexes.

1166. Landau, E. *On the Streets: The Lives of Adolescent Prostitutes.* New York: J. Messner, 1987.

Profiles young prostitutes from the perspective of the individual and discusses available social services.

1167. Lau, E. *Runaway: Diary of a Street Kid.* Toronto: Harper and Collins, 1989.

1168. Lloyd, R. *For Money or Love: Boy Prostitution in America.* New York: Vanguard Press, 1976; Reprint: New York: Ballantine, 1977.

Case histories furnish data on types of offenses, extent of problem, and social causes for the kind of lives led by boys aged eight to seventeen who sell themselves to adult males.

1169. Lloyd, R. *Playland: A Study of Boy Prostitution.* London: Blond and Briggs, 1977.

A somewhat revised and expanded American edition.

1170. Longres, J. "The Use of Survey Methods in Researching Parents of Adjudicated Teenage Prostitutes." *Journal of Sociology and Social Welfare* 14(3) (September 1987):65-86.

Suggests that researching parents of teenage prostitutes may be best done through an existing program. Finds, based on a survey utilizing this method, that many parents of these prostitutes are concerned for their daughters and willing to take part in a family-focused service.

1171. Lowen, J. *Juvenile Prostitution and Child Pornography.* Seattle: University of Washington Center for the Assessment of Delinquent Behavior and its Prevention, 1979.

Reviews literature on juvenile prostitution and child pornography. Describes current legislation and child abuse programs. Recommends experimental, nontraditional programs for runaways.

1172. Lowman, J. "Taking Young Prostitutes Seriously." *Canadian Review of Sociology and Anthropology (Revue Canadienne de Sociologie et d'Anthropologie)* 24(1) (February 1987):99-116.

Concludes that criminalization of juvenile prostitution is the only effective means of providing guidance and assistance.

1173. Lowman, J. "You Can Do It, But Don't Do It Here: Some Comments on Proposals for the Reform of Canadian Prostitution Law." *Regulating Sex.* Edited by J.Lowman, et al. Stoneham, MA: Butterworths, 1986.

Focuses on the Fraser Committee's recommendations for Canadian prostitution law reform and its disagreement with the Badgley Committee over the use of criminal law to check juvenile prostitution. Argues that social structures and attitudes permits prostitution to appear as an attractive occupational option to minors.

1174. MacDonnell, T. *Never Let Go: The Tragedy of Kristy McFarlane.* Toronto: McClelland-Bantam, 1988.

1175. MacVicar, K., and M. Dillon. "Childhood and Adolescent Development of 10 Female Prostitutes." *Journal of the American Academy of Child and Adolescent Psychiatry* 19(1) (1980):145-159.

Studies ten adolescent and young adult female prostitutes and makes the determination that three had schizophrenic psychoses and the remaining seven had borderline characteristics.

1176. Maiuro, R.D., E. Trupin, and J. James. "Sex-Role Differentiation in a Female Juvenile Delinquent Population: Prostitute vs. Control Samples." *American Journal of Orthopsychiatry* 53(2) (1983):345-352.

Studies the apparent lack of differentiation of sex role orientation among female juvenile delinquents. Finds that female subjects with a masculine sex role orientation have a higher incidence of prostitution. Questions the assumption of a postive relationship between androgyny and mental health.

1177. *Maltreatment of Children.* Baltimore: University Park Press, 1978.

1178. Maous-Chassagny, N. "'Ma mère est une putain': a propos d'une expérience avec des adolescents délinquantes." *Pratique des Mots* 33 (June 1980):18-24.

Presents case studies of female juvenile delinquents, whose female role models include mothers who are prostitutes. Advocates intervention, including individual psychotherapy, sex education, group therapy, and possible placement in foster care as a means of breaking the continuation of the same lifestyle by the daughters of prostitutes.

1179. Margolin, L. "Juvenile Sex Offender: Questionable Labeling." *Medical Trial Technique Quarterly* (1979):1-7.

Attacks the issue of definitional ambiguity of the term "sex offender" and illustrates the wide range of behaviors that are inappropriately categorized as sex offenses, including juvenile prostitution.

1180. Mathews, F. *Familiar Strangers: A Study of Adolescent Prostitution.* Toronto: Central Toronto Youth Services, 1987.

1181. McMullen, R.J. "Youth Prostitution: A Balance of Power?" *Journal of Adolescence* 10(1) (March 1987):35-43. (Also published in *International Journal of Offender Therapy and Comparative Criminology* 30(3) (1986):237-244.)

Portrays the behavioral dynamics of youth prostitution in London, England. Discusses society's projection of moral values, and the effectiveness of a therapeutic intervention program called Streetwise.

1182. Millhagen, S. *Gefühle kann man nicht kaufen: das Buch zum Thema Jugendprostitution.* Reinbek bei Hamburg: Rowohlt, 1986.

1183. Nelson, D. *Juvenile Prostitution in Minnesota.* Minneapolis: Enablers, 1978.

Describes the nature of juvenile prostitution in Minnesota. Provides information on number of prostitutes operating within the state and their experiences with law enforcement and juvenile justice system.

1184. Newman. F., and P.J. Caplan. "Juvenile Female Prostitution as Gender Consistent Response to Early Deprivation." *International Journal of Women's Studies* 5(2) (1982):128-137.

1185. Newton-Ruddy, L., and M.M. Handelsman. "Jungian Feminine Psychology and Adolescent Prostitutes." *Adolescence* 21(84) (Winter 1986):815-825.

Explores Jungian feminine psychology and its application to adolescent prostitution. Discusses Wolff's work on feminine functions and Leonard's work with father-daughter wounds in the treatment of adolescent prostitutes.

1186. Nightingale, R. "Adolescent Prostitution." *Seminars in Adolescent Medicine* 1(3) (September 1985):165-170.

1187. Padilla-Pimentel, M. de J. "Prostitution in Adolescence." *Revista de la Clinica de la Conducta* 6(13) (December 1973):10-18.

Delineates two categories of causality with respect to adolescent prostitution: social and individual. Discusses these factors and includes four cases. Suggests methods for prevention.

1188. Pospiszyl, K.   "Application of H.J. Eysenck's Maudsley Personality Inventory in the Study of Delinquent Youth." *Przeglad Psychologiczny* 16(2) (1973):193-209.

Investigates H.J. Eysenck's (1964) theory that criminals are predominantly extraverts, by comparing the mean averages of groups of delinquents and nondelinquents on the Maudsley Personality Inventory (MPI). Results indicate that seriously delinquent youths do show a higher degree of extraversion than nondelinquents. Demonstrates the usefulness of this tool as a comparative means of matching psychic features to involvement in specific crimes, such as prostitution.

1189. Price, V.A.   "Characteristics and Needs of Boston Street Youth: One Agency's Response."   *Children and Youth Services Review* 11(1) (1989):75-90.

Differentiates between homeless youth, runaway youth, and youth involved in prostitution. Describes the efforts of Bridge Over Troubled Waters, a multiservice agency in Boston, Massachusetts, which responds to the needs of street youth.

1190. Rabun, Jr., J.B.   "Combating Child Pornography and Prostitution: One County's Approach." *Child Pornography and Sex Rings*. Edited by A.W. Burgess and M.L. Clark. Lexington, MA: Lexington Books, D.C. Heath and Company, 1984.

Describes the success of the Task Force on Child Prostitution and Pornography in Jefferson County, Kentucky. Demonstrates that disparate organizations and agencies can unite to form an effective task force and that political and geographic boundaries can be crossed in the efforts to combat the sexual exploitation of juveniles.

1191. Saurel, R.   "The Boat People (Homosexuality, Sale and Prostitution of Children in South East Asia)"   (French) *Temps Modernes* 38(427) (1982):1446-1477.

1192. Schaffer, B., and R.R. DeBlassie. "Adolescent Prostitution." *Adolescence* 19(75) (Fall 1984):689-696.

Examines the conditions that foster teenage prostitution and discusses the role of the justice system.

1193. Schroeder, E.D. "Adolescent Women at Risk: Group Therapy for Increasing Self-Esteem." (Ph.D. Dissertation) University of Washington, 1983.

1194. Seng, M.J. "Child Sexual Abuse and Adolescent Prostitution: A Comparative Analysis." *Adolescence* 24(95) (Fall 1989):665-675.

Compares sexually abused children who have resorted to prostitution with sexually abused children who have not. Suggests that running away is an intervening variable in the link between sexual abuse and adolescent prostitution.

1195. Sereny, G. *The Invisible Children: Child Prostitution in America, West Germany, and Great Britain.* New York: Knopf, 1985; also published as, *The Invisible Children: Children "on the game" in America, West Germany and Great Britain.* London: Pan, 1986.

Includes interviews with hustlers from Great Britain and West Germany.

1196. Seymour, V.L. *Teenage Prostitution as a Product of Child Abuse.* (Research Report) Arlington, VA.: Eric Document Reproduction Service, 1977.

Profiles existing knowledge on juvenile prostitution and its relationship to abuse. Analyzes psychological evaluations of runaways and child abuse studies and proposes that new methods of intervention must be designed in light of this new research.

1197. Silbert, M.H., and A.M. Pines. "Sexual Child Abuse As an Antecedent to Prostitution." *Child Abuse and Neglect* 5(4) (1981):407-411.

Centers on underlying factors which influence behavior likely to bring youth in contact with the juvenile justice system, such as substance abuse, prostitution, suicide, and serious crime. Argues that these behaviors are considered by the juveniles as a logical alternative given their inability to achieve economic and social linkages to normative society.

1198. Smith, L.J., and S.A.B. Mitchell. *Juveniles in Prostitution: Facts Versus Fiction.* Saratoga, CA: R. & E. Publishers, 1984.

Describes and analyzes the characteristics and motivations of female juvenile prostitutes as well as the pimps who employ juveniles and the customers who seek them out. Examines the typical family background of the teenage prostitute and the treatment offered at a long-term residential facility.

1199. Sullivan, T. "Juvenile Prostitution: A Critical Perspective." *Marriage and Family Review* 12(1-2) (1987):113-134.

1200. Sullivan, T. "Juvenile Prostitution: An Unspoken Vocational Option." *School Guidance Worker* 40(5) (May 1985):31-34.

Argues that much of the contemporary discourse stems from an historic pattern of regulating family life through prescription and proscription of sexual behavior.

1201. Tappan, P.W. *Delinquent Girls in Court: A Study of the Wayward Minor Court of New York.* 1947. Reprint. Patterson Smith Reprint Series in *Criminology, Law Enforcement, and Social Problems.* No. 67. Montclair, NJ: Patterson Smith, 1969.

1202. Vitaliano, P., D. Boyer, and J. James. "Perceptions of Juvenile Experience-- Females Involved in Prostitution Versus Property Offenses." *Criminal Justice and Behavior* 8(3) (September 1981):325-42.

Investigates prostitutes as female criminals. Finds that prostitutes were significantly more deviant than other female criminals on five out of six variables but with fewer race and economic differences.

1203. Vitaliano, P., J. James, and D. Boyer. "Sexuality of Deviant Females: Adolescent and Adult Correlates." *Social Work* 26(6) (November

1981):468-72.

Shows the correlation between negative sexual experiences in adolescence and low self-image and a later deviant lifestyle. Determines that significantly more prostitutes had negative early sexual experiences than a corresponding sample of female offenders.

1204. Weininger, O.P. *Motherhood and Prostitution.* American Institute for Psychological Research, 1983.

1205. Weisberg, D.K. "Children of the Night: The Adequacy of Statutory Treatment of Juvenile Prostitution." *American Journal of Criminal Law* 12(1) (March 1984):1-67.

Criticizes federal and state laws on juvenile prostitution for not being gender neutral and ignoring the incidence of male juvenile prostitution. Recommends changes in existing legislation so that federal and state laws are more sensitive to this issue.

1206. Weisberg, D.K. *Children of the Night: A Study of Adolescent Prostitution.* Lexington, MA: Lexington, 1985.

Explores the relationship of juvenile prostitution and pornography to runaway behavior and the abuse and neglect which provide the incentive for the children to leave their homes. Discusses the dynamics of male juvenile prostitution and how it compares to female juvenile prostitution. Analyzes the recent statutory reforms at the federal and state levels.

1207. Wild, N.J. "Prevalance of Child Sex Rings." *Pediatrics* 83(4) (April 1989):553-558.

Studies the extent of child sex rings, the methods of victim recruitment, and the nature of the sex crimes against children that occur in sex rings.

1208. Wilson, P.R., and J. Arnold. *Street Kids: Australia's Alienated Young.* Blackburn, Victoria: Collins Dove, 1986.

1209. Wilson, V.W.   "A Psychological Study of Juvenile Prostitutes."
       International Journal of Social Psychiatry 5(1) (Summer 1959):61-73.

LEGAL

1210. Abramson, E.M. "A Note on Prostitution: Victims without Crime or There's No Crime but the Victim Is Ideology." *Duquesne Law Review* 17(1978-1979):355-80.

Comments on prostitution as a moral rather than criminal offense. Speculates that control efforts have failed because dealing with prostitution as a crime and jailing prostitutes fail to affect the causes of prostitution. Recommends that laws should emphasize therapy and training rather than prison.

1211. *The Administration of the Anti-Prostitution Law in Japan.* Japan: Ministry of Justice, 1960.

Reviews the history of legislation concerning prostitution in Japan after World War II and describes enforcement of the Anti-Prostitution Law which came into effect in 1958. Briefly outlines problems encountered by the Japanese government in the rehabilitation of prostitutes.

1212. American Bar Association. "Women and Criminal Law: A Symposium." *American Criminal Law Review* 11(2) (1973):291-558.

A feminist perspective on women as victims, accused, and prisoners in the criminal process. Examines laws against prostitution, sentencing of women, and the effect of the Equal Rights Amendment on such issues.

1213. Ansell, J. *A Century's Safeguards: The Criminal Law Amendment Act 1885.* Hatfield, UK: Josephine Butler Society, 1985.

This 6-page pamphlet describes prostitution and prostitution law in England.

1214. Antonini, C., and M. Buscarini. "Regulation of Prostitution in Post-Unified Italy." (Italian) *Rivista di Storia Contemporanea* 14(1) (1985):83-114.

1215. Archdale, R.L. *Prostitution and Persecution: Some Comments on the Street Offences Act, 1959.* Pall Mall Pamphlet, no. 8. London: Pall Mall, 1960.

1216. Arleff, W.P. "Die Prostitution im geltenden und zukünftigen Strafrecht: Zugleich ein Beitrag zur Bestimmung der Grenzen staatlicher Strafbefügnis." (Ph.D. Dissertation) Universität zu Köln, 1973?

1217. Bals, F.J. "Promotion of Prostitution." (German) *Kriminalistik* 31(6) (1977):273-274.

1218. Bason, J. "American Courts and Privacy of the Body." (Masters Thesis) North Texas State University, 1976.

Discusses right to privacy in personal and sexual matters. States that right of privacy now extends to private marital affairs, availability of contraceptives, abortion decision, and in some circumstances, employment of homosexuals, and the right to die. Distinguishes between public and private acts. Argues that the right to privacy does not extend to certain sexual activities of prostitutes and homosexuals considered to be forcible and/or public.

1219. Beaven, G.R. "Legislation of Morality." *Police Journal* 61(4) (October 1988):362-375.

Examines the history and problems of legislation in Great Britain and the United States against victimless crimes, including prostitution.

1220. Beotra, B.R. *The Suppression of Immmoral Traffic in Women and Girls Act, 1956, with State Rules.* 3rd ed. Revised by Devinder Singh. Allahabad: Law Book, 1981.

Complete text of the Suppression of Immoral Traffic in Women and Girls Act, passed by the Indian Parliament in 1956. Explains various provisions of the act along with specific case law examples. The third edition includes numerous amendments to the law which went into effect in 1970.

1221. Beretta Anguissola, P. *Prostituzione e legge merlin.* Firenze: L.

Pugliese, 1987.

1222. Bernat, F.P. "Gender Disparity in the Setting of Bail: Prostitution Offenses in Buffalo, NY, 1977-1979." *Journal of Offender Counseling Services, and Rehabilitation* 9(1-2) (Fall-Winter 1984):21-47. Also in *Gender Issues, Sex Offenses, and Criminal Justice--Current Trends.* Edited by S. Chaneles. New York: Haworth, 1984.

Examines court files of 809 defendants charged with prostitution or patronization to determine if gender classifications exist in pre-trial release decisions. Indicates that men are released more readily than women.

1223. Bernat, F.P. "New York State's Prostitution Statute: Case Study of the Discriminatory Application of a Gender Neutral Law." *Women and Politics* 4(3) (1984):103-120. Also in *Criminal Justice, Politics and Women.* Edited by C. Schweber and C. Feinman. New York: Haworth, 1985.

An analysis of prostitution/patronization arrest information in Buffalo, New York, from 1977-1980 reveals that despite equalization of patronization/prostitution statutes, enforcement of the statute is not gender neutral.

1224. Blackburn, E. *Discussion of the Neighborhood Crime Prevention Program.* Portland, OR: Office of Neighborhood Associations Crime Prevention Program, 1987.

Describes neighborhood organization efforts in Portland, Oregon, to control crimes, including prostitution.

1225. Blakey, G.R., L.D. Allard, et al. *Organized Crime in the United States.* Washington, DC: United States Department of Justice National Institute of Justice, 1982.

An overview of law enforcement of organized crime in the United States. Includes description of organized crime's involvement in prostitution.

1226. Blom-Cooper, L. "Prostitution: A Socio-Legal Comment on the Case of Dr. Ward." *British Journal of Sociology* 15(1) (March 1964):65-71.

Discussion of criminal proceedings brought against Dr. Stephen Ward, a British osteopath and artist brought to trial for living on the earnings of prostitution. Questions ambivalence in the British legal attitude toward prostitution in light of this trial.

1227. Blom-Cooper, L. "To Prosecute or Not to Prosecute." *Police We Deserve.* Edited by J.C. Alderson and P.J. Stead. London: Wolfe, 1973.

Argues that the police have wide discretionary powers in enforcing some proscribed behaviors and suggests decriminalization of victimless crimes, sexual offenses, and crimes against morality, such as prostitution, homosexuality, and pornography.

1228. Boles J., and C. Tatro. "Legal and Extra-Legal Methods of Controlling Female Prostitution: A Cross-Cultural Comparison." *International Journal of Comparative and Applied Criminal Justice* 2(1) (Spring 1978):71-85.

A cross-cultural examination of the legal and extra-legal methods used to control solicitation, police graft, neighborhood degeneration, and venereal disease which are viewed as problems associated with prostitution.

1229. Boruchowitz, R.C. "Victimless Crimes--A Proposal to Free the Courts." *Judicature* 57(2) (August-September 1973):69-78.

Discusses the impact and nature of victimless crimes such as prostitution, noting that victimless crimes constitute half of cases in United States courts. Asserts that more serious crimes could be handled if victimless crimes were decriminalized.

1230. Bottom, B. *Crime Rackets and Networks of Influence in Australia.* South Melbourne, Australia: Sun Books, 1987.

Discusses ties between organized crime in Australia and the United States and describes Australian criminal activities including prostitution.

1231. Bracey, D.H., and M. Neary, eds. *Prostitution: Is It a Victimless Crime?* New York: John Jay, 1979.

1232. Brannigan, A., L. Knafla, and C. Levy. *Street Prostitution: Assessing the Impact of the Law, Calgary, Regina, Winnipeg*. Ottawa: Communications and Public Affairs, Department of Justice Canada, 1989.

Describes the results of an inquiry into street soliciting, the adoption of a new law created to curb it and some of the intended and unintended consequences of the law. Covers patterns of enforcement of this bill, legal responses of criminal justice personnel, prostitution, soliciting, and escort services in three large Canadian cities.

1233. Breuer, T. "Problematics of Foreign Prostitutes on West Germany." (German) *Kriminalistik* 29(9) (1975):413-415.

1234. Brongersma, E. "Sexuality and the Law." *Journal of the American Institute of Hypnosis* 14(5) (September 1973): 210-221.

Examines legal aspects of sexual behavior and questions whether sexual morality can be legislated. Cites the Speijer report, an analysis of behavior in the Netherlands, as an enlightened approach to victimless crimes such as prostitution and pornography.

1235. Bruce, E.E. "Prostitution and Obscenity: A Comment Upon the Attorney General's Report on Prostitution." *Duke Law Journal* (1987)1:123-139.

Suggests that the Final Report of the U.S. Attorney General's Commission on Pornography (1986) offers a new approach to obscenity regulation. By relating prostitution to the production of obscene materials and emphasizing the ways in which prostitution can be regulated, the report offers a workable method of obscenity regulation.

1236. Bryant, M.A. "Prostitution and the Criminal Justice System." *Journal of Police Science and Administration* 5(4) (December 1977):379-389.

Examines nature, causes, and history of prostitution. Presents the benefits of decriminalization.

1237. Buckingham, H. "Prostitution Laws." (Letter) *New Society* 62(1049)
       (1982):530-531.

1238. Burnat, A. *Dossiers brûlants de la brigade des moeurs*. Paris: Presses
       de la Cité, 1976.

       Describes vice control and prostitution in France.

1239. Canada. Department of Justice. Policy Programs and Research Branch,
       Research and Statistics Section. "Pornography and Prostitution in the
       United States." Ottawa: The Department, 1984.

       Summarizes relevant U.S. federal, state, and local prostitution statutes as
       well as enforcement practices and public debates. The appendixes contain
       obscenity and prostitution laws from twelve key states and relevant
       excerpts from the Federal Code.

1240. Canada. Ministry of Justice. Special Committee on Pornography and
       Prostitution. "Pornography and Prostitution--Issues Paper." Vancouver,
       British Columbia, Canada: The Ministry, 1983.

       Identifies common elements in problems of pornography and prostitution.
       Poses questions regarding law reform efforts, impact on society, rights of
       the individual, criminalization, legalization, enforcement of morality, and
       decriminalization.

1241. Canada. Ministry of the Attorney-General Co-ordinated Law Enforcement
       Unit. *Organized Crime in British Columbia*. Victoria, British Columbia,
       Canada: The Ministry, 1979.

       Examines organized crime activities in British Columbia, including
       prostitution. Focuses on organization, ethnic background of participants,
       methods of control, achievements, and statistics.

1242. Canada. Quebec Commission de Police. *Organized Crime and the
       Business World*. 1977.

       Describes an investigation by the Quebec Police Commission into

Montreal's underworld activities from 1973-1977. Outlines the arrest and conviction of William Obront, a leading figure in Montreal's organized crime world. One section of the book is devoted to the story of Ziggy Wiseman, his extensive prostitution business, and how this business fell under the control of the underworld.

1243. Cao, L. "Illegal Traffic in Women: A Civil RICO Proposal." *Yale Law Journal.* 96(6) (May 1987):1297-1322.

Proposes that women in forced prostitution can be helped by a private right of action under the Racketeer Influenced and Corrupt Organizations Act.

1244. Cassels, J. "Prostitution and Public Nuisance--Desperate Measures and the Limits of Civil Adjudication." *Canadian Bar Review* 64(4) (1985): 764-804.

Attempts to define an appropriate legal response to the problem of street prostitution in Canada. Asserts that criminal law has failed to control public prostitution, and that common law may be a able to play a role.

1245. Caughey, M.S. "Criminal Law--Principle of Harm and its Application to Laws Criminalizing Prostitution Introduction." *Denver Law Journal* 51(2) (1974):235-262.

Discusses the principle of legal harm in relation to the criminalization of prostitution, and asserts that criminalization should not be allowed to stand constitutionally. Analyzes constitutional challenges to prostitution laws, including equal protection, right of privacy, and freedom of speech.

1246. Cooney, C.H., and J. Quint. *Prostitution in New York City: Answers to Some Questions.* New York: New York Women in Criminal Justice, 1977.

Examines the definition and legality of prostitution in New York City. Reviews research on men who engage prostitutes and discusses such problems as pimp conviction, prostitute victimization, prostitute drug use, venereal disease, and arrest and ages of prostitutes. Examines legal issues and the effectiveness of legal and social policies concerning prostitution in New York City. Lists penalties for prostitution and definitions of offenses. Addresses issues of decriminalization and legalization in a cross cultural context. Contains a brief discussion of juvenile prostitution.

1247. Costinew, B.A. "Education for Changing Public Policy: Decriminalization of Prostitution." (Ph.D. Dissertation) Wayne State University, 1983.

Discusses prostitution as a victimless crime and provides an overview and evaluation of enforcement methods that may be most effective. Covers the history of prostitution and enforcement attitudes and also provides definitions of specific types of prostitution activities and participants. Intended for law enforcement personnel and the general public, examines prostitution as it exists today, specifically in Detroit.

1248. Crites, L. *Female Offender.* Lexington, MA: D.C. Heath, 1976.

A collection of articles including historical treatment of female offenders, causes of female crime, impact of the legal system on female criminality, sentencing, children of prostitutes, juveniles in training schools, females in southern prisons, and the need for prison reform. Analyzes arguments for decriminalization of prostitution.

1249. Currie, A.J., and J.F. Decker. *The Prostitute: Regulation and Control: A Comparative Study.* [s.l.:s.n., 1971].

1250. Davis, N.J. *Cross-National Variation in Patterns of Control Over Prostitution.* (Asssociation paper) American Sociological Association, 1989.

Examines variations in control of prostitution among nations as related to legal, political, economic, cultural and social differences. Analyzes feminist, political, and equity models as alternatives to the present policy of enforcement which is alleged to isolate, degrade, and punish women.

1251. Decker, J.F. *Prostitution: Regulation and Control.* Littleton, CO: Rothman, 1979.

Provides historical analysis of the causes and control of prostitution from primitive societies to the present. Includes discussion of control of prostitution, motivation for control, roles of pimps, and patrons, and social and psychological problems. Discusses decriminalization and legalization and describes a detailed program for reform which advocates legalization and permits solicitation in some places but prohibits juvenile prostitution.

1252. DeCrow, K. "Criminal Law: Free Our Sisters, Free Ourselves." *Sexist Justice* by Karen DeCrow. New York: Random House, 1974.

Examines sex discrimination in criminal law, focusing on prostitution, rape, sentencing, economic discrimination, and treatment of female offenders in prisons. Argues that low-income women are often victimized and regarded as criminals rather than victims. Analyzes negative attitude toward women in prisons, and includes a list of grievances by women in House of Detention (New York).

1253. Dixon, O.F. *Action Taken by the Police Regarding Allegations of Graft and Corruption Within the Police Force and What Further Action Is Necessary Regarding Such Allegations.* Australia, 1982.

Reports on a case of police corruption in Western Australia involving prostitution where lack of evidence closed the inquiry.

1254. Doerkson, L. "Women and Crime: A Bibliography." *Resources for Feminist Research* 13/14(4):60-63.

Lists books and articles on women and crime.

1255. Edwards, S.M., and G. Armstrong. "Policing Street Prostitution: The Street Offences Squad in London." *Police Journal* 61(3) (July-September 1988):209-219.

Examines the implementation of current laws on prostitution by London police in the Metropolitan Police Street Offences Squad (SOS). Discusses the identification and arrest of prostitutes. Concludes that statutes covering street crime such as bail, vagrancy, and disruptive behavior make arrest and prosecution of prostitutes easier than arresting customers.

1256. Edwards, S.M. *Women on Trial: A Study of the Female Suspect, Defendant and Offender in the Criminal Law and Criminal Justice System.*

Manchester, UK: University Press, 1984.

Examines the impact of gender role stereotypes on legislation, enforcement, and administration of laws, particularly with regard to prostitution. Addresses plea negotiations, prosecution and sentencing. Based on two years of interviews with legal and law enforcement justice officials and female offenders.

1257. Ferguson, R.W. *Nature of Vice Control in the Administration of Justice.* St. Paul, MN: West, 1974.

A text for criminal justice students on the social, political, practical, and legal issues in vice control. Contains a chapter on prostitution.

1258. Flowers, R.B. *Women and Criminality: The Woman as Victim, Offender, and Practitioner.* Westport, CT: Greenwood, 1987.

Discusses women, including prostitutes, as victims, offenders, and "criminal justice practitioners".

1259. Fragoso, E. *Themes of the Modern Right: Prostitution, Noise Control, Abortion, Divorce.* Movimento cultural brasileiro. (French and Portuguese) Brasilia: Horizonte Editora, 1980.

1260. Galardo, A.T., L. Belzile, and E. Paradis. *New Orientation of Criminal Justice in Relation to Sexual Offenses.* (French) Montreal: Clinique Pinel, 1975.

Describes a study of 216 sexual offender cases referred by the courts to the Pinel External Treatment Hospital in Montreal. Contains data on frequency of incidence and offender characteristics. Surveys judges and outpatients and emphasizes the establishment of links between courts and treatment facilities for sexual offenders. Indicates that child molestation is the most frequent offense and links it to the spread of juvenile prostitution.

1261. Galliher, J.F., and J.R. Cross. *Moral Legislation without Morality: The Case of Nevada.* New Brunswick, NJ: Rutgers University Press, 1983.

Examines the pattern of vice control legislation in Nevada from the 1930s to the 1970s for prostitution, drug or alcohol abuse, gambling and quickie divorces. Speculates that the pattern of strict legislation versus the comparatively lenient enforcement of the legislation may stem from economic considerations, such as the desire to attract tourist trade while projecting an image of moral rectitude.

1262. Gemme, R., N. Payment, and L. Malenfant. *Street Prostitution: Assessing the Impact of the Law, Montreal.* Ottawa: Communications and Public Affairs, Department of Justice Canada, 1989.

Discusses prostitution laws and the legal status of prostitutes in Montreal and assesses the impact of Bill C-49, a 1985 amendment to the Canadian Criminal Code.

1263. Gilinskiy, Y. "Is the Prostitution Ban Effective?" (Russian) *Sotsiologicheskie Issledovaniya* 6 (1988):68-70.

1264. Gitchoff, G., and J. Ellenbogen. "Victimless Crimes: The Case Against Continued Enforcement." *Journal of Police Science and Administration* 1(4) (December 1973):401-408.

Argues against continued prosecution of victimless crimes, such as prostitution, homosexuality, obscenity, gambling and drug abuse. Refutes involvement of organized crime in such activities and discredits link between prostitution and drug use. Makes recommendations for control.

1265. Goldman, M. "Prostitution in America." *Crime and Social Justice* 2 (Fall/Winter 1974):90-93.

Describes a course on prostitution in America given at the University of California, Berkeley, School of Criminology. Issues include historical aspects, social causes, feminist issues, criminalization, and victimization.

1266. Graves, F. *Street Prostitution: Assessing the Impact of the Law, Halifax.* Ottawa, Ontario: Communications and Public Affairs, Dept. of Justice Canada, 1989.

Evaluates the impacts and effects of Bill C-49 on the control and practice of prostitution in Halifax, Nova Scotia. The bill, amending the Canadian Criminal Code in 1985, was intended to make it easier to enforce the law.

1267. Great Britain. Criminal Law Revision Committee. *Prostitution in the Street: Sixteenth Report*. London: HMSO, 1984.

1268. Great Britain. Criminal Law Revision Committee. *Prostitution: Off-Street Activities: Seventeenth Report*. London: HMSO, 1985.

1269. Great Britain. Criminal Law Revision Committee. *Working Paper on Offences Relating to Prostitution and Allied Offences*. London: HMSO, 1982.

1270. Green. J. "Is There a Case for the Legalization of Prostitution in Britain Today?" *Police College Magazine* 15(1) (Autumn 1978):51-53.

Uses a review of the history of prostitution and its legislative control to advocate the decriminalization of prostitution in Great Britain. Asserts that a need for the profession exists historically and argues that decriminalization would free prostitutes from the abuse and violence of professional criminals.

1271. Grittner, F.K. "White Slavery: Myth, Ideology, and American Law." (Ph.D. Dissertation) University of Minnesota, 1986.

Examines the historical, cultural, and legal aspects of white slavery in American from the late nineteenth century to the present as expressed in films, novels, government reports, and the history of the Mann Act. Attributes changes in enforcement attitudes to social changes of the times, such as immigration, urbanization, cultural unrest and, later, the sexual revolution.

1272. Guzman, R.F. "The Legal Regulation of Prostitution in Mexico." *Revista de la Facultad de Derecho de Mexico* 22(85/86) (1972):85-134.

Reviews Mexican prostitution law and the question of jurisdiction.

1273. Guzman, R.F. *La Prostitución*. Mexico: Editorial Diana, 1973.

Examines legal aspects of prostitution in Mexico.

1274. Haft, M.G. "Hustling For Rights." *Female Offender*. Edited by Laura Crites. Lexington, MA: D.C. Heath, 1976.

Cites four grounds on which prostitution laws should be declared unconstitutional: lack of equal protection of the laws for prostitutes, lack of privacy, the application of cruel and unusual punishment, and the lack of due process under the law. Describes the birth of prostitutes' rights organizations to combat unfair treatment.

1275. Halleck, C.W., et al. "Should Prostitution Be Legalized?" *Medical Aspects of Human Sexuality* 8(4) (April 1974):54-83.

Seven authors present their views on whether laws against prostitution should be abolished and discuss the implications of decriminalization for public health, constitutional and moral freedom, and social processes.

1276. Hamacher, W. "Supporters of Criminal Organizations." *Organized Crime: Conference Proceedings-West Germany, 1974.* (German) Wiesbaden, West Germany: Bundeskriminalamt, 1975.

1277. Hanna, R.E. "Combatting Prostitution: Salinas Police Curb City's Street Problem." *Police Chief* 46(6) (June 1979):62-66.

Outlines techniques used by the Police Department in Salinas, California, to combat prostitution in that city.

1278. Hardie, G.M., and G.F. Hartford. *Commentary on the Immorality Act (Act No. 23 of 1957).* Cape Town, South Africa: Juta, 1960.

1279. Heath, E.D. "Police Problems in Enforcement of Laws Pertaining to Obscenity and Sex-related Criminal Offenses." *Police Chief* 45(2) (1978):52-54.

Briefly outlines specific legal problems faced by police in enforcing various laws related to prostitution, promotion of prostitution, escort services, massage parlors, etc. Recommends regulatory legislation, the use of zoning restrictions, and licensing requirements to aid the police administrator.

1280. Hellebrand, H. "Kapitulation der Gerichte vor der Wirklichkeit? zur Förderung der Prostitution." *Kriminalistik* 32(2) (1978):61-64.

1281. Hewitt, W.H. "Nonvictim Crime: Some Police Perspectives." *Criminal Justice Planning.* Edited by Joseph E. Scott and Simon Dinitz. New York: Praeger, 1977.

Examines law enforcement aspects of victimless crimes, including prostitution. Concludes that sexual activity between consenting adults should not be prohibited by law.

1282. Hogan, B. "On Modernising the Law of Sexual Offenses." *Reshaping the Criminal Law.* Edited by P.R. Glazebrook. London: Stevens and Sons, 1978.

Comments on various areas of British law reform of sexual offenses, including prostitution. Recommends elimination of criminal prosecution for consensual sexual contact and suggests other changes in the existing laws.

1283. Holden, R.N. *A Comparative Analysis of White Slavery in the Modern World.* Paper presented at the Academy of Criminal Justice Sciences, Chicago, 1984.

Views white slavery as an international issue and suggests that the major obstacles to solving the problem include the lack of women's rights in many countries and the profit motive.

1284. Howard League for Penal Reform. "Street Offences: Statement to the Parliamentary Penal Reform Group on the Report of the Working Party on Vagrancy and Street Offences." London, 1976.

The Howard League for Penal Reform criticizes proposed legislative changes to combat street solicitation by prostitutes.

1285. Hubatka, W. "Fight Against the Excesses of Prostitution." (German) *Kriminalistik* 26 (March 1972):121-127.

1286. Hubner, K. "No Loopholes in Prostitution Laws." (Letter in German) *Kriminalistik* 41 (1987):245.

1287. Hughes, P. "Tensions in Canadian Society: The Fraser Committee Report." *The Windsor Yearbook of Access to Justice, v.6.* Edited by William A. Bogart. Windsor, Ontario: University of Windsor Press, 1988.

Criticizes Canada's Fraser Committee Report, which analyzes Canadian law pertaining to prostitution and pornography, and suggests various legal reforms.

1288. Hutchins, L.D. "Pornography: The Prosecution of Pornographers Under Prostitution Statutes--A New Approach." *Syracuse Law Review* 37(3) (1986):977-1002.

Highlights several cases in which photographers, producers, and distributors of pornography have been successfully prosecuted under prostitution statutes in several states.

1289. Institute of Criminology. Sydney University Law School, Sydney, Australia. *Street Offences: Proceedings of a Seminar.* Pyrmont, New South Wales, Australia: NSW Government Printing Office, 1983.

Includes papers by police officers, lawyers, and a community representative discussing the effectiveness of Australia's street offence laws, particularly the 1979 Offences in Public Places Act. Includes tables and a summary of the conclusions.

1290. International Criminal Police Organization (INTERPOL). *Exchange of Information on Persons Involved in Prostitution (Report submitted at the 43rd General Assembly Session).* Cannes, France, 1974.

Contains two information-exchange forms to be used by police to collect international data about the movements of prostitutes and their criminal contacts in one or more countries.

1291. International Criminal Police Organization (INTERPOL). *Traffic In Women (Report submitted at the 29th General Assembly Session).* Washington, DC, 1960.

Presents the results of a questionnaire focusing on international criminal cases which have resulted in convictions for trafficking in women. Few cases have come before the courts since 1950.

1292. Jackson, B. *Outside the Law: A Thief's Primer.* New Brunswick, NJ: Transaction Books, 1972.

First-person narrative of a criminal career; one chapter is devoted to an analysis of prostitution.

1293. Jacobs, J. *Deviance: Field Studies and Self-Disclosures.* Palo Alto, CA: National Press, 1974.

A collection of readings concerning the management of deviance in public, private, socio-legal and medical contexts. Most of the contributors are sociology students who have studied various forms of deviant behavior. Written from an interactionist perspective.

1294. James, J., et al. *The Politics of Prostitution: Resources for Legal Change.* 2nd ed. Seattle: s.n., 1977.

1295. Jennings, M.A. "The Victim As Criminal: A Consideration of California's Prostitution Law." *California Law Review* 64(5) (September 1976):1235-1284.

Examines the causes of prostitution and the reasons for retaining its criminal status in California. Concludes that attempts to suppress prostitution through criminal law have been unsuccessful because of the social, economic, and psychological pressures that perpetuate the activity. Analyzes current legislative reform efforts and suggests alternative legislation.

1296. Johnson, K.A. *Public Order Criminal Behavior and Criminal Laws: The Question of Legal Decriminalization.* Palo Alto, CA: R. and E. Research, 1977.

Reports on the extent of support for policies dealing with public order crimes and criminals in a non-metropolitan community. Concludes that decriminalization is more likely to be favored as community size and heterogeneity of the population increase.

1297. Johnson, W.C. "Policing a Town: Civilian by Day, GI by Night." *Police Chief* 42(3) (March 1975):57-58.

Briefly describes steps taken by the chief of police in Fayetteville, North Carolina, to handle prostitution and related problems. Notes that the city's proximity to several large military installations is one of the major reasons for the high rate of prostitution.

1298. Kaplan, J. "Edward G. Donley Memorial Lecture: Non-victim Crime and the Regulation of Prostitution." *West Virginia Law Review* 79 (Summer 1977):593-606.

Explores arguments against decriminalization and discusses the concept of regulating prostitution. Suggests that regulation is preferable to present laws and would make prostitution less of a social and moral problem.

1299. Kent, R.B., and D.J. Dingemans. "Prostitution and the Police: Patrolling the Stroll in Sacramento." *Police Chief* 44(9) (September 1977):64-65,73.

Reports that streetwalking activity is generally confined to a few geographically distinct areas within a specific city. Outlines the social and legal dilemma faced by officials in Sacramento, California, in dealing with streetwalking prostitutes.

1300. Kerner, H.J. *Professional and Organized Crime: A Stock-Taking and a Report on New Development Tendencies in the Federal Republic of Germany and in the Netherlands.* (German) Wiesbaden, West Germany: Bundeskriminalamt, 1973.

1301. Khan, M.Z., and D.R. Singh. "Prostitution, Human Rights, Law and Voluntary Action." *Indian Journal of Social Work* 47(4) (January 1987):443-453.

Examines the connection between prostitution and urbanization in India.

Discusses the concept of human rights and the legal and voluntary measures adopted to control prostitution. Argues that legal provisions against prostitution in India are insufficient and that their enforcement has been ineffective.

1302. Kiester, E. *Crimes with No Victims: How Legislating Morality Defeats the Cause of Justice.* New York: Alliance for a Safer New York, 1972.

Surveys the social and economic costs to society of several victimless crimes, including prostitution. Argues that social problems should not be addressed by the criminal law.

1303. Kretz, J. *Police Perception of Plaintiffless Crime: Preliminary Report of a Survey of the District of Columbia Metropolitan Police Department.* Washington, DC: Bureau of Social Science Research, 1974.

Attempts to explain the perceptions and attitudes held by police officers towards plaintiffless crimes such as Sunday liquor sales, numbers running, and prostitution. Argues that police officers perceive such crimes as a cluster distinct from other types of offenses.

1304. Kroll, B. *Night Asylum.* (German) Hamburg, West Germany: Stern-Bucher, 1981.

1305. Lazo, D.T. *Investigative Procedure and the Intelligence Function.* (Audiocassettes) San Jose, CA: Lansford, 1975.

Four tapes, a student handbook, and test materials describe the procedures used in all police investigations, including prostitution.

1306. Leng, R., and A. Sanders. "The CLRC Working Paper on Prostitution." *Criminal Law Review* (October 1983):644-655.

Comments on proposals contained in the Criminal Law Revision Committee's Working Paper on Offences Relating to Prostitution and Allied Offences (1982). Suggests that the law should not seek to eradicate prostitution but to penalize harmful activities associated with it.

1307. Leone, B. *Should Prostitution Be a Crime?* St. Paul, MN: Greenhaven, 1983.

1308. Leonhardt, F. *Prostitution: Alternatives to Prohibition.* Salem, OR: Oregon Legislative Research, 1981.

Discusses policies to legalize prostitution in several European countries, including West Germany, Great Britain, the Netherlands and the Soviet Union. Compares these policies to U.S. laws prohibiting prostitution.

1309. Lermack, P. "Hookers, Judges, and Bail Forfeitures: The Importance of Internally Generated Demands on Policy-implementing Institutions." *Administration and Society* 8(4) (February 1977):459-468.

Analyzes bail forfeitures and other aspects of bail administration. Notes that accused prostitutes jump bail more than other offenders and have the ability to raise money easily. Concludes that the informal pressures in the bail administration should be examined.

1310. Lesce, T. "The Anatomy of a Vice Operation: 'Operation Cold Shower'."*Law and Order* 33(8) (August 1985):51-56.

Outlines steps taken by the Sheriff's Office in Maricopa County (Arizona) to close 14 escort services which operated as fronts for prostitution. The round-up, known as "Operation Cold Shower," took many months of planning and investigation, culminating in a series of raids.

1311. Lidz, C.W. "Cop-Addict Game: A Model of Police-Suspect Interaction." *Journal of Police Science and Administration* 2(1) (March 1974):2-10.

Asserts that although vice squad personnel believe strongly in professional police ideology, their daily work involves them in competitive games with suspects. Argues that these games violate the legal restrictions on police-suspect interaction.

1312. Lindquist, J.H., et al. "Judicial Processing of Males and Females Charged With Prostitution." *Journal of Criminal Justice* 17(4) (1989):277-291.

Studies variables related to case disposition, judgment, and sentence length, based on the experience of Bexar County, Texas, from 1973 to 1985.

1313. Lindquist, J.H. *Misdemeanor Crime: Trivial Criminal Pursuit.* Newbury Park, CA: Sage, 1988.

Discusses misdemeanor crime, its offenders, victims, and management.

1314. Lipetz, M.J. "Routine Justice: The Impact of the Courtroom Workgroup on the Processing of Cases in Women's Court." (Ph.D. Dissertation) Northwestern University, 1980.

Analyzes work patterns of personnel at the Chicago Women's Court to show how the group accomplishes institutional goals. Concludes that the court manages control of prostitution activities without ever facing the issue of decriminalization versus meaningful enforcement.

1315. Livesey, S. *Survey of the Legal Literature on Women Offenders.* Pittsburgh, PA: Entropy, 1975.

Selection of annotated and unannotated legal sources dealing with women and the criminal law, prostitution, rape, and the Equal Rights Amendment.

1316. Lowman, J., et al. eds. *Regulating Sex: An Anthology of Commentaries on the Findings and Recommendations of the Badgley and Fraser Reports.* Stoneham, MA: Butterworths, 1986.

Contains 12 papers that explain and critique Canada's Badgley and Fraser Reports.

1317. Lowman, J., and L. Frazer. *Street Prostitution: Assessing the Impact of the Law, Vancouver.* Ottawa: Communications and Public Affairs, Department of Justice Canada, 1989.

Examines prostitution laws and the legal status of prostitutes in Vancouver, British Columbia, following the implementation of Bill C-49, the 1985 amendment to the Canadian Criminal Code.

1318. MacMillan, J. "Rape and Prostitution." *Victimology: An International Journal* 1(3) (Fall 1976):414-420.

Outlines theories which ascribe a causal relationship between rape and prostitution. Based on a comparative analysis, questions whether legalizing prostitution would decrease the rape rate.

1319. Malik, V. *Mazhar Husain's The Suppression of Immoral Traffic in Women and Girls Act, 1956: With Critical Commentary, Case Law and States' Rules.* 3rd ed. Lucknow: Eastern Book, 1978.

Provides the complete text of the 1956 law designed to control and limit prostitution in India. The law covers issues such as punishment for living on the earnings of prostitution, prostitution in public places, and protective homes.

1320. Marx, G.T. "New Police Undercover Work." *Urban Life* 8(4) (January 1980):399-446.

Describes tactics used in police undercover activity and examines the implications of such tactics as used in a variety of crimes, including prostitution. Finds no evidence that undercover work reduces crime rate.

1321. Mathews, R. "Streetwise? A Critical Review of the Criminal Law Revision Committee's Report on Prostitution in the Street." *Critical Social Policy* 4(3) (Spring 1985):103-111.

Reviews existing British laws on public solicitation for sexual purposes and discusses three proposed reforms designed to curb solicitation.

1322. McLeod, E. "A Fresh Approach? A Critique of the Criminal Law Revision Committee's Working Paper on Offences Relating to Prostitution and Allied Offences." *Journal of Law and Society* 10(2) (1983):271-279.

Criticizes recommendations made by the British Home Office committee paper of 1982. Suggests that laws to control prostitution do little to address the roots of prostitution as a social problem. Concludes that criminal law in this area is neither appropriate nor effective.

1323. McLeod, E. "Working With Prostitutes: Probation Officers' Aims and
       Strategies." *British Journal of Social Work* 9(4) (1979):453-469.

       Examines the strategy of probation officers to define and respond to
       prostitutes' legal, emotional, and material problems on an individual basis.
       Reports that strategies are ineffective and recommends alternatives.

1324. McPherson, M. *Controlling Vice in Minneapolis During the 1970's.*
       Minneapolis, MN: Minnesota Crime Prevention Center, 1980.

       Examines the Minneapolis municipal government's public debate on
       strategies for dealing with prostitution. Argues that although the control
       of prostitution and pornography became one of the most controversial
       issues to be publicly debated in Minneapolis from 1972 to 1979, it did not
       lead to effective reform.

1325. Megino, G.R. *Prostitution and California Law: An Interim Study.*
       Sacramento, CA: California Legislature, Senate Committee on Judiciary,
       1977.

       Considers various alternatives to prostitution law in light of the spread of
       venereal disease, increase in drug abuse, and involvement of organized
       crime. Highlights decriminalization, legalization, and various other
       alternatives.

1326. Montreal Association of Women and the Law. *Position Paper of the
       Montreal Association of Women and the Law on Soliciting.* Montreal: The
       Association, 1980.

1327. Morris, N. "Overreach of the Criminal Law: Main Paper." *Crime, Law
       and the Community.* Capetown, South Africa: Juta, 1976.

       Recommends decriminalization and regulation for victimless crimes,
       including prostitution.

1328. Moyer, S. *Street Prostitution: Assessing the Impact of the Law, Toronto.*
       Ottawa: Communications and Public Affairs, Department of Justice
       Canada, 1989.

Presents an evaluation of Bill C-49 for Metropolitan Toronto. Covers Ottawa, Niagara Falls and London, Ontario in lesser detail. Describes the implementation of the legislation by police and the courts and reviews the impact of the law on street prostitution.

1329. National Task Force of Prostitution. *Decriminalization of Prostitution: A Position Paper.* San Francisco: National Task Force of Prostitution, 1980.

Suggests that prostitution laws should be replaced with business codes in order to control exploitation. Recommends applying pressure on law enforcement agencies, district attorneys, public defenders, and judges to improve treatment of victims until laws can be changed.

1330. Neave M. "The Failure of Prostitution Law Reform: The John Barry Memorial Lecture." *Australian and New Zealand Journal of Criminology* 21(4) (December 1988):202-213.

Examines the nature and effects of Australian prostitution law and proposes four main principles which should guide reform.

1331. New York City Commission to Investigate Allegations of Police Corruption. *Knapp Commission Report on Police Corruption.* New York: The Commission, 1973.

Covers findings of the commission appointed to determine the incidence, prevalence, and causes of police corruption in New York City. Covers the patterns of gambling, narcotics, prostitution, and other elements involving graft and corruption. Discusses methods used, reason for payoffs, and interrelationships of factors.

1332. New York Civil Liberties Union. *How Not To Get Hooked By the New Prostitution Law.* New York: New York Civil Liberties Union, 1976.

1333. Noble, H.B. "Sweeping the Streets: A Return to the Old Morality Puts New Pressure on City Police." *Police Magazine* 2(2) (March 1979):54-62.

Outlines problems faced by urban police in attempting to control prostitution and commercial sex establishments in Boston and New York City.

1334. O'Donnell, M. J., and G.M. Bicek. "Massage Parlor Problem." *FBI Law Enforcement Bulletin* 46(6) (June 1977):16-20.

Discusses steps taken by authorities in Chicago, Illinois, to combat the growing number of massage parlors. Argues that most massage parlors are houses of prostitution whose owners use loopholes in the legal system to circumvent the laws. Describes licensing requirements and an ordinance which limits the types of activities in massage parlors.

1335. Olson-Raymer G., and B. Fisher. *Definitional, Programmatic, and Statutory Issues Confronting Enforcement Response to Runaways.* Sacramento, California: American Justice Institute. National Juvenile Justice System Assessment Center, 1984.

Describes federal, state and local responses to runaways and services provided to homeless youth involved in prostitution. Includes case studies of juvenile prostitution programs in Seattle, San Francisco, Minneapolis, and Louisville.

1336. Pace, D.F. *Handbook of Vice Control.* Englewood Cliffs, NJ: Prentice-Hall, 1971.

Includes guidelines for the enforcement of sex-related offenses.

1337. Pace, D.F., and J.C. Styles. *Organized Crime: Concepts and Control.* 2nd ed. Englewood Cliffs, NJ: Prentice-Hall, 1983.

Includes a discussion of prostitution.

1338. Parnas, R.I. "Legislative Reform of Prostitution Laws: Keeping Commercial Sex Out of Sight and Out of Mind." *Santa Clara Law Review* 21(3) (1981):669-696.

Proposes a reform bill which would add controls to some types of prostitution activities and eliminate controls on others in an attempt to appease competing interest groups. Notes that courts and legislatures increasingly recognize that prostitution as commercial sex is distinguished from other types of sexual behavior and that it should be treated differently.

1339. Pateman, C. *The Sexual Contract.* Oxford, England: Stanford University Press, 1988.

Covers contradictions and paradoxes surrounding women and contracts, including marriage, employment, and prostitution.

1340. Pathak, B.C. *Rape: Law and Flaw, Along With Immoral Traffic (Prevention) Act, 1956.* Allahabad: Gogia Law House, 1988.

1341. Pearl, J. "The Highest Paying Customers: America's Cities and the Costs of Prostitution Control." *Hastings Law Journal* 38(4) (1987):769-800.

Measures the dollar cost of prostitution enforcement through analysis of police, judicial and correction costs. Assesses the non-monetary costs of prostitution enforcement as well.

1342. Pennsylvania. Pennsylvania Crime Commission. *Decade of Organized Crime, 1980 Report.* Linglestown, PA: The Commission, 1980.

Documents the growing problems caused by various forms of organized crime in Pennsylvania. Argues that organized criminal activities, including prostitution, have generated huge profits and recommends a series of actions.

1343. Pennsylvania Program for Women and Girl Offenders. *Decriminalization of Prostitution.* (Microfiche) Rockville, MD: National Institute of Justice. National Criminal Justice Reference Service Microfiche Program, 1975.

Briefly summarizes the laws against prostitution, arguments for and against decriminalization, constitutional arguments, and myths about prostitution.

1344. Pheterson, G., ed. *A Vindication of the Rights of Whores: The International Struggle for Prostitutes' Rights.* Seattle, WA: Seal, 1989.

Contains transcriptions of several international conferences on prostitute rights. Most of the speakers and their audience are or have been prostitutes.

1345. Police Science Services, Inc. *Sex Crimes.* (Audiocassette kit.) Niles, IL: Police Science Services, 1978.

An audiocassette and slide presentation which outlines various types of sex crimes. Highlights problems encountered by law enforcement officers during the investigation of sex crimes, including public pressure to eliminate prostitution and difficulties in identifying witnesses and obtaining evidence.

1346. Powis, D. *Signs of Crime: A Field Manual for Police.* New York: John Jay, 1978.

Includes a chapter on tracking and arresting prostitutes and their employers.

1347. "Privacy and Prostitution: Constitutional Implications of State v. Pilcher." *Iowa Law Review* 63(1) (1977):248-265.

Examines prostitution statutes in Iowa which have come under constitutional challenges for reasons of vagueness, overbreadth, equal protection and the right to privacy. Defines and evaluates state interests that have been or may be advanced to support the use of criminal penalties in the control of prostitution.

1348. *Prostitution in Canada.* (Ottawa): Canadian Advisory Council on the Status of Women, 1984.

Describes prostitution legislation in Canada.

1349. *Prostitution--Is It a Victimless Crime? Professional Law Enforcement Problem Series.* Transcript of the Symposium on Prostitution held at John Jay College of Criminal Justice, New York City, 1977. University City, MO: American Academy for Professional Law Enforcement.

Examines prostitution from the legal, sociological, and law enforcement perspectives. Participants address the relationship between crime and prostitution, and describe the difficulties involved in legalizing prostitution.

1350. Quigley, J. "Response to Professor Schwartz's Analysis." *Criminal Law Reporter: Federal Criminal Code Reform* 23(11) (June 14, 1978):30-40.

1351. Reid, E.L. "Prostitution and the Law: A Descriptive and Analytical Study of Prostitution." (Thesis) Kansas State College of Pittsburgh, 1974.

Analyzes the role of prostitution in Western society and examines the existing regulation of prostitution through the passage and enforcement of laws. Includes an analysis of the attitudes and practices of law enforcement officials.

1352. Rich, R.M. *Crimes Without Victims: Deviance and the Criminal Law.* Lanham, MD: University Press of America, 1978.

Examines forms of social deviance commonly thought of as victimless crimes, and presents arguments for and against decriminalization. Each chapter deals with specific forms of social deviance. Includes legal history, definitions, statutory provisions, enforcement practices, and characteristics of offenders.

1353. Richards, D.A.J. "Commercial Sex and the Rights of the Person: A Moral Argument for the Decriminalization of Prostitution." *University of Pennsylvania Law Review* 127(5) (May 1979):1195-1287.

Explores concepts of human rights and public morality as a basis for the decriminalization of prostitution. Suggests that in order to understand the criminal prohibitions against prostitution, four arguments should be considered: criminogenesis, the control of venereal disease, the intrinsic immoral and degrading nature of commercial sex, and the self-destructive and debilitating nature of prostitution. Examines three legal approaches to prostitution.

1354. Richards, D.A.J. *Sex, Drugs, Death, and the Law: An Essay on Human Rights and Overcriminalization.* Totowa, NJ: Rowman and Littlefield, 1982.

Analyzes the way in which the American criminal justice system has overcriminalized sex, drug use, and the right to die. Advocates decriminalization of consensual adult sexual relations among homosexuals and with prostitutes. Discusses the morality of prostitution and the constitutional right to privacy and argues that decriminalization of specified acts is an extension of the basic American value of human rights.

1355. Riggs, J. "Prostitution Bill Drives 'Oldest Profession' Underground." *Perception* 9(5) (1986):51-52.

Discusses implications of Bill C-49, which amended the Canadian Criminal Code and targeted prostitutes with six-month jail terms and fines of up to $2,000. Suggests that by making prostitution a criminal offence, the bill makes it harder for prostitutes to get different jobs and that it does not address the economic and social causes of prostitution.

1356. Roby, P.A. "Politics and Criminal Law: Revision of the New York State Penal Law on Prostitution." *Criminal Justice: Law and Politics*. Edited by George F. Cole. 3rd ed. North Scituate, MA: Duxbury, 1980.

Examines the process by which behavior is classified as criminal or noncriminal in a study of the revision of New York State's prostitution law. Argues that the formulation and enforcement of the New York prostitution law are political processes involving numerous interest groups.

1357. Roby, P.A. "Politics and Prostitution: A Case Study of the Revision, Enforcement, and Administration of the New York State Penal Laws on Prostitution." *Crime and Justice, 1971-72: An AMS Anthology*. Edited by J. Susman. New York: AMS, 1974. Also published in *Criminology* 9(4) (1972):425-447.

Explores the political processes and reform efforts which affected the formulation, enforcement, and judicial administration of New York State's prostitution laws from 1960 to 1970. Traces the social and political pressures against the revised law initiated by citizens, businesses, and special interest groups.

1358. Romenesko, K., and E.M. Miller. "The Second Step in Double Jeopardy: Appropriating the Labor of Female Street Hustlers." *Crime and Delinquency* 35(1) (January 1989):109-135.

Documents life histories of female street hustlers who are members of a pseudofamily, i.e., a family made up of one man and the women who work for him. Characterizes the pseudofamily as a heteropatriarchal mechanism that traps female members in a tangled web of conflicting emotions and motives.

1359. Rounthwaite, A. *Issues Paper, Prostitution: Prepared for the Law Reform Commission of Canada.* (Microfiche) Kanata, Ontario: Micro-Can, 1985.

1360. Rowe, S. "Prostitution and the Criminal Justice System: An Analysis of Present Policy and Possible Alternatives". *Critical Issues in Criminal Justice 1979.* Edited by R.G. Iacovetta and D.H. Chang. Durham, NC: Carolina Academic Press, 1979.

Discusses the prostitute in society, law enforcement policies, and decriminalization and legalization efforts. Argues that, although present enforcement policies have been ineffective, law enforcement agencies insist that prostitution remain illegal in order to control associated crimes. Urges a comprehensive study before policy alternatives are chosen.

1361. Russell, J.S. "Offence of Keeping a Common Bawdy-House in Canadian Criminal Law." *Ottawa Law Review* 14(2) (1982):270-313.

Suggests that the Canadian government should change its definition of a bawdy-house (brothel) if it wants to protect the individual's right to private consensual sexual activity. Asserts that keeping bawdy-houses is victimless since neither keepers nor clients sustain serious harm.

1362. Russell, K.V., and C. Owen. "Prostitution: Women, Clients and the Law." *Police Journal* 57(1) (Jan./Mar. 1984):68-99.

A British study analyzing the socioeconomic and educational backgrounds of prostitutes prior to their becoming prostitutes. Assesses client backgrounds, prostitute-patronage patterns, and the criminal processing of prostitutes. Finds discrimination against the prostitutes on grounds of sex, social origin, and socioeconomic status at all stages of criminal process.

1363. Samuels, A. "Prostitution and Planning Law." *Journal of Planning and Environment Law* (September 1980):578-582.

1364. Saney, P. "In Praise of Organized Crime." *Rutgers Law Journal* 16(3-4)
       (Spring-Summer 1985):853-867.

       Suggests that organized crime persists in the U.S. because it meets social
       and economic needs. Favors government regulation rather than
       proscription of gambling, prostitution, and drug use.

1365. Sartoriust, R.E. "Enforcement of Morality." *Yale Law Journal* 81(5)
       (April 1972):891-910.

       Critically examines Mill's principle that only self-preservation of society
       warrants interference with absolute individual freedom through a
       discussion of the enforcement of sexual morality by criminal law.

1366. Schantz, M.E. "Survey of Iowa Criminal Law." *Drake Law Review* 26
       (1) (1976/1977):116-158.

       Examines major Iowa State Supreme Court decisions from July 1975
       through June 1976 in the context of developing doctrines in criminal law
       in Iowa and elsewhere. The section on substantive law covers
       constitutional challenges to statutes in the area of prostitution as well as
       decisions related to specific offenses. Concludes that the Iowa court
       continues to follow a moderately conservative course.

1367. Scharbert, J. "Communal Dwellinghouses for Prostitutes: Solution of the
       Problem of Prostitutes?" (German) *Kriminalistik* 28 (August 1974):337-
       341.

1368. Schmidt, V. "The Love Industry: Prostitution, the Law on Aliens, and
       Police Practice." (German) *Kriminalistik* 43 (1989):423-428.

1369. Schnitzler, P., T.J. Weingarten, and B.J. Bernstein. *Prostitution Issues
       in Sexual Behavior Series*. New York: Harper and Row, 1976.

       Slides and printed material pose questions about the morality of
       prostitution and whether it should be decriminalized. Includes interviews
       with prostitutes, their clients, psychiatric personnel, and others. Discusses
       decriminalization versus legalization.

1370. Schreiber, M. "Strategy of Combatting Organized Crime from the Point of View of a Big City Police Force." (German) *Organized Crime Conference Proceedings*. Wiesbaden, West Germany: Bundeskriminalamt, 1974.

1371. Schroeder, F.C. "New Empirical Research on Pandering." (German) *Monatsschrift fur Kriminologie und Strafrechtsreform* 61(1) (January 1978):62-67.

1372. Schuster, J.F. "Not So Seamless Web: Some Thoughts on 'Victimless Crime'." *Journal of Contemporary Criminal Justice* 3(1) (February 1987):27-37.

Presents arguments for and against decriminalizing victimless crimes such as prostitution. States that arguments for decriminalization should focus on specific crimes rather than the broad category of victimless crimes.

1373. Schwartz, L.B., and S.R. Goldstein. "Vice and Organized Crime." *Police Guidance Manuals*. Edited by L.B. Schwartz and S.R. Goldstein. Pennsylvania State University, 1968.

Guidelines and advice designed to familiarize members of the Philadelphia police department with the laws, directives, policies, and investigative techniques used against such offenses as gambling, drugs, and prostitution.

1374. Schweber, C., and C. Feinman, eds. *Criminal Justice, Politics, and Women: The Aftermath of Legally Mandated Change*. New York: Haworth, 1985.

Covers areas of corrections, domestic violence, sexual assault, and prostitution.

1375. Scibelli, P. "Empowering Prostitutes: A Proposal for International Legal Reform." *Harvard Women's Law Journal* 10 (Spring 1987):117-157.

Examines legalization and deregulation of prostitution in light of present legal approaches in the U.S., Thailand, and France. Contends that criminalization or regulation of prostitution leaves prostitutes vulnerable to police harassment and abuse by pimps and clients.

1376. Shaver, F.M. "Prostitution: A Critical Analysis of Three Policy Approaches." *Canadian Public Policy* 11(3) (1985):493-503.

Compares three different legal approaches to the problem of prostitution in Canada: criminalization, decriminalization, and legalization. Uses arguments and evidence from both Canadian and international sources.

1377. Shekar, S. "The Legal Processing of the Prostitute: A Self-Defeating Exercise." *Indian Journal of Social Work* 47(3) (October 1986): 335-340.

Discusses the implementation of some provisions for the arrest and processing of prostitutes by law enforcement agencies in India and examines some of the assumptions behind these provisions. Suggests realistic and limited goals within the framework of the present socio-economic situation and legal framework.

1378. Sheley, J.F., ed. *Exploring Crime: Readings in Criminology and Criminal Justice*. Florence, KY: Wadsworth, 1987.

Intended as a text for courses in introductory and advanced criminology and criminal justice. Includes readings on prostitution.

1379. Sion, A.S. *Prostitution and the Law*. London: Faber and Faber, 1977.

Surveys female prostitution in England, including the laws controlling it and the difficulties of enforcement. Discusses various systems for regulating prostitution. Includes extensive footnotes and a table of judicial cases.

1380. Skolnick, J.H. *Justice Without Trial: Law Enforcement in Democratic Society*. 2nd ed. New York: John Wiley, 1975.

Examines patterns of police behavior in various areas of law enforcement, including traffic violations, prostitution, and narcotics. Concludes that tension between the operational goals of order, efficiency, and initiative versus the legal rights of individual citizens constitutes the principal problem.

1381. Skolnick, J.H., and J. Dombrink. "The Legalization of Deviance." *Criminology: An Interdisciplinary Journal* 16(2) (August 1978):193-208.

Compares the use of criminal law versus government regulation to control vice. Suggests that the concept of victimless crimes must be more clearly defined in order to determine the most appropriate regulation model.

1382. Skousen, W.C. "Perennial Problem of Prostitution: How to Beat the Call Girl Racket." *Law and Order* 22(5) (May 1974):8-15.

Outlines the efforts of a newly appointed police chief to end prostitution in his city of 200,000 by utilizing community involvement and the cooperation of motel owners, cabdrivers, and bartenders.

1383. Smith, A.B., and H. Pollack. "Crimes Without Victims." *Case and Comment* 77(4) (July/August 1972):9-15.

Calls for repeal of the current victimless crime laws since many behaviors once considered unacceptable are now considered normal by large segments of society. States that laws against prostitution, gambling, and drug use are difficult to enforce, consume enormous police resources, and are a major cause of crime in themselves.

1384. Smith, R.W. "Legalized Recreation As Deviance." *Quarterly Journal of Ideology* (10)1 (January 1986):37-42.

Describes Nevada's economy which is supported by gambling and prostitution. Argues that awareness of economic costs and benefits of these activities has formed the basis of most decisions on legal policy in the state and that these decisions are supported by the majority of the residents.

1385. Stoddard, E.R., ed. *Prostitution and Illicit Drug Traffic on the U.S.-Mexico Border.* El Paso, TX: State University Consortium for Latin America, 1971. Microfiche.

1386. Strom, F.A. *Zoning Control of Sex Business: The Zoning Approach to Controlling Adult Entertainment.* New York: Clark Boardman, 1977.

Compares zoning to more traditional methods of controlling the growth of pornography and commercial sex establishments. Reviews various legal and practical drawbacks to traditional approaches and attempts to convey useful information to both proponents and opponents of adult zoning legislation.

1387. Sumner, M. "Prostitution and the Position of Women: A Case for Decriminalisation." *Women and Crime*. Edited by A. Morris and L. Gelsthorpe. Cambridge: University of Cambridge, Institute of Criminology, 1981.

Concludes that British law regarding prostitution discriminates against women. The legal repression of prostitution is specifically directed against working-class women as shown by an analysis of prostitution laws in both the nineteenth and twentieth centuries.

1388. Swigert, V.L. "Public Order Crime." *Major Forms of Crime*. Edited by R.F. Meier. Newbury Park, CA: Sage, 1984.

Discusses the nature of "mala prohibita offenses" which include a wide range of behaviors known as crimes against the public or moral order. Raises questions about the nature of law in society and about society's reaction to those who violate the laws. Notes that the extent and nature of deviant behavior suggest that the focus should shift to the laws that proscribe these activities.

1389. Taschner, J., and A.R. Eberhart. "Criminal Codes and Ciphers: What Do They Mean?" *FBI Law Enforcement Bulletin* 54(1) (January 1985):18-22.

Explains how cryptanalysts in the FBI laboratory can decode clandestine suspected criminal documents relating to gambling, drug, and prostitution cases. Examples of criminal codes and ciphers accompany the text.

1390. Tegel, H. "Prostitution, Match-making, Pimps." (German) *Kriminalistik* 26 (September 1972):449-452.

1391. Teske, Jr., R.H.C., and N.L. Powell. *Texas Crime Poll--Spring 1978, Survey*. Huntsville, Texas: Sam Houston State University Criminal Justice Center, 1978.

Reports results of a survey of Texas residents dealing with fear of crime, punishment, and the operation of the criminal justice system. The data reveal a definite fear of crime and a strong punishment orientation toward the criminal. 44% of those surveyed wanted more severe laws for prostitution.

1392. Til, J.V. "Shortening the Long Arm of the Criminal Law: Toward a Strategy for Decriminalization." *Pennsylvania Association on Probation, Parole, and Correction Quarterly* 31(3) (Autumn 1974).

Reviews the case for the decriminalization of nine victimless crimes, including prostitution. Argues that all of the offenses examined should be decriminalized, and that most of them should be regulated and/or legalized as well.

1393. University of Queensland. *Two Faces of Deviance: Crimes of the Powerless and the Powerful.* St. Lucia, Queensland, Australia: University of Queensland Press, 1978.

Considers methods and mechanisms by which the powerful in society use their positions of privilege to engage in exploitive and illegal acts. Suggests that relatively minor forms of lawbreaking such as prostitution are differentially enforced against powerless people.

1394. Wade, D.E. "Prostitution and the Law: Emerging Attacks on the 'Women's Crime'". *UMKC Law Review* 43(3) (Spring 1975):413-428.

Reviews constitutional challenges to prostitution laws with specific attention paid to the Kansas City, MO, ordinance used to combat prostitution. Argues that enforcement of the Kansas City ordinance violates the equal protection clause of the fourteenth amendment as well as the guarantee of free speech and the right to privacy.

1395. Wandling, T.M. "Decriminalization of Prostitution: The Limits of the Criminal Law." *Oregon Law Review* 55(4) (1976):553-566.

Examines the Oregon prostitution laws and proposes that they be repealed. Suggests that enforcement of the laws is an inappropriate and inefficient use of government resources. Argues for legalization and/or decriminalization of prostitution.

1396. Weissman, J.C., and K.N. File. "Criminal Behavior Patterns of Female Addicts: A Comparison of Findings in Two Cities." *Drug Abuse: Modern Trends, Issues, and Perspectives*. Edited by Arnold Schecter, et al. New York: Marcel Dekker, 1975. (Also published in *International Journal of Addictions* 11(6) (1976):1063-77.)

Compares two studies which document the characteristics and criminal backgrounds of drug-addicted female arrestees in Philadelphia, PA, and Denver, CO. Data refute the common belief that most female addicts are prostitutes. Finds an association between race and the incidence of prostitution arrests in both cities.

1397. Welsh, T.E. "Organized Crime Committee." *Canadian Police Chief* 69(4) (October 1980):46-47.

Presents the 1979 report of Canada's Organized Crime Committee. Describes the involvement of various gangs in several aspects of organized crime, including prostitution, drugs, and gambling.

1398. Western Australia. Royal Commission into Matters Surrounding the Administration of the Law Relating to Prostitution. *Report*. Perth: Government of Western Australia, 1976.

1399. Williams, J.B. *Vice Control in California*. Encino, CA: Glencoe Publishing Co., 1972.

Describes practices of prostitutes, pimps, and homosexuals with suggested techniques for their detection and apprehension. Includes California laws, leading appellate cases, and state supreme court decisions.

1400. Wilson, G.P., et al. "State Intervention and Victimless Crimes: A Study of Police Attitudes." *Journal of Police Science and Administration* 13(1) (March 1985):22-29.

Examines police attitudes toward control of victimless crime from questionnaires completed by 88 police officers. Results indicate that most officers do not view vice as a serious problem but believe current surveillance procedures are adequate and that it is generally impossible to control victimless crimes.

1401. Wilson, R. "Corruption and Reform." *Police Magazine* 2(3) (May 1979):6-9.

Describes reform efforts initiated by new police chiefs in three cities as the result of local government corruption. Provides details of the situations in Stamford, CT, New Orleans, LA, and Charlestown County, SC.

1402. Winterton, M.J. "Collation of Crime Intelligence with Regard to Chinese Triads in Holland." *Police Journal* 54(1) (Jan.-Mar. 1981):34-57.

Examines the organization, history, and operations of the Chinese Triads in Amsterdam, Holland. These groups are characterized as criminal associations operating in the Chinese community, and they are active in various illegal activities, such as prostitution and narcotics.

1403. Woetzel, R.K. Organized Crime and Criminal Law Reform. *Criminal Justice Planning*. Edited by J.E. Scott and S. Dinitz. New York: Praeger, 1977.

Studies the relationship between law reform and the involvement of organized crime in the gambling, prostitution, and narcotics trade. Recommends amending penal laws to permit prostitution within certain bounds and without organizational ties. Suggests establishment of an organized crime law enforcement investigation section with offices in every police department.

1404. *Women and Law: Prostitution*. Berkeley, CA: Women's History Research Center, 1975. Microfilm, Reel no. 3.

Microfilm of a clipping archive produced by the Women's History Research Center. Contains clippings gathered from newspapers, newsletters, speeches, flyers, research papers, etc., documenting the women's rights movement during the 1970s.

1405. Women Endorsing Decriminalization. "Prostitution: Non-Victim Crime?" *Issues in Criminology* 8(2) (Fall 1973):137-162.

Considers three methods of dealing with prostitution: illegalization, which penalizes the prostitute but not the customer; legalization, which would legitimate the exploitation of women; and decriminalization, viewed as the most favorable short-term solution, since it would end exploitation and discrimination. Highlights existing California prostitution laws which are being challenged on constitutional grounds.

1406. Yondorf, B. "Prostitution as a Legal Activity: The West German Experience." *Policy Analysis* 5(4) (Fall 1979):417-433.

Discusses whether prostitution should be legalized in the U.S. by analyzing the impact of legalized prostitution in West Germany. Studies the effects of legalized prostitution on crime, the incidence of venereal disease, and the prevalence of the pimp. Concludes that prostitution should be legalized.

MALES AND PROSTITUTION

MALES: JOHNS, PIMPS, ET AL.

1407. Acosta Patiño, R. "Proxenetismo." (Doctoral Thesis no. 22/83) Madrid: Facultad de Derecho, Universidad Complutense de Madrid, 1983.

A study of Spanish pimps.

1408. Allaman, J.L. "The Crime, Trial, and Execution of William W. Lee of East Burlington, Illinois." *Western Illinois Regional Studies* 6(23) (1983):49-66.

Lee, who ran a house of prostitution, was hanged for murdering a prostitute, Jessie McCarty. Author argues the well publicized trial and execution in 1875-76 were an attempt to stem post-Civil War vice in western Illinois.

1409. Amelunxen, C. *Der Zuhälter: Wandlungen eines Tätertyps.* Hamburg: Kriminalistik Verlag, 1967.

A study of West German pimps.

1410. Angenent, H.L. "Characteristics of a Pimp." (Dutch) *Nederl. T. Psychol.* 24 (1969):207-26.

1411. Armstrong, E.G. "Pondering Pandering." *Deviant Behavior* 4(2) (January-March 1983):203-17.

Examination of pandering activities of pimps through interviews with 18 Port Authority police officers. Popular assumptions checked by having a female researcher set herself up for wandering pimps at Port Authority bus terminal. Question of whether prostitutes are victims or volunteers discussed and perspectives on social construction of pandering summarized. The results challenge the popular press conception of pimps as panderers leading others into prostitution. Earlier version presented at

1980 meeting of Society for the Study of Social Problems.

1412. Bargon, M.   *Prostitution und Zuhälterei: Zur kriminologischen und strafrechtlichen Problematik mit einem geschichtlichen und rechtsvergleichenden Überblick.* Lübeck: Schmit-Romhild, 1982.

Pimps and prostitutes in West Germany.

1413. Barry, K.   "The Underground Economic System of Pimping." *Journal of International Affairs* 35(1) (1981):117-27.

Argues that the highly profitable and widespread financial network based on buying, selling, and brutal use of women's bodies is a result of a lack of enforcement of laws against rape, murder, pimping, and involuntary servitude.

1414. Beatty, Jr., R.   "Netting Mackerel: The Pimp Detail." *The Police Journal* 53(3) (July 9, 1980):257-65. Illustrated.

1415. Beck, R.   *The Naked Soul of Iceberg Slim.* Los Angeles: Holloway House, 1971.

Several autobiographies and biographies of Iceberg Slim, some under a pseudonym. This is an autobiographical account.

1416. Beck, R.   *Trick Baby: The Biography of a Con Man [by Iceberg Slim].* Los Angeles: Holloway House, 1967.

1417. Boggs, V.W.   "A Swedish Dilemma: Scandinavian Prostitutes and Black Pimps." (Ph.D. Thesis) City University of New York, 1979. (Microfiche: Ann Arbor, MI: University Microfilms, 1979.)

1418. "Canada: Naming Hookers' 'Johns'." *Law and Order* 36(12) (December 1980):7.

Practice of publishing names of clients in newspapers.

1419. Chapman, B., and J.T. Landa. "Prude, Prostitute, Pimp." *Philosophy* 60 (1985):525-531.

1420. Donaldson, W. *Don't Call Me Madam: The Life and Hard Times of a Gentleman Pimp.* New York: Mason/Charter, 1975.

The life of a London pimp.

1421. Geis, G. "Why Prostitutes Support Pimps?" *Medical Aspects of Human Sexuality* 8(10) (October 1974):98, 103.

Argues that the pimp does the woman a great favor by allowing her sexual access to him and giving other rewards as well as providing protection.

1422. Gokhale, B.B., R.S. Master, and S.C.S. Master. "The Visiting Client (A Pilot Study on the Client of the Prostitute)." *Indian Journal of Psychiatry* 4(1) (January 1962):39-45.

1423. Hall, P., and D.J. Birch. "Case and Comment: Prostitution." *Criminal Law Review* 6 (1983):401-402.

Refers to pimps.

1424. Hall, S. *Gentlemen of Leisure: A Year in the Life of a Pimp.* New York: New American Library, 1972.

Now regarded as a classical study.

1425. Hardy, A. *The Autobiography of a Pimp.* [S.l.: s.n., 194-?].

1426. Heusinger, R. "Der Tätertyp des Zuhälters in seiner kriminologischen und dogmatischen Bedeutung." (Thesis) Erlangen-Nürnberg University, 1976.

Pimps in West Germany.

1427. Holzman, H.R., and S. Pines. "Buying Sex: The Phenomenology of Being a John." *Deviant Behavior* 4(1) (October-December 1982):29-116.

Thirty customers of prostitutes were interviewed to determine the feeling and perceptions involved in being a "John." Argues for four phases of involvement: conception of intent, pursuit of the encounter, the encounter, and aftermath. Holds that image of the John differed from that typically found in literature of prostitituion.

1428. Iceberg Slim. *Pimp: The Story of My Life*. Los Angeles: Holloway House, 1967.

Claims to be the autobiography of a black pimp who felt he had only two ways of surviving in a white society, crime or pimping. He chose pimping as the lesser of two evils. After some twenty years, he gave up that occupation to become a respectable family man.

1429. James, J. "Prostitute-Pimp Relationships." *Medical Aspects of Human Sexuality* 7(11) (November 1973):140-63.

Argues that pimps do not force women to work, seduce young girls, or turn women into dope addicts. Pimps cannot prevent a woman from leaving since pimps and prostitutes are not married. There are comments on this article by C. Winick, J.K. Schimel, and H. Greenwald to which the author responds.

1430. Kennedy, L.H.C. *The Trial of Stephen Ward*. London: V. Gollancz, 1964.

Ward, 1912-1963, was accused of using his escort service to gain classified information for the Russians. It was a major political scandal which threatened the then-conservative government.

1431. Leonard, T.L., M. Freund, and J.J. Platt. "Behavior of Clients of Prostitutes." *American Journal of Public Health* 79(9) (1989):1309-10.

Based on participant observation study in Camden, NJ.

1432. Lewis, D. *The Prostitute and Her Clients: Your Pleasure Is Her*

Business. Springfield, IL: Charles C. Thomas, 1985.

1433. Mancini, J.G. *Prostituées et proxénètisme*. Paris: Universitaires de France, 1962. *Prostitutes and Their Parasites*. Translated in English by D.G. Thomas from the French. London: Elek Books, 1963.

1434. Milner, C. *Black Players: The Secret World of Black Pimps*. (Ph.D. Dissertation) Boston: Little, Brown, 1973.

Classical study of the black pimp based upon the author's 1971 Ph.D. dissertation at the University of California. Examines the organization and value system of a ghetto occupational subculture.

1435. Reitman, B.L. *The Second Oldest Profession: A Study of the Prostitute's Business Manager*. New York: Vanguard, 1931.

A pioneering study listed here because it is apparently the first such study.

1436. Scarlet, I. *The Professionals: Prostitutes and Their Clients*. London: Sidgwick and Jackson, 1972.

A British sociological study which includes discussion of clients.

1437. Stein, M.L. *Lovers, Friends, Slaves: Nine Male Sexual Types: Their Psycho-Sexual Transactions with Call Girls*. New York: G.P. Putnam's Sons, 1974.

An outstanding study. Stein observed the encounters of 1,230 men with call girls. Categorized nine types of clients: opportunists, fraternizers, promoters, adventurers, lovers, friends, slaves, guardians, and juveniles. Regardless of type, all wanted sex needs met conveniently and professionally without obligations other than monetary payment.

1438. Stewart, G.I. "On First Being a John." *Urban Life Culture* 1 (October 1972):255-74.

1439. Suárez Danero, E.M. *El cafishio*. Buenos Aires: Fontefrida Editora,

1971.

Argentine pimps and their prostitutes.

1440. Watts, M.H. *The Men in My Life*. New York: L. Stuart, 1960.

A biography of a London prostitute focusing on her clients.

1441. Wepman, D., R.B. Newman, and M.B. Binderman. *The Life: The Lore and Folk Poetry of the Black Hustler*. Philadelphia: University of Pennsylvania Press, 1976.

1442. Winick, C. "Prostitutes' Clients' Perception of the Prostitutes and Themselves." *International Journal of Social Psychiatry* 8(4) (Autumn 1962):289-97.

MALE PROSTITUTES

1443. Adam, C. "A Special House in Hamburg." *New Statesman* 85 (April 13, 1973):521-22.

Describes a male brothel in West Germany where they were legally permitted.

1444. Allen, D.M. "Young Male Prostitutes: A Psychosocial Study." *Archives of Sexual Behavior* 9(5) (October 1980):399-426.

Makes a typological classification into four distinct categories of 98 male prostitutes in the Boston area: full time street walkers and bar hustlers, "call boys" and "kept boys," part-time prostitutes seeking extra money, and delinquents who exploit through threats and assaults. Semi-structured interviews reveal similarities and differences between groups and concludes that there is no one "typical" profile of the male prostitute.

1445. Augras, M. "Poder do desejo, ou desejo de poder?" (The power of desire, or the desire for power?). *Arquivos Brasileiros de Psicologia* 37(2) (April-June 1985):106-109.

Discusses an article on male prostitution by Perlongher (see below) and compares it with research on female prostitution. Holds that the same mechanisms of alienation and depersonalization appear in both situations.

1446. Boyer, D. "Male Prostitution: A Cultural Expression of Male Homosexuality." (Ph.D. Dissertation) Seattle, WA, University of Washington, 1986.

1447. Boyer, D. "Male Prostitution and Homosexual Identity." *Journal of Homosexuality* 17(1-2) (1989):151-84.

Examines 47 male adolescent prostitutes and compares with 50 controls (male adolescent delinquents) and holds that gay male adolescents who are exposed to public forms of homosexuality may develop a self-understanding linking their homosexual identity with prostitution.

1448. Bray, Jr., H.F. "Comparison of Male and Female Prostitution on Levels of Hostility." (Ph.D. Dissertation) United States International University, 1981.

1449. Brule, C. *Nom: toxicomane; sexe: masculin; profession: prostitué; specialité: hommes.* Versailles: Association d'aide aux jeunes en difficulté, 1984.

Discusses drug problems among French hustlers.

1450. Bullinga, M., et al. *Van de liefde kun je niet leven: Interviewsmet hoeren en hoerenjongens.* Nijmegen: SOF, 1982.

Interviews with Dutch male and female prostitutes and an analysis of the social world of homosexual prostitution.

1451. Calhoun, R., and V. Pickerill. "Young Male Prostitutes: Their Knowledge of Selected Sexually Transmitted Diseases." *Psychology: A Journal of Human Behavior* 25(3-4) (1988):1-8.

Interviewed 18 male street prostitutes and found they knew more about symptoms of gonorrhea and syphilis than of herpes and AIDS, but at best knowledge was limited and fragmentary.

1452. Caplan, G.M. "Policing Boy Prostitution." *Crime Control Digest* 15(8) (September 21, 1981):3-5.

1453. Carney, R.J. "The Other Prostitutes: A Review of the Literature on Male Prostitution." (M.A. Thesis) Rutgers University, 1978.

1454. Cates, J.A. "Adolescent Male Prostitution by Choice." *Child and Adolescent Social Work Journal* 6(2) (Summer 1989):151-56.

Presents case study of two male adolescents who are active as male prostitutes. Examines male prostitutes in a middle-sized Midwestern city, and claims that hierarchy, typology, and social network of hustlers found in larger cities were lacking. Suggests possible interventions.

1455. Caukins, S.E., and N.R. Coombs. "The Psychodynamics of Male Prostitution." *American Journal of Psychotherapy* 30(3) (July, 1976):441-51.

Interviewed 33 Los Angeles male prostitutes and 22 male customers. Found there is a hierarchy of occupational levels: street hustler, bar hustler, call boy, and kept boy. Each type is illustrated with case histories. Most hustlers do not regard themselves as homosexuals and relationships with customers involve considerable mutual hostility. Money exchange reduces guilt and limits the terms of the association.

1456. Chappel, H. "The Rent a Boy Scene." *New Society* 78(1244) (October 31, 1986):8-9.

Case study of an eighteen-year-old is presented to illustrate growing problems of "rent a boy" teenage male prostitution in the Piccadilly area of London.

1457. Cohen, M.I. "Soliciting by Men." *Criminal Law Review* 6 (1982):349-62.

Examines homosexual prostitution in terms of laws, legal status, and attitudes of judges.

1458. Coleman, E. "The Development of Male Prostitution Activity Among Gay and Bisexual Adolescents." *Journal of Homosexuality* 17(1-2) (1989):131-49.

Attempts to develop a theoretical understanding based on reviews of current research literature. Gives a clinical case study of a twenty-one-year-old undergoing treatment to illustrate development of activity.

1459. Coombs, N.R. "Male Prostitution: Psychosocial View of Behavior." *American Journal of Orthopsychiatry* 44(5) (1974):782-89.

Based on study of 41 hustlers in Los Angeles, age twelve to twenty-eight, shows that a majority exhibited a constellation of negative traits. Concluded that the group contained men for whom the competition for economic survival had proven overwhelming.

1460. Craft, M. "Boy Prostitutes and Their Fate." *British Journal of Psychiatry* 112(492) (November 1966):111-14.

Study based on life histories of 33 apprehended and treated British hustlers, many of whom transacted business in movie houses.

1461. Davies, P.M., and P.J. Simpson. *On the Contemporary Forms of Male Homosexual Prostitution in London.* Cardiff: University College, 1987.

Includes a discussion of AIDS.

1462. "Defense Counsel Successfully Argues Men Were Not Arrested for Wearing Women's Clothing, but for Illicit Behavior." *AELE Liability Reporter* 152 (August 1985):6-71.

Transsexuals and prostitution.

1463. Deisher, R.W. "The Young Male Prostitute." *Pediatrics* 45(1) (January 1970):153-54.

This article is a rebuttal to criticism of the paper listed below. Critics complained about the failure of the paper to elaborate a psychopathology of the study sample. Deisher argues that speculation about the psychopathological aspects without understanding the psychiatry would be misleading.

1464. Deisher, R.W., V. Eisner, and S.I. Sulzbacher. "The Young Male Prostitute." *Pediatrics* 43 (1969):936-41.

A report on the findings of interviews with 63 males prostitutes from San Francisco. Report emphasizes the limited education, high mobility, unstable home environment, and lack of social and vocational skills. At time of interview most were unemployed.

1465. Dietz, P.E. "Medical Criminology Notes No. 5: Male Homosexual Prostitution." *Bulletin of the American Academy of Psychiatric Law* 6(4) (1978):468-71.

Brief overview of existing literature.

1466. Drew, D., and J. Drake. *Boys for Sale: A Sociological Study of Boy Prostitution.* New York: Brown Book, 1969.

1467. Duarte, A., and H. Clemente. *Prostituição masculina em Lisboa.* Lisboa: Contra-Regra, 1982.

Journalistic view of the life of hustlers in Lisbon. Interviews and photographs.

1468. Dunne, G. "The Male Street-Walker: A Sydney Report." *Forum: The Australian Journal of Interpersonal Relations* 7 (1979):7-12.

Reports Australian pattern similar to European.

1469. Dynes, W.R. *Homosexuality: A Research Guide.* New York: Garland, 1987.

The best overall bibliographical guide to homosexuality. Includes a section on male prostitution, pp. 479-87.

1470. Earls, C.M., and H. David. "A Psychosocial Study of Male Prostitution." *Archives of Sexual Behavior* 18(5) (October 1989): 401-19.

Administered a semistructured questionnaire to 50 male prostitutes and 50 nonprostitutes matched for age, sex, and socio-economic status. 35 subjects from each group also given Beck Depression Inventory and Tennessee Self-Concept Scale. Findings suggest that factors related to family background may be less important as potential determinants than influences related to financial gain, sexual orientation, and early sexual experiences.

1471. Erickson, R.A. "Entrepreneurs of the Night: A Psychosocial Study of the Adolescent Male Prostitute." (Ph.D. Dissertation) Union of Experimenting Colleges and Universities, 1986.

1472. Estep, R.E., and D. Waldorf. *Safe Sex Among Male Street Hustlers and Call Men.* (Unpublished paper) American Sociological Association, 1989.

Two samples, each including 189 male prostitutes, obtained by chain referral method. Street hustlers engaged in more unsafe sex acts than call men. Significant variables included general knowledge about AIDS, number of customers serviced, and social class of prostitute.

1473. Feschet, J., J. Brouchon, and M. Bluteau. *Garçon pour trottoir.* Paris: Éditions la Découverte, 1986.

1474. Fisher, B., D. K. Weisberg, and T. Marotta. *Report on Adolescent Male Prostitution.* San Francisco: Urban and Rural Systems Associate, 1982.

A report prepared under contract for HEW. Original in Rutgers University Library; microfiche in University Microfilms International.

1475. *Flame: A Life on the Game.* London: Gay Men's Press, 1984.

Working-class Liverpool youth who became a hustler in London reminiscences about his experience.

1476. Gandy, P., and R.W. Deisher. "Young Male Prostitutes: The Physician's

Role in Social Rehabiliation." *JAMA* 212(10) (June 8, 1970):1661-66.

Reports on an experimental fifteen-month intervention program for vocational retraining. Concludes prospects of success are poor given the number of psychopathic personalities and very successful hustlers.

1477. Gauthier-Hamon, C., and R. Teboul. *Entre père et fils: la prostitution homosexuelle des garçons*. Paris: Presses Universitaires de France, 1988.

Includes a section devoted to psychoanalytic analysis and a section devoted to history.

1478. Ginsburg, K.N. "The 'Meat-Rack': A Study of the Male Homosexual Prostitute." *American Journal of Psychotherapy* 21(2) (April 1967):170-85.

Theorizes that hustler's family constellation engenders a pathological state characterized by an unstable self-identity, an inadequate evaluation of self, and little learned interaction potential or alternatives for action.

1479. Handzel, Z.T., R. Burstein, J. Cohen, et al. "Absence of T Cell Impairments in a Unique Group of Anal-Receptive Transvestite and Male Prostitutes in Israel." *Israel Journal of Medical Sciences* 26(1) (1990):26-31.

1480. Harlan, S., et al. *Male and Female Adolescent Prostitution: Huckleberry House Sexual Minority Youth Services Project*. Washington, DC: Youth Development Bureau, U.S. Department of Health and Human Services, 1981.

Study essentially based on runaways. Also see J. James.

1481. Harris, M. *The Dillyboys: The Game of Male Prostitution in Piccadilly*. Rockville, MD: New Perspectives, 1973.

Ethnographic account of teenage male prostitution.

1482. Hennig, J-L. *Les garçons de passe: enquête sur la prostitution masculine*.

Paris: Hallier, 1978.

Interviews by a French journalist with Paris hustlers. Often insightful.

1483. Hoffman, M. "The Male Prostitute." *Sexual Behavior* 2 (1972):16-21.

Compares two groups of hustlers. One group was composed of teenagers who though they sold their bodies did not regard themselves as hustlers while the second group consisted of an older group who regarded themselves as hustlers but not as homosexuals. Concludes that there are some hustlers who are homosexuals and some who are not.

1484. James, J. "Entrance into Juvenile Male Prostitution." *NIMH* Rockville, MD NIMH-83-216 (November 1982).

Comparative study of 46 juvenile male prostitutes and 50 juvenile male non-prostitute delinquents to examine the process of entrance into prostitution. Dependency status increased the possibility of entrance into prostitution as did negative early sexual experience and exposure to prostitution. Relationship between drug abuse and associated criminal behavior was inconclusive.

1485. James, J. "Male Prostitutes for Women." *Medical Aspects of Human Sexuality* 8(2) (February 1974):163.

A non-scholarly summary of the types of prostitution available for women: gigolo, professional companions or escorts, masseurs, and male prostitutes.

1486. Janus, M.D. "On Early Sexual Victimization and Adolescent Male Prostitution." *SIECUS Report* 13 (1983):1, 8-9.

1487. Kamel, G.W.L. *A Phenomenological Study in Retrospect: The Methodological and Ethical Aspects of Field Research with Male Street Prostitutes.* (Unpublished paper) Society for the Study of Social Problems, 1983.

After observing environment and activities of male prostitutes (hustlers) for several months a phenomenological research design was developed that included residing in the setting and implementing participant-observation procedures including a conversational interview which conformed to the guidelines of the Committee on Investigations Involving Human Subjects. Interviews were taped when permission was granted and data analysis procedures engineered to assure the anonymity of research participants. Study available from Thomas Weinberg, SUNY College at Buffalo, Buffalo, NY. 14214.

1488. Kearns, M. *The Happy Hustler: My Own Story.* By Grant Tracy Saxon [pseudonym]. New York: Warner, 1975.

An "autobiography" of a successful male prostitute; it is a takeoff of Xaviera Hollander's *The Happy Hooker.* How much is fiction and how much reality is unclear. Has some insightful passages.

1489. Klein, A.M. "Managing Deviance: Hustling, Homophobia, and the Bodybuilding Subculture." *Deviant Behavior* 10(1) (1989):11-27.

Subculture of southern California bodybuilding examined through 55 formal and 120 informal interviews. Special attention paid to hustling as an economic and psychological strategy. Sees a crisis of hustling in which homosexual behavior is juxtaposed to homophobic behavior viewed as a necessity in order to maintain an alleged heterosexual identity.

1490. Levine, E.J., D. Gruenewald, and C.H. Shaiova. "Behavioral Differences and Emotional Conflict among Male-to-Female Transsexuals." *Archives of Sexual Behavior* 5(1) (1976):81-86.

Interview data used to study aspects of transsexualism and homosexuality, prostitution and employment, and other factors in eighteen male transsexuals. Those transsexuals who worked in gainful employment and led more stable lives developed a stronger self-system enabling them to more effectively deal with emotional conflicts than those engaged in prostitution.

1491. Luckenbill, D.F. "Deviant Career Mobility: The Case of Male Prostitutes." *Social Problems* 33(4) (April 1986):283-96.

Interviewed 28 male prostitutes and identified three modes of operation: street hustling, bar hustling, and escort prostitution. These were ranked according to income levels and safety from arrests. Most respondents moved from street hustling to bar hustling and a few moved up to escort prostitution. Changes affecting this mobility were analyzed.

1492. Luckenbill, D.F. "Dynamics of the Deviant Sale." *Deviant Behavior* 5(1-4) (1984):337-53.

Examined dynamics of male prostitution through interviews of 25 male prostitutes in Chicago to identify principal characteristics of deviant sale. Identified seven stages of sale and compared this with an ideal-typical model of respectable sale. Deviant sale more tenuous and dangerous.

1493. Luckenbill, D.F. "Entering Male Prostitution." *Urban Life* 14(2) (July 1985):131-53.

Found through open-ended interviews of 26 male prostitutes that entry into male prostitution proceeded through two stages: (1) initial and (2) regular involvement. Initial involvement can be a defensive act in which boys turn to prostitution as a solution to desperate living and financial problems or an adventurous act to earn extra money and sometimes obtain sexual satisfaction. First group moves to regular involvement shortly after first sale; second group takes longer to become regulars depending on life situation contingencies.

1494. MacKay, J.H. *The Hustler.* Translated by H. Kennedy. Boston: Alyson, 1985.

A German novel published under the title *Der Puppenjunge* in 1926 that documents, although in fictional terms, the milieu of the teenage hustlers in Berlin of the Weimar era.

1495. "Male Prostitution Seen Partly as Just Becoming More Visible." *Crime Control Digest* 10(32) (August 9, 1976):81.

1496. Markham, F. "Fred's Piece." *Fag Rag* 30 (1982):4-8.

A 1950s hustler from Seattle recalls his youth.

1497. Marlowe, K. *Mr. Madam: Confessions of a Male Madam*. Los Angeles: Sherbourne, 1964.

A Hollywood transvestite describes his career as the operator of a call boy service in Los Angeles. Reader should probably be skeptical of some details.

1498. Mathews, P.W. "On 'Being a Prostitute.'" *Journal of Homosexuality* 15(3-4) (1988):119-35.

Review essay of R. Perkins and G. Bennett, *Being a Prostitute: Prostitute Women and Prostitute Men* (Sydney: Allen and Unwin, 1985), argues that certain categories of male prostitutes have been excluded.

1499. Mathews, P.W. *Male Prostitution: Two Monographs*. Sydney: Australian Book, 1987.

Includes the article cited above as well as "Some Preliminary Observations of Male Prostitution in Manila."

1500. McMullen, R.J. *Enchanted Boy*. London: Gay Men's Press, 1989.

Male homosexuality in England.

1501. Nery, L.C. "The Covert Subculture of Male Homosexual Prostitutes in Metro-Manila." *Philippine Journal of Psychology* 12(1) (January-June, 1979):27-32.

Interviewed six call boys at a brothel/gay bar and found they came from poor homes in which parents were separated or father deceased. All had homosexual experiences before they were out of school. Found that male homosexual prostitute subculture functioned through informal and simple mutual cooperation.

1502. Nicosia, G., and R. Roffe. *Bughouse Blues: An Intimate Report of Gay Hustling*. New York: Vantage, 1977.

A composite portrait derived from interviews of Chicago male prostitutes operating in Washington Square (Bughouse Square).

1503. Panajian, A.Y. "Psychological Study of Male Prostitutes." (Ph.D. Dissertation) United States International University, 1983.

1504. Paperny, D.M., and R.W. Deisher. "Maltreatment of Adolescents: The Relationship to a Predisposition Toward Violent Behavior and Delinquency." *Adolescence* 18(71) (Fall 1983):499-506.

A study conducted on 21 adolescent male prostitutes found a history of physical abuse by parents or authors. Found two types of prostitutes, those who prostitution activities and criminal offenses tended to be situational, and those who were professionals with histories of victimizing their clients.

1505. Perlongher, N.O. "O contrato da prostituição viril." (On the 'virile prostitution' contract). *Arquivos Brasileiros de Psicologia* 37(2) (April-June 1985):94-105.

Empirical observations and interviews of varying depth with 20 male prostitutes, clients, and gay men about the special type of contract governing services given by young and hypermasculine prostitutes to homosexual clients (virile prostitution). Implies that violence is implicit in the nature of the transaction and is inherent in the sale of masculinity.

1506. Pieper, R. "Identity Management in Adolescent Male Prostitution in West Germany." *International Review of Modern Sociology* 9(2) (July-December 1979):239-59.

Scattered reports from five western European countries along with results of research in Hamburg are drawn together for a description of the adolescent male prostitute. Argues for four types and gives model of the process of development and stabilization of deviant identities.

1507. Pitman, D.J. "The Male House of Prostitution." *Trans-Action* 8(5-6) (March-April, 1971):21-27.

Describes a male house of prostitution catering to male homosexuals, managed by a male homosexual, and located in a residential area of single-family dwellings, duplexes, and apartment houses. There is a core group of 15 full time models and a fringe group of 20 models who supplement their income by doing modeling. Recruitment of models, socialization of models, types of sexual activities, and models' disenchantment are described.

1508. Price, V.A., B. Scanlon, and M.D. Janus. "Social Characteristics of Adolescent Male Prostitution." *Victimology* 9(2) (1984):211-21.

Based on interviews of 28 adolescent male prostitutes, holds that prostitution is not the principal issue in therapy. Instead the fundamental issues are of arrested development.

1509. Rechy, J. *City of Night*. New York: Grove, 1963.

A fictional but realistic account of a hustler's life in New York City, California, and New Orleans. In the 1985 edition of the book, Rechy describes how he came to write it and how much it corresponds to real life.

1510. Rechy, J. *The Sexual Outlaw: A Documentary*. New York: Grove, 1985.

1511. Reim, R. *Una questione diversa*. Cosenza: Lerici, 1978.

A series of interviews with Italian hustlers is included.

1512. Reiss, A.J. "The Social Integration of Queers and Peers." *Social Problems* 9(2) (1961):102-20.

A classic study demonstrating the dissonance between sexual identity and behavior in lower-class boys in Nashville, Tennessee, and how potential image problems are regulated in transactions with clients.

1513. Russell, D.H. "On the Psychopathology of Boy Prostitutes." *International Journal of Offender Therapy* 15 (1971):49-52.

Holds that early maternal deprivation is the root cause of much of boy prostitution.

1514. Salamon, E. "The Homosexual Escort Agency: Deviance Disavowal." *British Jounal of Sociology* 40(1) (March 1989):1-21.

Explores, by interviewing owner of London escort agency and 28 male escorts, how stigmatizing sexual liaisons are routinely managed. Focus is on management of deviance disavowal and neutralization of moral disapproval.

1515. Salvaresi, E.T. *Travelo*. Paris: Les Presses de la Renaissance, 1982.

A study of French cross dressing prostitutes with personal biographies.

1516. Schickedanz, H-J. *Homosexuelle Prostitution: Eine empirische Untersuchung der sozial-des-kriminiertes Verhalten bei Strichjungen und Callboys*. Frankfurt am Main: Campus Verlag, 1979.

Empirical study of street hustlers and call boys.

1517. Schmidt-Relenberg, N., et al. *Strichjungen Gespradche: Zur Soziologie jugendlicher homosexuellen Prostitution*. Darmstadt: Luchterhand, 1975.

Interviews and quotations with young German hustlers set into a sociological analysis.

1518. Stone, C.B. "Psychiatric Screening for Transsexual Surgery." *Psychosomatics* 18(1) (1977):25-57.

After screening 60 candidates for surgery between twenty-three and thirty-two years of age, 13 were selected. Most of candidates had many arrests and convictions for prostitution.

1519. Traverso, G.D. "Criminological Relevance of Two Cases of Male Homosexual Prostitution Associated with Drug Use." *Rassegna di Criminologia* 6(1-2) (1975):235-45.

Holds that prostitution is the the final link in a cause and effect chain which begins in childhood and early adolescence. Argues that homosexual prostitution, drug addiction, and crime linkage have to be viewed in a larger socio-economic context if problems are to be addressed.

1520. Truong, T.D. *Sex, Money and Morality in South-east Asia*. London: Zed,

1990.

1521. Tsoi, W.F., L.P. Kok, and F.Y. Long. "Male Transsexualism in Singapore: A Description of 56 Cases." *British Journal of Psychiatry* 131(10) (October 1977):405-09.

Claims that 82% of 56 cases had been prostitutes. Most felt by age of five they were females and most began taking female hormones early. Only 32 underwent sex reassignment.

1522. *Urban and Rural Systems Associates (URSA): An Annotated Bibliography on Adolescent Male and Female Prostitution and Related Topics.* Washington, DC: Youth Develolpment Bureau, U.S. Department of Health and Human Services, 1981.

One of a number of official government publications indicating concern with juvenile prostitution by both sexes.

1523. Vignoli, G. *Contributo ad una indagine sulla prostituzione maschile.* Savona: 1973.

A pamphlet on theoretical and practical considerations of male prostitution.

1524. Visano, L.A. "Staging a Deviant Career: The Social Organization of Male Prostitution." (Ph.D. dissertation) University of Toronto.

Published as *This Idle Trade: The Occupational Patterns of Male Prostitution.* Concord, ON, Canada: Vita Sana, 1987.

1525. Waldorf, D., S. Murphy, D. Lauderback, et al. "Needle Sharing Among Male Prostitutes: Preliminary Findings of the Prospero Project." *Journal of Drug Issues* 10(2) (1990):309-34.

A study of 178 San Francisco male prostitutes which showed a high incidence of intravenous drug use among them. Needle sharing was part of socializing but also important was convenience.

1526. Weeks, J. "Inverts, Perverts, and Mary-Annes: Male Prostitution and the Regulation of Homosexuality in England in the Nineteenth and Early Twentieth Centuries." *Journal of Homosexuality* 6(1-2) (1980-81):113-14.

Looks at changing patterns of legal and ideological control in England and how the social and legal context dictated the close relationship between the homosexual subcultures and prostitution. Differences between female and male prostitution are also discussed.

1527. Weiss, J. *Arraché au trottoir: le drame de la prostitution masculine.* Paris: Garancière, 1985.

An account of one male prostitute whom the author helped to leave his profession.

1528. Wilson, D.C. "Night Acts: An Analysis of the Street Working Male Prostitutes of Denver, CO." (M.A. Thesis) University of New Mexico, 1983. Microfiche, University Microfilms International, 1985.

1529. Wiltfang, G.L. "New Faces in the World's 'Oldest Profession': The Emergence of Male Heterosexual Prostitution." (Ph.D. Dissertation) University of Arizona, Tucson, AR, 21985.

Examines male heterosexual prostitution where women pay men for sexual services. Argues there has been an increase in this form of prostitution as the number of women entering the work force has increased. Examines the typology of the prostitute roles based on type of payment and organizational affiliation.

MEDICINE

MEDICINE AND SEXUALLY TRANSMITTED DISEASES

1530. Adam, E., F.B. Hollinger, J.L. Melnick, et al. "Type B Hepatitis Antigen and Antibody Among Prostitutes and Nuns: A Study of Possible Venereal Transmission." *Journal of Infectious Diseases* 129(3) (March 1974):317-21.

Finds that in Cali, Colombia, venereal transmission is not a major mode of spread of type B hepatitis.

1531. Barton, S.E., D. Taylor-Robinson, and J.R. Harris. "Female Prostitutes and Sexually Transmitted Diseases." *British Journal of Hospital Medicine* 38(1) (July 1987):34, 36, 40.

Asserts that the epidemiology of HIV infection makes communication between the health care system and prostitutes a high priority in order to screen and prevent the spread of all STDs.

1532. Bchir, A., L. Jemni, M. Saadi, et al. "Markers of Sexually Transmitted Diseases in Prostitutes in Central Tunesia." (Letter) *Genitourinary Medicine* 64(6) (December 1988):396-7.

1533. Bell, T.A., J.A. Farrow, W.E. Stamm, et al. "Sexually Transmitted Diseases in a Juvenile Detention Center." *Sexually Transmitted Diseases* 12(3) (July-September, 1985):140-4.

Indicates similar rate of genital infections for prostitutes as well as non-prostitutes held in a juvenile detention center. 68% use no contraception. Recommends health education for STDs and family planning for this population.

1534. Bisno, A.L., I. Ofek, E.H. Beachey, et al. "Human Immunity to Gonococci: Studies of Opsonization by Sera of Prostitutes and Nuns." *Transactions of the Association of American Physicians* 87 (1974):

195-204.

Reports that opsonic antibodies to N. gonorrhea in sera is present in a prostitute population but not in the sera of Catholic nuns. Recommends further investigation of the biologic significance of opsonic antibodies as a possible step in developing effective immunizing agents.

1535. Bradbeer, C.S. "Diaphragms and Condoms for Prostitutes." (Letter) *British Journal of Hospital Medicine* 38(4) (October 1987):385.

1536. Bradbeer, C.S., R.N. Thin, T. Tan, et al. "Penicillin Treatment for Gonorrhoea in Relation to Early Syphilis in Prostitutes." *Genitourinary Medicine* 64(1) (February 1988):7-9.

Suggests that penicillin derivatives in doses sufficient to treat gonorrhea will also prevent early syphilis.

1537. Bradbeer, C.S., R.N. Thin, T. Tan, et al. "Prophylaxis against Infection in Singaporean Prostitutes." *Genitourinary Medicine* 64(1) (February 1988):52-3.

Interviews of one hundred prostitutes show significantly fewer gonococcal infections with the use of contraceptive diaphragms and antibiotics.

1538. Chan, S.H., T. Tan, A. Kamarudin, et al. "HLA and Sexually Transmitted Diseases in Prostitutes." *British Journal of Venereal Diseases* 55(3) (June 1979):207-10.

Compares HLA profile of 148 Chinese prostitutes with control subjects. Recommends that an identical study be done with other groups of prostitutes of same and different ethnic origins due to statistical uncertainty.

1539. Chavers, C.R. "A Longitudinal Study of the Incidence of Hepatitis B Markers in Nevada Prostitutes." (Thesis) UCLA, 1981.

1540. Conrad, G.L., G.S. Kleris, B. Rush, et al. "Sexually Transmitted Diseases among Prostitutes and Other Sexual Offenders." *Sexually Transmitted Diseases* 8(4) (October-December, 1981):241-4.

Discusses the relationship between prostitution and venereal disease. Traces the belief held since the nineteenth-century that prostitution is a direct factor in the spread of venereal disease and concludes that this theory is still valid today.

1541. Curran, W.J. "Venereal Disease Detention and Treatment: Prostitution and Civil Rights." *American Journal of Public Health* 65(2) (February 1975):180-1.

Discusses the public health law decision handed down in the mid-1970s in the case of Reynolds v. McNichols, in which the U.S. Court of Appeals for the Tenth Circuit held that the city of Denver ordinance forcing treatment of known prostitutes for venereal disease is constitutional. Argues that this important decision in the field of public health was upheld in spite of the civil rights movement.

1542. Dannenmaier, B., W. Alle, E.W. Hoferer, et al. "Incidences of Antibodies to Hepatitis B, Herpes Simplex and Cytomegalovirus in Prostitutes." *Zentralblatt für Bakteriologie, Mikrobiologie, und Hygiene Series A* 259(2) (April 1985):275-85.

Confirms that prostitutes must be considered a risk group for the transmission of hepatitis BV and CMV- and HSV 2-caused diseases.

1543. da Paz, A.C., L. Cardeman, T.D. Ricciardi, et al. "Cytologic Study of 1,607 Prostitutes--Dysplasias and Carcinoma 'In Situ' of the Uterine Cervix in Young Women." (Meeting Abstract) *Acta Cytologica* 25(1) (1981):41.

Determines that this group had a higher incidence of carcinoma of the uterine cervix. Suggests that certain practices characteristic of the lifestyle of prostitutes, including high frequency of intercourse and induced abortion, are decisive factors.

1544. Darougar, S., B. Aramesh, J.A. Gibson, et al. "Chlamydial Genital Infection in Prostitutes in Iran." *British Journal of Venereal Diseases* 59(1) (February 1983):53-5.

Suggests that Iranian prostitutes are a major source of chlamydial genital infection.

1545. Darrow, W.W. *Venereal Disease and Victimless Crime*. (Association Paper) *Society for the Study of Social Problems*. Atlanta, Georgia: Center for Disease Control, 1978.

Defines the types of prostitution that are more susceptible to infection of venereal disease. Also suggests that some areas of the country are more highly infected than others.

1546. Day, S. "Prostitute Women and the Ideology of Work in London." *Culture and AIDS*. Edited by Douglas A. Feldman. New York: Praeger, 1990.

Studies the relationship between life-style and sexually transmitted infections in a cohort of 112 prostitute women in London. Observes that condoms are used with clients to separate work from private life but that infection may come from unprotected sex with boyfriends. Suggests that health programs promote universal condom use.

1547. Day, S., H. Ward, and J.R. Harris. "Prostitute Women and Public Health." *BMJ* 297(6663) (December 1988):1585.

Asserts that there is no evidence that the female prostitute is at an added risk of HIV infection only due to a greater number of sexual partners. Finds that in the West the sharing of IV drug equipment constitutes the single most important risk factor and recommends that the use of condoms should be encouraged, not only with clients but also with boyfriends.

1548. D'Costa, L.J., F.A. Plummer, I. Bowmer, et al. "Prostitutes Are a Major Reservoir of Sexually Transmitted Diseases in Nairobi, Kenya." *Sexually Transmitted Diseases* 12(2) (April-June 1985):64-7.

STDs have been ranked as the sixth most important health problem in Africa. Shows that upper-, middle-, and lower-social strata prostitutes in Niarobi are a readily identifiable group of transmitters of gonococcal infection and that control programs must also take into account the high rate of reinfection. Argues that prostitution in Africa differs from that of Western countries since there are few ways in which unmarried or abandoned women can participate in the economy other than through prostitution, and that the central role of prostitutes must be taken into account in designing strategies to control STDs.

1549. de Hoop, D., W.J. Anker, R. van Strik, et al. "Hepatitis B Antigen and Antibody in the Blood of Prostitutes Visiting an Outpatient Venereology Department in Rotterdam." *British Journal of Venereal Diseases* 60(5) (October 1984):319-22.

Shows that prostitutes had a significantly higher prevalence of antibodies to hepatitis B surface antigens (anti-HBs). Argues that prostitutes should be screened for the presence of both hepatitis B surface antigens and antibodies, and those with no anti-HBs should be vaccinated.

1550. Deisher, R.W., J.A. Farrow, K. Hope, et al. "The Pregnant Adolescent Prostitute." *American Journal of Diseases of Children* 143(10) (1989):1162-5.

Describes the pregnancy and early postpartum experiences of a group of teenage prostitutes. Discusses subjects' environment, prenatal care, drug use, contraceptive practices, repeated pregnancies, and the risk of sexually transmitted diseases. Determines that pregnant adolescent prostitutes constitute a high risk group, and recommends more professional investigations into the subject as well as sensitive clinical approaches.

1551. Donovan, B. "Gonorrhea in a Sydney House of Prostitution." *Medical Journal of Australia* 140(5)(March 3, 1984):268-71.

This is a one year study of the presence of sexually transmitted diseases in a Sydney house of prostitution. Conclusions indicate that contraceptive use was unsatisfactory and the presence of a high incidence of pelvic inflammatory disease. Recommendations are made for infection control.

1552. Donovan, B. "Prostitution and STD." (Letter) *Medical Journal of Australia* 140(9) (April 28, 1984):561.

1553. Donovan, B. "Prostitution and STD--Reply." (Letter) *Medical Journal of Australia* 140(12) (1984):738-9.

1554. Duenas, A., E. Adam, J.L. Melnick, et al. "Herpesvirus Type 2 in a Prostitute Population." *American Journal of Epidemiology* 95(5) May 1972:483-9.

Determines that the frequency of herpesvirus type 2 antibodies is dependent on the age of the woman and the duration of prostitution. Also suggests that the greater occurence of carcinoma of the cervix in prostitutes could be attributed to the early onset of sexual activity and the increased number of sex partners.

1555. Edwards, W.M. "A Study of Progonasyl Using Prostitutes in Nevada's Legal Houses of Prostitution." *Journal of Reproductive Medicine* 11(2) (August 1973):81.

Discusses the efficiency of progonasyl, a contraction of prophylaxis against gonorrhea and syphilis, as a preventive measure against venereal disease. Concludes that there were significantly fewer instances of gonorrhea when the product was used.

1556. Farrow, J.A. and T.A. Bell. "Penicillinase-producing Neisserie-gonorrhoeae Infection in Adolescent Prostitutes in Detention." *Journal of Adolescent Health Care* 5(2) (1984):120-3.

Finds that young prostitutes are at high risk of being infected with PPHG, and suggests specific treatment.

1557. Fernandez, H., and C. Guevara. "Genital Mycoplasmas and N-Gonorrhea in Prostitutes." (Spanish) *Revista Medica de Chile* 108(9) (1980):814-17.

1558. Fitzpatrick, C., B.M. Coughlan, R. Hamill, et al. "Prostitutes and Screening for STD." (Letter) *Irish Medical Journal* 82(4) (1989):180.

1559. Goh, C.L., P. Meija, E.H. Sng, et al. "Chemoprophylaxis and Gonococcal Infections in Prostitutes." *International Journal of Epidemiology* 13(3) (September 1984):344-6.

Demonstrates that chemoprophylaxis reduces risk of gonococcal infections and that those who take penicillin chemoprophylaxis have a higher risk of Penicillinase Producing Neisseria Gonorrhoeae (PPNG).

1560. Goh, C.L., V.S. Rajan, S.H. Chan, et al. "Hepatitis B Infection in Prostitutes." *International Journal of Epidemiology* 15(1) (March 1986):112-5.

Supports early immunization against Hepatitis B infection of prostitutes since they must be considered a high risk group. Shows correlation between presence of HBV markers and duration of prostitution.

1561. Goh, C.L., A. Kamarudin, S.H. Chan, et al. "Hepatitis B Virus Markers in Prostitutes in Singapore." *Genitourinary Medicine* 61(2) (April 1985):127-9.

Proves that hepatitis B markers are significantly more prevalent in men than in women prostitutes, and that compared with other people, prostitutes have significantly higher incidence of hepatitis B markers. Suggests that sexual transmission of Hepatitis B infection is an important factor in the spread of the disease in areas where it is endemic.

1562. Haug, M. *The Ladies and Gentlemen of the Night and the Spread of Sexually Transmitted Diseases.* Ottawa: Department of Justice Canada, Policy, Programs and Research Branch, Research and Statistics Section, 1984.

1563. "An Historical Vignette: From House of Infection to Hospital for Control of Venereal Disease." *Journal of the American Venereal Disease Association* 2(1) (September 1975):31-32.

1564. Jones, R. "STD in Prostitutes." (Letter) *Medical Journal of Australia* 140(5) (March 3, 1984):303-4.

1565. Kaklamani, E., Z. Zhong-Tang, D. Trichopoulos, et al. "Hepatitis B Surface Antigen and Alphafetoprotein Levels in the Serum of Healthy Women." *Oncology* 41(3) (1984):176-9.

Supports the view that the oncogenic potential of the hepatitis B virus may be related to the induction of alphafetoprotein synthesis in apparently healthy HBsAg-positive individuals (including prostitutes).

1566. Keighley, E. "Carcinoma of the Cervix Among Prostitutes in a Women's Prison." *British Journal of Venereal Diseases* 44(3) (September 1968):254-5.

Investigates the incidence of carcinoma of the cervix among a group of incarcerated prostitutes. Finds that prostitutes over the age of 25 are at an increased risk of developing this disease.

1567. Krogsgaard, K., C. Gluud, C. Pedersen, et al. "Widespread Use of Condoms and Low Prevalence of Sexually Transmitted Diseases in Danish Non-Drug Addict Prostitutes." *British Medical Journal* 293(6560) (1986):1473-4.

1568. Leeb, B.O., J.A. Sebastian, and R. See. "Gonorrhea Screening in a Prostitute Population." *Obstetrics and Gynecology* 51(2) (February 1978):229-32.

Finds that the risk of gonorrhea infection in a prostitute population in Taiwan is directly related to exposure rate, and that the use of oral contraceptives did not increase the risk of infection. Concludes that the role of mechanical barriers in the prevention of gonorrhea infection needs futher study.

1569. Lim, K.B., V. Srivasin, S.L. Gan, et al. "Chlamydial Infection in Female Prostitutes in Singapore." *Singapore Medical Journal* 30(3) (June 1989):263-4.

Recommends chlamydial control programs for prostitutes following a study indicating that 8 to 9% of prostitutes tested for gonorrhoea were also infected with chlamydia and that 9 to 12% harbored chlamydia trachomatis.

1570. Lim, K.B., S.N. Tham, T. Tan, et al. "Screening for Cervical Cancers in Prostitutes." *Singapore Medical Journal* 28(4) (August 1987):300-3.

Analyzes the results of cytologic screening in prostitutes for a three year period in order to determine the importance of the number of sexual partners as an indicator of high risk for cervical carcinoma. Concludes that multiple sexual consorts are an important risk factor, and that cervical carcinoma behaves like a sexually transmitted disease.

1571. Maggi, L., R. Rodrigues, and M. Suarez. "Genital Herpes in Prostitutes." (Spanish) *Revista Medica de Chile* 114(4) (1986):291-7.

1572. Marchand, D. "Paying the Price of Prostitution: Gonorrhea in Thailand." *IDRC Reports* 16(2) (April 1987):20-1.

1573. Medina, R., L. Mella, H. Espoz, et al. "Venereal-disease Prevalence in Prostitutes from Santiago." (Spanish) *Revista Medica de Chile* 117(9) (1989):1063-67.

1574. Meheus, A., A. De Clerco, and R. Prat. "Prevalence of Gonorrhoea in Prostitutes in a Central African Town." *British Journal of Venereal Diseases* 50(1) (February 1974):50-2.

Attempts to determine the prevalence of gonorrhea in a group of prostitutes in Africa, in order to give evidence to support or contradict the theory that there is a high occurence of gonorrhea in tropical Africa and the emphasis of the importance of prostitution in transmission. Finds that in this study of 100 prostitutes prevalence of gonorrhea was 51.8% and that among the rest of the population the prostitutes were nearly always cited as the source of infection.

1575. Moraitis, S. "Prostitution and STD." (Editorial) *Medical Journal of Australia* 140(12) (1984):738.

1576. Nayyar, K.C., M. Cummings, J. Weber, et al. "Prevalence of Genital Pathogens among Female Prostitutes in New York City and in Rotterdam." *Sexually Transmitted Diseases* 13(2) (April-June, 1986):105-7.

Compares the prevalence of genital microorganisms among 300 female prostitutes in New York City and 60 female prostitutes in Rotterdam, the Netherlands, and finds some variation in rates of specific STDs.

1577. Nedoma, K., and I. Sipova. "A General Gynecological Study of Prostitutes." *Ceskoslovenska Gynekologie* 38(6) (1973):425-7.

1578. Nielsen, R. "Sensitivity of Gonococci to Antibiotics in Strains Isolated From 'Prostitutes' in Copenhagen." *British Journal of Venereal Diseases* 46(2) (April 1970):153-5.

Finds that strains of gonococci isolated from prostitutes did not include a higher proportion less sensitive to antibiotics than those of control cases.

1579. Papaevangelou, G., D. Trichopoulos, T. Kremastinou, et al. "Prevalence of Hepatitis B Antigen and Antibody in Prostitutes." *British Medical Journal* 2(913) (May 1974):256-8.

Supports the hypothesis that hepatitis B infection is sexually transmitted. Concludes that the prevalence of hepatitis B antibody is age related, based on evidence indicating the incidence of infection significantly increases with the number of years in prostitution.

1580. Papaevangelou, G., D. Trichopoulos, G. Papoutsakis, et al. "Hepatitis B Antigen in Prostitutes." *British Journal of Venereal Diseases* 50(3) (June 1974):228-31.

Suggests that sexual transmission may be a significant factor in the spread of hepatitis B in urban populations. Tests this hypothesis by studying the carrier rate of prostitutes in a high HBAg prevalence urban area, since they constitute a high risk group for sexually transmitted diseases.

1581. Patterson, W.H. "Prostitution and Sexually Transmitted Disease." *Medical Journal of Australia* 140(5) (March 3, 1984):252-3.

Reviews the findings of Basil Donovan concerning the hyperendemicity of sexually transmitted diseases among prostitutes. Considers possible methods for reducing the incidence of STDs among prostitutes and their consorts.

1582. Phaosavasdi, S, W. Snidvongs, P. Thasanapradit, et al. "Syphilis among Pregnant Thai Prostitutes." *Journal of the Medical Association of Thailand* 70(4) (April 1987):217-22.

Examines the medical problems faced by fourteen pregnant prostitutes in Bangkok who had contracted syphilis. Demonstrates the importance of close follow up in the treatment of syphilis during pregnancy in prostitutes who are at risk of reexposure.

1583. Philpot, C.R. "STD and Prostitution." (Letter) *Medical Journal of Australia* 140(7) (March 31, 1984):442.

1584. Potterat, J.J., R.B. Rothenberg, and D.C. Bross. "Gonorrhea in Street Prostitutes: Epidemiologic and Legal Implications." *Sexually Transmitted Diseases* 6(2) (April-June, 1979):58-63.

Shows that prostitutes have a substantially higher risk of contracting gonorrhea than non-prostitutes and that the risk of both groups decreases over a two-year period when control measures are applied.

1585. Rajakumar, M.K., S.H. Ton, K.F. Lim, et al. "Hepatitis B Markers in Heterosexuals Involved in Promiscuous Sexual Activity." *Medical Journal of Malaysia* 39(1) (March 1984):65-8.

Shows a higher than normal incidence of hepatitis B among a group of 179 heterosexuals, mainly prostitutes, involved in promiscuous sexual activity in Malaysia. Risk of infection increases considerably with number of sexual partners.

1586. Ranney, E.K. "Role of Prostitution in Sexually Transmitted Diseases." (Letter) *Canadian Medical Association Journal* 129(8) (1983):798.

1587. Reeves, W.C., J.R. Arosemena, M. Garcia, et al. "Genital Human Papillomavirus Infection in Panama City Prostitutes." *Journal of Infectious Diseases* 160(4) (October 1989):599-603.

Indicates that most prostitutes in the city are infected with genital HVPs and that multiple sampling is necessary to estimate accurately the infection rate.

1588. "Relationship of Syphilis to Drug Use and Prostitution--Connecticut and Philadelphia, Pennsylvania." (from Morbidity Mortality Weekly Report) *JAMA* 261(3) (1989):353.

1589. Requena Caballero, L., C. Requena Caballero, I. Requena Caballero, et al. "Prevalence and Risk Factors of Hepatitis B in Spanish Prostitutes." *Epidemiology and Infection* 99(3) (December 1987):767-74.

Shows that Hepatitis B markers are more prevalent in prostitutes than in the general population. Determines factors related to the prevalence of these markers, including age, history of sexually transmitted diseases, drug abuse, and promiscuity.

1590. Richter, J., B. Donovan, J. Gerofi, et al. "Low Condom Breakage Rate in Commercial Sex." (Letter) *Lancet* 2(8626-8627) (December 24-31, 1988):1487-8.

1591. Ruijs, G.J., I.K. Schut, J. Schirm, et al. "Prevalence, Incidence, and Risk of Acquiring Urogenital Gonococcal or Chlamydial Infection in Prostitutes Working in Brothels." *Genitourinary Medicine* 64(1) (February 1988):49-51.

In addition to showing the prevalence, incidence, and risk of gonococcal or chlamydial infections in 24 prostitutes, considers the epidemiological importance of prostitutes as a reservoir of infection.

1592. Sastrowidjojo, H., and A. Idajadi. "Penicillinase-producing Neisseria Gonorrhoeae among Prostitutes in Surabaya." *British Journal of Venereal Diseases* 59(2) (April 1983):98-9.

Indicates that the high prevalence of PPNG among high-class prostitutes in Surabaya, Indonesia is due to the importation of PPNG strains from abroad.

1593. Schulte, R.M. "Drug-Prostitution--Psychosocial and Medical Aspects." (German) *Medizinische Welt* 40(49-5) (1989):1395-7.

1594. Schwimmer, W.B., K.A. Ustay, and S.J. Behrman. "Sperm-agglutinating Antibodies and Decreased Fertility in Prostitutes." *Obstetrics and Gynecology* 30(2) (August 1967):192-200.

Confirms that prostitutes have a poor reproductive history. Suggests that the presence of high sperm-agglutinating antibodies may contribute to a low conception rate among prostitutes. Finds that these antibodies have no relationship to the increased abortion rate, also characteristic of prostitutes.

1595. Sebastian, J.A., B.O. Leeb, and R. See. "Cancer of the Cervix--a Sexually Transmitted Disease. Cytologic Screening in a Prostitute Population." *American Journal of Obstetrics and Gynecology* 131(6) (July 15, 1978):620-3.

Attempts to separate the variables of frequent intercourse with multiple partners and multiple infections from early coital experience in 750 Taiwan prostitutes. Concludes promiscuity and infection rates are not significant epidemiologically if they occur after the first pregnancy or early adolescence.

1596. Skrabanek, P. "Cervical Cancer in Nuns and Prostitutes: a Plea for Scientific Continence." *Journal of Clinical Epidemiology* 41(6) (1988):577-82.

Shows there is no basis for the hypothesis that carcinoma of the cervix is rare among nuns and common in prostitutes. Traces the research from 1842 to the present, arguing that the epidemiological evidence does not conclusively support nor contradict the theory that cervical cancer is venereal disease.

1597. Stary, A., W. Kopp, W. Gephart, et al. "Culture Viruses Direct Specimen Test--Comparative Study of Infections with Chlamydia Trachomatis in Viennese Prostitutes." *Genitourinary Medicine* 61(4) (1985):258-60.

Shows that the incidence of chlamydial infections in Viennese prostitutes decreased from 1980 to 1984 indicating greater patient awareness and more efficient treatment. Concludes that both direct specimen test and culture tests are adequate in detecting infection. While conceding that the second is more sensitive, advocates the direct specimen test for screening of large groups for chlamydial infection due to lower cost, more rapid and simplified handling and high specificity.

1598. Tantivanich, S., and B. Udomratana. "Prevalence of Hepatitis B Virus Among Hospitality Girls in Bangkok." *Southeast Asian Journal of*

Tropical Medicine and Public Health 16(1) (March 1985):127-8.

1599. Teoh, S.K., and N.F. Ngeow. "Sexually Transmitted Diseases in Teenage Girls from a Remand Home." *Medical Journal of Malaysia* 35(2) (December 1980):109-11.

Explores the incidence of STDs among thirty young girls detained in a remand home on suspicion of prostitution and finds that 63% were infected with one or more STDs. Recommends that regular and comprehensive screening be carried out on high risk women.

1600. Urabe, S., S. Yoshida, and Y. Mizuguchi. "Sexually Transmitted Diseases among Prostitutes in Fukuoka, Japan." *Japanese Journal of Medical Science and Biology* 41(1) (February 1988):15-20.

Shows the prevalence of various STDs among prostitutes in Fukuoka, Japan.

1601. Urmil, A.C., P.K. Dutta, K. Basappa, et al. "A Study of Morbidity Patterns among Prostitutes Attending a Municipal Clinic in Pune." *Journal of the Indian Medical Association* 87(2) (February 1989):29-31.

Reports that more than 80% of 200 prostitutes tested suffered from STDs and many from other communicable diseases as well. Recommends continuous surveillance, early diagnosis and appropriate treatment in addition to health education among sexually promiscuous individuals.

1602. Van den Hoek, J., M.M.D. van der Linden, and R.A. Coutinho. "Increase in Infectious Syphilis among Heterosexuals in Amsterdam--Its Relationship to Drug Use and Prostitution." *Genitourinary Medicine* 66(1) (1990):31-32.

Reports an increase in heterosexually acquired syphilis since 1986 in Amsterdam similar to that of the U.S.. Links findings to prostitution and drug use. Recommends intensifying STD programs for addicted prostitutes, since studies have found that STDs causing genital ulcers facilitate transmission of HIV.

1603. van Ulsen, J., M.F. Michel, R. van Strik, et al. "Experience with a

Modified Solid-phase Enzyme Immunoassay for Detection of Gonorrhea in Prostitutes." *Sexually Transmitted Diseases* 13(1) (January-March, 1986):1-4.

High predictive value makes this test suitable for elimination of gonorrhea from this pool of patients.

1604. Velaso, M., and C. Delafuente. "Hepatitis B Surface Antigen in 489 Prostitutes in Santiago, Chile." (Spanish) *Revista Medica de Chile* 111(5) (1983):461-2.

1605. Waugh, M. "Sexually Transmitted Diseases and Prostitution." *Journal of the Royal Society of Medicine* 82(6) (June 1989):319-20.

Traces the historic links between prostitutes, their clients, and venereal disease from the mid-sixteenth-century to the present day. Reports that prostitutes and their clients are at an increased risk today due to intravenous drug abuse and sexual transmission of HIV infection. Establishes a link between prostitutes and the spread of HIV infection. Argues that education and laws prohibiting prostitution are not enough and that alternative means for making a living are necessary in order to reduce prostitution and the spread of AIDS.

1606. White, F.M. "Role of Prostitution in Sexually Transmitted Disease." (Letter) *Canadian Medical Association Journal* 130(3) (February 1, 1986):253.

1607. World Forum on Syphilis and Other Treponematoses, Washington, D.C., 1962. *Proceedings*. Atlanta, U.S. Department of Health, Education, and Welfare, Public Health Service, Communicable Disease Center, Venereal Disease Branch; for sale by the Superintendent of Documents, U.S. Government Printing Office, 1964.

1608. Yates, G.L., et al. "A Risk Profile Comparison of Runaway and Non-Runaway Youth." *American Journal of Public Health* 78(7) (July 1988):820-1.

Reveals that run-away youths are at a greater risk for developing medical problems and health-compromising patterns of behavior, including prostitution.

MEDICINE AND AIDS

1609. Adams, R., C. Johnson, and U. Smith. "The Role of Prostitution in AIDS and Other STDs." *Medical Aspects of Human Sexuality* 21(8) (August 1987):27-33.

Examines the role of prostitution in the spread of AIDS and other STDs. Reports on the findings of the use of prostitutes by middle-class males and stresses the importance of "safe sex" practices.

1610. "AIDS: Kids, Prostitutes and Drug Abusers." (Audiocassette) National Public Radio.

Produced by the National Council on Family Relations, this audiocassette examines the impact of AIDS on one community.

1611. "AIDS: Prevention, Policies, and Prostitutes." (Editorial) *Lancet* 1(8647) (May 20, 1989):1111-3.

1612. Aim, G., I. Devincenzi, R. Ancellepark, et al. "HIV Infection in French Prostitutes." (Letter) *AIDS* 3(11) (1989):767-8.

1613. Barton, S.E., G.S. Underhill, C. Gilchrist, et al. "HTLV-III Antibody in Prostitutes." (Letter) *Lancet* 2(8469) (1985):1424.

1614. Bayik, M.M., et al. "Cellular and Humoral Immunity in Prostitutes in Istanbul." *Japanese Journal of Experimental Medicine* 58(4) (August 1988):185-8.

Shows a significant correlation between the number of partners in a given week and the mean number of E rosettes, EAC rosette forming cells, and cells expressing surface immunoglobulins in a study of 34 prostitutes.

1615. Bergman, B. "AIDS, Prostitution, and the Use of Historical Stereotypes to Legislate Sexuality." *John Marshall Law Review* 21(4) (Summer 1988):777-830.

Examines public health response to prostitution in the nineteenth century and compares it to current treatment of AIDS patients. Argues that public policy should focus on education, not scapegoating.

1616. Brandt, A.M.   "AIDS and Metaphor: Toward the Social Meaning of Epidemic Disease." *Social Research* 55(3) (Autumn 1988):413-432.

1617. Brenkyfaudeux, D., and A. Fribourgblanc.   "HTLV-III Antibody in Prostitutes." (Letter) *Lancet* 2(8469) (1985):1424.

1618. Brokensha, D.   "Overview: Social Factors in the Transmission and Control of African AIDS." *AIDS in Africa: the Social and Policy Impact.* Edited by Norman Miller and Richard C. Rockwell. Lewiston, New York: Edwin Mellen, 1988, pp. 167-73.

1619. Calabrese, L.H., and K.V. Gopalakrishna.   "Transmission of HTLV-III Infection from Man to Woman to Man." (Letter) *New England Journal of Medicine* 314(15) (April 10, 1986):987.

1620. Caldwell, J.C., et al.   "The Social Context of AIDS in Sub-Saharan Africa." *Population and Development Review* 15(2) (June 1989):185-234.

Within a broader context, discusses prostitution in Sub-Saharan Africa. Addresses the difficulty of labeling a particular form of behavior as prostitution. Identifies the type of woman who becomes a prostitute as well as her clients. Considers the link between prostitution and sexually transmitted diseases, especially AIDS, within the framework of social structure.

1621. Cameron, D.W., L.J. D'Costa, G.M. Maitha, et al.   "Female to Male Transmission of Human Immunodeficiency Virus Type 1: Risk Factors for Seroconversion in Men." *Lancet* 2(8660) (August 19, 1989):403-7.

A prospective study of 422 men who had acquired a SDT from a group of prostitutes indicates a high rate of female to male transmission of

HIV-1 in the presence of STD. Demonstrates a causal relation between lack of male circumcision, genital ulcer disease, and susceptibility to HIV-1 infection.

1622. Carael, M., and P. Piot. "HIV Infection in Developing Countries." *Journal of Biosocial Science* 21, supplement 10 (1989):35-50.

Discusses seroprevalence rates for HIV antibodies in developing countries. Concludes that heterosexual activity is the major mode for transmission and that female prostitutes are a high risk group. Shows that seroprevalence rate correlates to pattern of sexual behavior.

1623. Chen, C.J. "Seroepidemiology of Human T Lymphotropic Viruses and Hepatitis Viruses among Prostitutes in Taiwan." *Journal of Infectious Diseases* 158(3) (September 1988):633-5.

1624. Chikwem, J.O., et al. "Human Immunodeficiency Virus Type 1 (HIV-1) Infection among Female Prostitutes in Borno State of Nigeria: One Year Follow-up." *East African Medical Journal* 66(11) (November 1989):752-6.

Shows an increase of almost 10% of HIV-1 infection among prostitutes tested in Borno State, Nigeria. Concludes that a continuous sharp rise in the rate of infection will continue unless serious efforts are made to intensify health education campaigns.

1625. Chikwem, J.O., et al. "Impact of Health Education on Prostitutes' Awareness and Attitudes to Acquired Immune Deficiency Syndrome (AIDS)." *Public Health* 102(5) (September 1988):439-45.

1626. Cohen, J.B. et al. "Antibody to Human Immunodeficiency Virus in Female Prostitutes." *MMWR. Morbidity and Mortality Weekly Report* 36(11) (March 27, 1987):157-61.

1627. Cooper, D.A. "Aids and Prostitutes." (Letter) *Medical Journal of Australia* 145(1) (1986):55.

1628. Coutinho, R.A., R.L. van Andel, and T.J. Rijsdijk. "Role of Male

Prostitutes in Spread of Sexually Transmitted Diseases and Human Immunodeficiency Virus." (Letter) *Genitourinary Medicine* 64(3) (June 1988):207-8.

1629. Dan, M., M. Rock, and S. Barshani. "HIV Antibodies in Drug Addicted Prostitutes." (Letter) *JAMA* 257(8) (1987):1047.

1630. Day, S. "Prostitute Women and AIDS: Anthropology." *AIDS* 2(6) (December 1988):421-8.

Examines the role of prostitutes in the transmission of HIV. Distinguishes between prostitution in the West, in Asia, and in Sub-Saharan Africa, and argues that the variables associated with prostitution derive from the wider society. Concludes that preventive programs must be based on understanding of the local organization of prostitution.

1631. Decker, J.F. "Prostitution as a Public Health Issue." *AIDS and the Law: A Guide for the Public.* Edited by H.L. Dalton, S. Burris, and the Yale AIDS Law Project. New Haven, CT: Yale University Press, 1987.

Reframes an argument often conducted in moral rather than rational terms. Argues that without a clear analysis, irrational beliefs could become the justification for an oppressive social policy.

1632. Elifson, K.W., J. Boles, M. Sweat, et al. "Seroprevalence of Human Immunodeficiency Virus among Male Prostitutes." (Letter) *New England Journal of Medicine* 321(12) (September 21, 1989):832-3.

1633. Elizalde Sagardia, B. "Profile of a Population Tested for HIV Antibodies at the Latin American Center for Sexually Transmitted Diseases, 1986." *Boletin--Asociación Medica de Puerto Rico* 79(1) (January 1987):2-6.

1634. Gagnon, J.H. "Disease and Desire." *Daedalus* 118(3) (Summer 1989):47-77.

Explores the effect of the AIDS epidemic on female prostitutes, as well as other groups. Stresses the need for more AIDS research and more public health education, particularly in high risk areas.

1635. Golenbock, D.T., et al. "Absence of Infection with Human Immunodeficiency Virus in Peruvian Prostitutes." *AIDS Research Human Retroviruses* 4(6) (December 1988):493-9.

Demonstrates that none of the 140 female prostitutes from the port city of Callao, Peru, tested for evidence of HIV infection was seropositive despite the use of unsterile needles for injection of vitamins, antibiotics, or steroids. Concludes that HIV infection has not yet been introduced to prostitutes in this port city but that the use of unsterile needles represents a serious health threat in developing countries.

1636. Gongora-Biachi, R.A., and P. Gonzales-Martinez. "Human Immunodeficiency Virus (HIV) Antibodies in a Population of Prostitutes from Merida, Yucatan, Mexico." (Spanish) *Revista de Investigacion Clinica* 39(3) (July-September 1987):305-6.

1637. Harcourt, C.L., C.R. Philpot, and J.M. Edwards. "Human Immunodeficiency Virus Infection in Prostitutes." (Letter) *Medical Journal of Australia* 150(9) (May 1, 1989):540-1.

1638. Hillman, R., D. Tomlinson, D. Taylor-Brown, et al. "Risk of AIDS Among Workers in the 'Sex Industry'." (Letter) *British Medical Journal* 299(6699) (September 2, 1989):622-3.

1639. "HTLV-III Antibody in Prostitutes." (Letter) *Lancet* 2(8469-70) (December 21-28, 1985):1424.

1640. Hyams, K.C., J. Escamilla, T.J. Papadimos, et al. "HIV Infection in a Non-drug Abusing Prostitute Population." (Letter) *Scandinavian Journal of Infectious Disease* 21(3) (1989):353-4.

1641. Jayaraman, K.S. "Pool of Infected Women? AIDS In India." (News item) *Nature* 321(6066) (May 8-14, 1986):103.

1642. John, T.J., P.G. Babu, H. Jayakumari, et al. "Prevalence of HIV Infection in Risk Groups in Tamilnadu, India." (Letter) *Lancet* 1(8525) (January 17, 1987):160-1.

1643. Kanki, P., R. Marlink, S. Mboup, et al. "Epidemiology of HIV-2 in Prostitutes in Senegal." (Meeting Abstract) *AIDS Research and Human Retroviruses* 6(1) (1990):76.

Finds that the epidemiology of HIV-2 in a population of 1394 female prostitutes in Senegal differs significantly from that of HIV-1. Differences include age-specific seroprevalence, risk factors for infection, rate of sexual transmission, and clinical outcome.

1644. Kant, H.S. "The Transmission of HTLV-III." (Letter) *JAMA* 254(14) (October 11, 1985):1901.

1645. Khabbaz, R.F., et al. "Seroprevalence and Risk Factors for HTLV-I/II Infection among Female Prostitutes in the United States." *JAMA* 263(1) (January 5, 1990):60-64.

Shows that rates among black, Hispanic, and American Indian prostitutes from eight areas of the United States are significantly higher that for white or Asian Americans with or without a history of intravenous drug use. Recommends futher studies to evaluate patterns of transmission and long-term health effects.

1646. Koenig, E.R. "International Prostitutes and Transmission of HIV." (Letter) *Lancet* 1(8641) (April 8, 1989):782-3.

1647. Kraiselburd, E.N., et al. "Interactions of HIV and STDs in a Group of Female Prostitutes." *Archives of AIDS Research* 3(1-3) (1989):149-57.

1648. Kreiss, J.K., et al. "AIDS Virus Infection in Nairobi Prostitutes. Spread of the Epidemic to East Africa." *New England Journal of Medicine* 314(7) (February 13, 1986):414-8.

Demonstrates that AIDS has spread across the African continent in a study of 90 female prostitutes, 40 men treated at a clinic for sexually transmitted diseases, and 42 medical personnel in Nairobi, Kenya.

1649. Kreiss, J.K., et al. "Isolation of Human Immunodeficiency Virus from Genital Ulcers in Nairobi Prostitutes." *Journal of Infectious Diseases*

160(3) (September 1989):380-4.

Shows that genital ulcers in seropositive patients are a potential source of HIV infections, and recommends that public health measures aimed at controlling genital ulcer diseases be an integral part of AIDS prevention programs.

1650. Landers, R.K. "AIDS Dilemma for Health Policy Makers." *Editorial Research Reports* 6 (1987):578-87.

Discusses conflicts between the patients' rights and the public's right to be protected. Recommends specific prevention measures, including education of teenagers.

1651. Lange, W.R., et al. "HIV Infection in Baltimore: Antibody Seroprevalence Rates among Parenteral Drug Abusers and Prostitutes." *Maryland Medical Journal* 36(9) (September 1987):757-61.

Finds a prevalence of HIV infection of 34% among a subsample of prostitutes in Baltimore with histories of heavy drug use in 1986. Determines that the rate of HIV infection is highest in predominently black neighborhoods in the center of the city. Concludes that HIV has penetrated the Baltimore addict community, including drug users engaged in prostitution as a means of supporting their habit.

1652. Larranaga, J.R., T. Ardiz, D. Delblanco, et al. "Incidence of Hepatitis B Virus Among the Prostitutes of Vigo." (Spanish) *Revista Clínica Española* 185(1) (1989):44.

1653. Leonard, T., et al. "The Prevalence of Human Immunodeficiency Virus, Hepatitis B, and Syphilis among Female Prostitutes in Atlanta." *Journal of the Medical Association of Georgia* 77(3) (March 1988):162-4, 167.

Addresses the rate of infection of HIV, hepatitis B virus, and syphilis among prostitutes in Atlanta. Suggests that prostitutes constitute a high risk group of HIV infection unless precautionary measures are taken. Finds that prostitutes have a high prevalence for HBV (Hepatitis B) markers, intravenous drug use, and unsafe sex practices.

1654. Luthy, R., et al. "Prevalence of HIV Antibodies among Prostitutes in Zurich, Switzerland." *Klinische Wochenschrift* 65(6) (March 16, 1987):287-8.

Shows no correlation between HIV infection and race, number of clients, or sexual practices in a study of 123 prostitutes in Zurich. Demonstrates that intravenous drug users are a risk.

1655. McAnally, J.S. "Prostitutes and AIDS." (Letter) *Sciences* 24(5) (1984):12.

1656. Mann, J., T.C. Quinn, P. Piot, et al. "Condom Use and HIV Infection among Prostitutes in Zaire." (Letter) *New England Journal of Medicine* 316(6) (February 5, 1987):345.

1657. Mann, J., et al. "HIV Infection and Associated Risk Factors in Female Prostitutes in Kinshasa, Zaire." *AIDS* 2(4) (August 1988):249-54.

Out of 377 prostitutes in Kinshasa, Zaire, 27% tested seropositive. Indicates that the number of lifetime sexual partners, and factors which interfere with the integrity of the vaginal or cervical mucosa increase the risk of HIV infection acquired through heterosexual contact.

1658. Nahmias, S. "A Model of HIV Diffusion from a Single Source." *Journal of Sex Research* 26(1) (February 1989):15-25.

Studies the transmission of HIV infection from one prostitute to her clients and to their sexual partners using a mathematical model. Concludes that in 5 years, a single prostitute can be expected to infect about 20 men and 0.8 unborn children.

1659. Nahmias, S. "A Model of HIV Diffusion from a Single Source: A Scholium." *Journal of Sex Research* 26(4) (November 1989):510-513.

Modifies the model discussed in the entry above from a geometric distribution to a normal distribution, and shows how the expected number of infected clients will change.

1660. Ngugi, E.N. "Prevention of Transmission of Human Immunodeficiency Virus in Africa: Effectiveness of Condom Promotion and Health Education Among Prostitutes." *Lancet* 2(8616) (October 15, 1988):887-90.

Assesses condom use after an educational program about AIDS and STDs among a prostitute population in Nairobi. Finds a striking increase in condom use after the program, especially in view of a general reluctance to accept condoms as a method of contraception in Africa. Provides evidence that education programs can effect changes in sexual behavior.

1661. Padian, N.S. "Prostitute Women and AIDS; Epidemiology." *AIDS* 2(6) (December 1988):413-9.

Considers role of female prostitutes in the AIDS pandemic. Examines epidemiologic data from prostitute surveys from around the world and finds that prevalence of infection varies according to geographic area. Argues that the geographic diversity should be interpreted with caution. Concludes that intravenous drug use and varied sexual exposure put prostitutes at significant risk for HIV infection but that the role of prostitutes in spreading the disease is less certain.

1662. Palacio, V., S. Vazques, R. Quiros, et al. "Incidence of HIV in Prostitutes in Oviedo, Spain." (Letter) *AIDS* 3(7) (July 1989):461-2.

1663. Papaevangelou, G., et al. "Education in Preventing HIV Infection in Greek Registered Prostitutes." *Journal of Immune Deficiency Syndrome* 1(4) (1988):386-9.

Three hundred and fifty registered prostitutes were screened for anti-HIV in 1984 and 1985. Attributes failure to detect further HIV infections in a follow-up study to avoidance of clients from Central Africa and to almost universal use of condoms following an intensive educational campaign.

1664. Papaevangelou, G., A. Roumeliotou-Karayannis, G. Kallinikos, et al. "LAV/HTLV-III Infection in Female Prostitutes." (Letter) *Lancet* 2(8462) (November 2, 1985):1018.

1665. Perkins, R. "AIDS and Prostitution." (Letter) *Medical Journal of*

Australia 143(9) (October 28, 1985):426.

1666. Philpot, C.R., et al. "Human Immunodeficiency Virus and Female
Prostitutes, Sydney 1985." *Genitourinary Medicine* 64(3) (June
1988):193-7.

Finds both groups of 132 female prostitutes and 55 non-prostitutes
surveyed in Sydney at risk of HIV infection due to intravenous drug use,
unprotected sexual intercourse with men using IV drugs and with bisexual
men, and to exposure to several STDs.

1667. Piot, P., et al. "Prostitutes: a High Risk Group for HIV Infection?" *Soz
Praventivmed* 33(7) (1988):336-9.

Asserts that prevalence of HIV infection among prostitutes varies
geographically, the highest rates occurring in Africa and in areas with
large numbers of HIV-infected intravenous drug users. Recommends that
HIV infection in prostitutes be monitored and that health education on
AIDS prevention be available to prostitutes and their clients.

1668. Plant, M. *AIDS, Drugs, and Prostitution.* London: Routledge, 1990.

Describes the interrelations between prostitution, HIV infection, and AIDS
and the use and abuse of drugs and alcohol. Contains studies of AIDS
risks among prostitutes and their clients compiled to provide an
introduction to the AIDS/sex work/drug connection. Identifies the
objectives, scope, and preliminary results of various initiatives around the
world. Concludes that AIDS is a much larger threat to society than either
drugs or prostitution and must be treated accordingly.

1669. Plant, M., et al. "Sex Industry, Alcohol and Illicit Drugs: Implications
for the Spread of HIV Infection." *British Journal of Addiction* 84(1)
(January 1989):53-59.

Links alcohol and illicit drugs to high risk sexual behavior. Calls for more
research to determine how much prostitutes know about AIDS and its
prevention since an increasing number of female prostitutes in Western
countries test seropositive for AIDS.

1670. Plummer, F.A., J.N. Simonsen, E.N. Ngugi, et al. "Incidence of Human Immunodeficiency Virus (HIV) Infection and Related Diseases in Cohort of Prostitutes." (Meeting Abstract) *Clinical and Investigative Medicine/Medecine Clinique et Experimentale* 10(4) (1987):B91.

1671. Quero, M.S., M. Suarez, J. Uribe, et al. "HIV Infection in Prostitutes-- Markers and Risk Factors." (Spanish) *Revista Medica de Chile* 117(6) (1989):624-8.

1672. Randal, J.H. "Local Communities Take the Lead in Coping with AIDS. Acquired Immune Deficiency Syndrome." *Governing* 1(2) (November 1987):34-40.

Contends that coping with the AIDS pandemic has fallen to local governments with little help from the Washington. The incidence is mainly concentrated in 10 metropolitan centers, and the localities are facing problems dealing with the crisis. In New York City 17% of the prostitutes tested seropositive for AIDS and 30% were intravenous drug users. Presents recommendations to handle the crisis more effectively.

1673. Ratham, K.V. "Awareness of AIDS among Transsexual Prostitutes in Singapore." *Singapore Medical Journal* 27(6) (December 1986):519-21.

Evaluates AIDS awareness among Singapore transsexual prostitutes and the extent to which this group adopts precautionary measures. Assesses the effectiveness of these measures and suggests improvements.

1674. Richardson, D. *Women and AIDS*. New York: Methuen, 1988.

Includes discussion of prostitution. Analyzes from a feminist perspective the misunderstandings about the role of prostitutes in the spread of AIDS. Argues that it is premature and sexist to implicate prostitution as a major factor in the spread of the disease.

1675. Rose, D.B. "AIDS in a Canadian Woman Who Had Helped Prostitutes in Port-Au-Prince." (Letter) *Lancet* 2(8351) (September 17, 1983):680-681.

1676. Rosenberg, M.J., et al. "Prostitutes and AIDS; a Health Department Priority?" *American Journal of Public Health* 78(4) (April 1988):418-23.

Indicates that HIV infection in prostitutes follows a different pattern than for STDs, and that infection in non-drug using prostitutes is low or absent. Recommends that health departments place high priority on preventive measures directed towards prostitutes since they often are drug users and are easily reachable.

1677. Ross, M.W. "Prevalence of Classes of Risk Behaviors for HIV Infection in a Randomly Selected Australian Population." *Journal of Sex Research* 25(4) (1988):441-450.

A random survey of 2600 individuals in Australia suggests that the prevalence of homosexual behavior and contact with prostitutes is substantially lower than estimated by Kinsey in 1948 and 1953. Discusses the implication of the data for HIV prevention programs.

1678. Roumeliotou, A., G. Papoutsakis, G. Kallinikos, et al. "Effectiveness of Condom Use in Preventing HIV Infection in Prostitutes." (Letter) *Lancet* 2(8622) (1988):1249.

1679. Schoub, B.D., et al. "Absence of HIV Infection in Prostitutes and Women Attending Sexually-transmitted Disease Clinics in South Africa." *Transactions of the Royal Society of Tropical Medicine and Hygiene* 81(5) (1987):874-5.

Attributes the absence of HIV infection among prostitutes and women attending sexually-transmitted disease clinics in South Africa to the relatively low rate of contact between South African populations and those of other African countries.

1680. Seidlin, M., et al. "Prevalence of HIV Infection in New York Call Girls." *Journal of Acquired Immune Deficiency Syndrome* 1(2) (1988):150-4.

Indicates that despite their promiscuity HIV infection is still uncommon among 78 call girls in New York City.

1681. Setters, J. "Alcohol and Drug Use Among Prostitutes and Their Clients--
Implications for the Spread of HIV Infection." (Meeting Abstract) *British
Journal of Addiction* 83(12) (1988):1476.

1682. Simoes, E.A., et al. "Evidence for HTLV-III Infection in Prostitutes in
Tamil Nadu (India)." *Indian Journal of Medical Research* 85 (April
1987):335-8.

1683. Simonsen, J.N., F.A. Plummer, E.N. Ngugi, et al. "HIV Infection
Among Lower Socioeconomic Strata Prostitutes in Nairobi." *AIDS* 4(2)
(1990):139-44.

1684. Singh, Y.N., A.N. Malaviya, S.P. Tripathy, et al. "HIV Serosurveillance
among Prostitutes and Patients from a Sexually Transmitted Diseases
Clinic in Delhi, India." *Journal of Acquired Immune Deficiency
Syndromes* 3(3) (1990):287-9.

1685. Smith, G.L. and K.F. Smith. "Lack of HIV Infection and Condom Use
in Licensed Prostitutes." (Letter) *Lancet* 2(8520) (December 13,
1986):1392.

1686. Smith, R.D. "Prostitutes and AIDS - Reply." (Letter) *Sciences* 24(5)
(1984):12.

1687. Spitzer, P.G. and Neil, J. "Transmission of HIV Infection from a
Woman to a Man by Oral Sex." *New England Journal of Medicine* 320(4)
(January 1989):251.

Indicates that a sixty-year-old man with diabetes mellitus was infected with
HIV following oral sex with an intravenous drug-using female prostitute.

1688. Sterk, C. "Cocaine and HIV Seropositivity." (Letter) *Lancet* 1(8593)
(May 7, 1988):1052-3.

1689. Tan, M., A. Deleon, B. Stoltzfus, et al. "AIDS as a Political Issue--
Working with the Sexually Prostituted in the Philippines." *Community
Development Journal* 24(3) (1989):186-93.

1690. Thomas, R.M., et al. "Risk of AIDS among Workers in the Sex Industry: Some Initial Results from a Scottish Study." *British Medical Journal* 299(6692) (July 15, 1989):148-9.

Reports that one in twelve sex workers in Edinburgh is found seropositive for AIDS, and that one fifth use intravenous drugs. Calls for health education among people engaged in buying or selling sexual services.

1691. Tirelli, U. "HIV Antibodies in Drug Addicted Prostitutes--Reply." (Letter) *JAMA* 257(8) (1987):1047.

1692. Tirelli, U., G. Rezza, M. Giuliani, et al. "HIV Seroprevalence among 304 Female Prostitutes from Four Italian Towns." (Letter) *AIDS* 3(8) (August 1989):547-8.

1693. Tirelli, U., E. Vaccher, P. Bullian, et al. "HIV-1 Seroprevalence in Male Prostitutes in Northeast Italy." (Letter) *Journal of Acquired Immune Deficiency Syndrome* 1(4) (1988):414-5.

1694. Tirelli, U., E. Vaccher, A. Carbone, et al. "HTLV-III Antibody in Prostitutes." (Letter) *Lancet* 2(8469) (1985):1424.

1695. Tirelli, U., E. Vaccher, R. Sorio, et al. "HTLV-III Antibodies in Drug Addicted Prostitutes Used by United States Soldiers in Italy." (Letter) *JAMA* 256(6) (1986):711-2.

1696. Valls, E.V., M.B. Torres-Mendoza, M.N. Ayalachavira, et al. "To Evaluate the Prevalence of HIV Antibodies and Their Risk Factors in Prostitutes from Guadalajara." (French) *Contraception, Fertilité, Sexualité* 17(3) (1989):265-8.

1697. Van de Perre, P. "Female Prostitutes: a Risk Group for Infection with Human T-Cell Lymphotropic Virus Type III." *Lancet* 2(8454) (September 7, 1985):524-7.

Demonstrates that Central African prostitutes are a high-risk group for HTLV-III infection based on a study of 33 female prostitutes and 25 male customers in Rwanda.

1698. Van den Hoek, J.A., et al. "HIV Infection and STD in Drug Addicted Prostitutes in Amsterdam: Potential for Heterosexual HIV Transmission." *Genitourinary Medicine* 65(3) (June 1989):146-50.

Finds antibody to HIV in 30% of 117 prostitutes, 82% of whom are intravenous drug users. Despite frequent condom use, 81% contract one or more STDs in the six-month period preceding the study. Concludes that given the high incidence of HIV and STD and other studies showing the presence of STD may facilitate the transmission of HIV, both clients and prostitutes are at high risk for HIV transmission.

1699. Van den Hoek, J.A., et al. "Prevalence and Risk Factors of HIV Infections among Drug Users and Drug-using Prostitutes in Amsterdam." *AIDS* 2(1) (February 1988):55-60.

Risk factors reported in this study of drug users and drug-using prostitutes include frequency of borrowing needles or syringes, date of first intravenous drug use, time living in Amsterdam and German nationality as well as an attack of herpes zoster in the previous 5 years.

1700. Viljoen, A.T. "Apartheid and AIDS." (Letter) *Lancet* 2(8674) (November 25, 1989):1280.

1701. Wallace, J.I., J. Downes, A. Ott, et al. "T-cell Ratios in New York City Prostitutes." (Letter) *Lancet* 1(8314-5) (January 1, 1983):58-9.

1702. Wallace, J.I. "T-cell Ratios: Sperm and Asialo GM1 Antibody Levels in New City Prostitutes." *Annals of the New York Academy of Sciences* 437 (1984):568-75.

Finds that promiscuous women are a lower risk for AIDS than promiscuous men and presents a multifactorial explanation. Recommends studies comparing risk of women who are promiscuous to women who practice rectal sex, and to women who are sexual partners of intravenous drug users.

1703. Yoshida, S., et al. "Prevalence of Hepatitis B Markers, Antibodies to Adult T Cell Leukemia/Lymphoma Virus and Antibodies to Human Immune Deficiency Virus in Prostitutes in Fukuoka, Japan." *Japanese Journal of Medical Science and Biology* 40(5-6) October-December 1987):171-4.

Indicates that no seropositive case for HIV infection was found among 237 prostitutes in a study conducted in the Kyushu district in 1986.

PORNOGRAPHY

1704. Boivin, S.P. *Soliciting for the Purpose of Prostitution: A Brief Presented Before the Special Committee on Pornography and Prostitution.* Ottawa: National Association of Women and the Law--Association nationale de la femme et la droit, 1984.

1705. Burgess, A.W., C.R. Harman, M.P. McCausland, and P. Powers. "Response Patterns of Children and Adolescents Exploited Through Sex Rings and Pornography." *American Journal of Psychiatry* 141(5) (1984):656-62.

A study of 66 children and adolescents exploited by adults through sex rings and pornography shows that three-fourths of the victims demonstrated patterns of negative psychological and social adjustments after rings were exposed. Identified four patterns of reponse: integration of the event, avoidance of the event, repetition of symptoms, and identification with the exploiter.

1706. Canada. Special Committee on Pornography and Prostitution. *Pornography and Prostitution in Canada: Report of the Special Committee on Pornography and Prostitution: Summary.* Ottawa, Ontario: Communications and Public Affairs, Department of Justice Canada, 1985.

1707. Casini, C. *Porno prostituzione: analisi dei rapporti tra stampa, pornografia e prostituzione.* Roma: La parola, 1981.

1708. El Komos, M. *Canadian Newspaper Coverage of Prostitution and Pornography, 1978-1983.* (Microform) Ottawa: Department of Justice Canada, Policy, Programs and Research Branch, Research and Statistics Section, 1984. Reproduction of original in the Rutgers University Library. Ann Arbor, MI: University Microforms International, 1986.

1709. *Ett Onödigt ont: en antologi mot porr och prostitution.* Edited by G. Fredelius. Stockholm: Ordfront, 1978.

1710. Hoddeson, B. *The Porn People: A First Person Documentary Report.* Photos by the author except whereas otherwise credited. Watertown, MA: American Pub. Corp, 1974.

1711. Huston, N. *Mosaïque de la pornographie: Marie Thérèse et les autres.* Paris: Denoël: Gonthier, 1982.

1712. Janus, M.D. "Youth Prostitution." *Child Pornography and Sex Rings.* Edited by A.W. Burgess. Lexington, MA: Lexington, 1984, pp. 127-46.

Describes various types of hustlers found in metropolitan Boston; gives their backgrounds and other information.

1713. Jayewardene, C.H.S, T.J. Julianai, and C.K. Talbot. *Prostitution and Pornography in Selected Countries.* (Microform) Ottawa: Department of Justice Canada, Policy, Programs, and Research Branch, Research and Statistics Section, 1984. Reproduction of original in the Rutgers University Library. Ann Arbor, MI: University Microfilms International, 1986.

1714. Kiedrowski, J., and S. Dijk. *Pornography and Prostitution in France, The Netherlands, West Germany, Denmark and Sweden.* (Working Papers on Pornography and Prostitution - Report N 1) Ottawa, Canada: Canada Department of Justice, 1984.

A working paper of Canada's Special Committee on Pornography and Prostitution, appointed to review Canada's criminal code in specific areas, by examining the European experience with pornography and prostitution. Information for the report was obtained through questionnaires completed by known authorities in each country on the various aspects of prostitution.

1715. Kutchinsky, B. *Experience with Pornography and Prostitution in Denmark.* Copenhagen: Kriminalistisk Institut, Københavns Universitet, 1985.

1716. McCormack, T. "Pornography and Prostitution in Canada. Report of the Special Committee on Pornography and Prostitution." *Atlantis* (Canada)

13(1) (1987):160-163.

Links pornography with patriarchy and inequality in Canada, instead of social pathology.

1717. Peat, Marwick, and Partners. *A National Population Study of Prostitution and Pornography*. (Microform) Ottawa: Department of Justice Canada, Policy, Programs, and Research Branch, Research and Statistics Section, 1984. Reproduction of the original in the Rutgers University Library. Ann Arbor, MI: University Microfilms International, 1986.

1718. *Pornography and Prostitution: Issues Paper: This is a Discussion Paper Prepared by the Special Committee on Pornography and Prostitution Appointed by the Minister of Justice for Canada.* Ottawa, Canada: Department of Justice, Communications and Public Affairs, 1983.

1719. Restif de La Bretonne. *Le pornographe, ou, idées d'un honnête homme: sur un projet de règlement pour les prostituées, propre à prevenir les malheurs qu'occasionne le publicisme des femmes.* Paris: Éditions d'Aujourd'hui, 1983.

Numerous editions in French and English.

1720. San Francisco Committee on Crime. *A Report on Non-Victim Crime in San Francisco: Part II: Sexual Conduct, Gambling, Pornography.* San Francisco: The Committee, 1971.

1721. Sansfacon, D. *Pornography and Prostitution in the United States.* (Microform) Ottawa: Department of Justice Canada, Policy, Programs and Research Branch, Research and Statistics Section, 1984. Reproduction of the original in the Rutgers University Library. Ann Arbor, MI: University Microfilms International, 1986.

1722. Sansfacon, D. *Prostitution in Canada: A Research Review Report.* (Microform) French title: La prostitution au Canada: Une synthèse des résultats de recherche. Reproduction of original in the Rutgers University Library. Ottawa: Department of Justice Canada, Policy Programs and Research Branch, Research and Statistics Section, 1985. Ann Arbor, MI:

University Microfilms International, 1987.

1723. Sansfacon, D. *United Nations Conventions, Agreements, and Resolutions on Prostitution and Pornography*. (Microform) Ottawa: Department of Justice Canada, Policy, Programs and Research Branch, Research and Statistics Section, 1984. Reproduction of original in the Rutgers University Library. Ann Arbor, MI: University Microfilms International, 1986.

1724. Saskatchewan. *Respecting Human Dignity*. Presentation by the Government of Saskatchewan to the Special Committee on Pornography and Prostitution, Regina, April 5, 1984. Regina, Saskatchewan: The Government, 1984.

1725. Schetky, D.H. "Child Pornography and Prostitution." *Child Sexual Abuse: A Handbook for Health Care and Legal Professionals*. Edited by D.H. Schetky, et al. New York: Brunner/Mazel, 1988, pp. 153-65.

1726. Silbert, M.H., and A.M. Pines. "Pornography and Sexual Abuse of Women." *Sex Roles* 10(11 & 12) (June 1984):857-68.

Interviews of 200 juvenile and adult, current and former female prostitutes, aged 10-46, indicated a "clear relationship" between violent pornography and sexual abuse.

1727. *Ta strid för kärleken: kamp mot porr och prostitution: en antologi*. Edited by J. Gentele. Stockholm: Ordfront, 1979.

1728. United States. Congress. House Committee on Education and Labor. Subcommittee on Select Education. *Teenage Prostitution and Child Pornography; Hearings Before the Subcommittee on Select Education of the Committee on Education and Labor, House of Representatives, Ninety-seventh Congress, Second Session, Hearings held in Pittsburgh, PA, April 23; and Washington, DC, June 24, 1982*. Washington, DC: United States Government Printing Office, 1982.

PSYCHOLOGY AND PSYCHIATRY

1729. Agassi, J. "Institutional Individualism." *British Journal of Sociology* 26(2) (June 1975):144-155.

Presents a philosophical discussion of several approaches, within the social science disciplines, to prostitution. Discusses the distinctions between "holism" and "individualism" and between "institutionalism" and "psychologism."

1730. Alvarez, V. "Políticas nacionales de juventud en América Latina. (National youth policies in Latin America)." *De Juventud Revista de Estudios e Investigaciónes* (9) (March 1983):53-71.

Outlines the United Nations' plan for the coordination of national youth policies in Latin America; including the establishment of a network of youth centers to help prevent juvenile delinquency, protect the mental and physical health of the young, and eliminate problems such as substance abuse and prostitution.

1731. Atwan, R. "Physiognomy, Photography, and Prostitution: Cesare Lombroso and the Female Offender." *Research Communications in Psychology, Psychiatry and Behavior* 9(4) (1984):353-364.

Describes attempts to use physiognomy scientifically, to determine the facial characteristics of criminals, including prostitutes by photography. Lombroso suggests that women show less deviation in physical appearance than do men engaged in crime.

1732. Berchat, M.I. "How Do Prostitutes See Themselves?" (French with English Abstract) *Revue Internationale de Criminologie et de Police Technique* 32(1) (January-March 1979):62-66.

Explores the numerous lifestyles of prostitutes and the attitudes of French prostitutes. Concludes that the prostitutes' work reflects the degradation of society, and that the negative effects are incompatible with human dignity, resulting in the endangerment of individual, family, and community well-being.

1733. Bourgeois, M., et al. "Incestuous Behavior and Psychopathology."
      Annales-Medico-Psychologiques 137(10) (December 1979):1008-1017.

      Proposes that information about the frequency of incestuous behavior and
      its implications for psychopathology be updated. Suggests that current
      sources provide biased samples; postulates that incest appears to be less
      influential on personality development than earlier supposed.

1734. Burgess, A.W., and A. Lazare. "The Prostitute." *Community Mental
      Health: Target Populations*. Edited by A.W. Burgess, and A. Lazare.
      Englewood Cliffs, NJ: Prentice-Hall, 1976, pp. 264-72.

      Discusses the clinical aspects of counseling prostitutes who have been
      victimized. Stresses the importance of listening for evidence of a crisis
      situation, encouraging dialogue, and providing emotional support.

1735. Caracushansky, S., and A. Giampeitro. "The Use of Myths and Fairy
      Tales in a Bernian Approach to Psychotherapy." *Transactional Analysis
      Journal* 17(1) (January 1987):277-285.

      Clinical case study of a nineteen-year-old female prostitute with suicidal
      tendencies and the use of myths and fairy tales in transactional analysis as
      a technique for script diagnosis. Illustrates diagnostic and therapeutic
      procedures.

1736. Corbett-Qualls N. *The Sacred Prostitute: Eternal Aspects of the Feminine*.
      Toronto: Inner City, 1988.

      Discusses the instinctive, erotic, and dynamic facet of feminine nature,
      with an emphasis on the positive aspects inherent in the archetypal image
      of the prostitute. Provides a Jungian perspective of the paradoxical nature
      of the sacred prostitute, as it relates to the Collective Unconscious and the
      promise of this conceptual framework for healing the split between
      sexuality and spirituality.

1737. De Schampheleire, D. "MMPI Characteristics of Professional Prostitutes
      --A Cross Cultural Replication." *Journal of Personality Assessment*

54(1-2) (1990):343-350.

Compares personality characteristics of 41 professional prostitutes in Belgium with 96 non-prostitute women using the Minnesota Multiphasic Personality Inventory (MMPI). The results show significant deviation on indicators of psychopathology for the prostitute group.

1738. Deusinger, I.M. "The Personality Structure of Delinquents." *Psychologische Beitrage* 15(3) (1973):408-418.

A comparative study between 20 females jailed for criminal offenses, such as prostitution or vagrancy, with 20 non-offenders, utilizing the Rosenzweig Picture Frustration Test and the Eysenck Maudsley Personality Questionnaire. There was significant variance between the two groups on both tests.

1739. Dezcallar, A., et al. "Aproximación a la delincuencia a través de un cuestionario de opinión. (Perceptions of delinquency using a questionnaire)." *Anuario de Sociología y Psicología Jurídicas* (9) (1982):45-91.

Postulates that higher levels of education and socio-economic status are associated with a more liberal attitude toward various forms of criminal sexual behavior. A questionnaire was distributed to a random sample of people, selected from a university directory. Results indicate that respondents from lower socio-economic backgrounds exhibit more rigidity in their attitudes toward "criminal" acts such as sexual misconduct, rape, homosexual behavior, exhibitionism, nudity, prostitution and abortion. Individuals from upper socio-economic backgrounds are more liberal in their attitudes.

1740. Diederich, N., A. Karenberg, et al. "Psychopathologische Bilder bei der HIV-Infektion: AIDS-Lethargie und AIDS-Demenz." (Psychopathological manifestations associated with the HIV infection: AIDS lethargy and AIDS dementia) *Fortschritte der Neurologie-Psychiatrie* 56(6) (June 1988):173-85.

Studies lethargy and dementia in patients with acquired immunodeficiency syndrome in deviant groups, including prostitutes, intravenous drug users, infants, and a hemophiliac.

1741. Durban, P. *La psychologie des prostituées*. Paris: Maloine, 1969.

1742. Eschenbach, U. "The Meaning of Consciousness Development for the Woman." *Analytische-Psychologie* 8(3) (1977):245-261.

Focuses on the contemporary woman's development of identity and advocates an archetypal model for self-development as a means for women to find their own creative possiblilities. Discusses the dangers of role models such as prostitutes.

1743. Exner, J. E., J. Wylie, A. Leura, et al. "Some Psychological Characteristics of Prostitutes." *Journal of Personality Assessment* 41(5) (October 1977):474-485.

Examines intra-occupational categories of prostitutes with demographically matched controls utilizing interviews, WAIS Vocabulary subtest, the MMPI, and the Rorschach. Concludes that street walkers appear to be less mature and more dependent than their control group counterparts and part time prostitutes yielded major indices of psychopathology.

1744. Foster, D. "A Treatment Approach for Women Escaping Prostitution." (Thesis) University of Wisconsin-Stout, 1989.

A study on the rehabilitative process of prostitutes, utilizing group psychotherapy methodology.

1745. Foster, H.H. "The Devil's Advocate." (Editorial) *Bulletin of the American Academy of Psychiatry and Law* 5(4) (1977):470-3.

1746. Gilman, S.L. "Freud and the Prostitute: Male Stereotypes of Female Sexuality in Fin-De-Siècle Vienna." *Journal of the American Academy of Psychoanalysis* 9(3) (July 1981):337-360.

Discusses the historical basis of Freud's theory of female sexuality, which stated that most women were capable of prostitution. Presents fictional and nonfictional accounts of young female prostitutes in Vienna.

1747. Glover, E. *The Psychpathology of Prostitution*. London: Institute for the

Study and Treatment of Delinquency, 1969.

Presents a psychopathologist's perspective on prostitution and the social sanction of a pathological condition. Provides suggestions for preventive measures including individual treatment and reform of the law.

1748. Goldman, E. "Prostitution Diversion Program: A Program Evaluation." (Ph.D. Thesis) California School of Professional Psychology, Los Angeles, 1978.

1749. Gonzalez, J.M. "Comportamiento sexual del universitario." (Sexual behavior of the university student). *Revista Latinoamericana de Psicología* 17(1) (1985):7-56.

A survey of sexual behavior, administered to 611 women and 486 men, in the young adult age group. It includes questions on masturbation, petting, sexual intercourse, homosexuality, prostitution, sexual relations with animals, sexually transmitted diseases, and use of contraceptives. A comparative analysis of the results was conducted using previous studies done in other countries.

1750. Greenwald, H. *The Call Girl: A Social and Psychoanalytic Study.* California: Libra, 1987.

Describes the emotional poverty of the high-class call girl and a lifestyle that perpetuates the self-contempt which predisposes individuals to this profession.

1751. James, J., and N.J. Davis. "Contingencies in Female Sexual Role Deviance: The Case of Prostituion." *Human Organization* 41(4) (Winter 1982):345-350.

Studies the role of contingencies in female sexual development which result in a devalued self, utilizing the frequency of 8 events in the lives of the two groups being compared. Suggests a series of unplanned events or contingencies may weaken conventional controls on behavior.

1752. James, J., and J. Meyerding. "Early Sexual Experience as a Factor in Prostitution." *Archives of Sexual Behavior* 7(10) (January 1978):31-42.

Compares the pattern of early sexual experience among prostitutes with nonprostitute women. Analysis of the data focuses on abusive sexual experiences such as incest and rape. Results indicate that an abusive sexual self-identity relates to the development of an adult female pattern of occupational deviance such as prostitution.

1753. Kestenberg, J.S.   "Der komplexe Charakter weiblicher Identität. Betrachtungen zum Entwicklungsverlauf." (The complex nature of female identity: Reflections on the course of its development). *Psyche Zeitschrift für Psychoanalyse und ihre Anwendungen* 42(4) (April 1988):349-364.

Traces the female psychosexual development, focusing on the maternal phase and the contradictory female personality traits, which cause the female to be perceived as goddess and whore.

1754. Klein, J.   "The Mother-Child Relationship in the Present-Day world." *Bulletin de Psychologie Scolaire et d'Orientation* 26(1) (Janurary 1977):25-29.

Suggests that the absence of rapport between a mother and child from 6 to 15 months of age may result in problems for the child such as apathy, loss of appetite, verbal and intellectual retardation, delinquency, prostitution, and maladaptation.

1755. Krevelen, D.A.   "Analysis of a Prostitute." *Acta Paedosychiatrica* 33(4) (April-May 1966):109-17.

Presents a case study of a nineteen-year-old prostitute's life and provides a psychodynamic explanation for her behavior.

1756. Laplante, J.   "The Sexual Offender: Its Constant Redefinition." *Vie médicale au Canada français* 6(2) (February 1977):211-227.

Discusses the psychopathology of the sexual offender, such as the prostitute; includes the development of laws based on the social milieu related to their activities.

1757. Maerov, A.S.   "Prostitution: A Survey and Review of 20 Cases." *Psychiatric Quarterly* 39(4) (October 1965):674-701.

Attempts to expose weaknesses inherent in the legalistic and moralistic handling of prostitutes, while proposing some psychological factors that might be utilized in dealing with the problem more effectively.

1758. Miksik, O. "On the Personality Profile of Women with Specific Manifestations in Sexual Behavior." *Ceskoslovenska-Psychologie* 20(6) (1976):495-513.

Hypothesizes that basic components of personality form the foundation for the development of certain types of sexual behavior. Data from the IHAVEZ Inventory indicate personality differences in the two groups studied.

1759. Nedoma, K., and I. Sipova. "Heterosexual Relations of Prostitutes." (Czechoslovakian with Russian and English Abstracts) *Ceskoslovenska-Psychiatrie* 68(1) (February 1972):23-26.

Investigates the nature and development of the heterosexual behavior of 100 women ordered hospitalized for diagnosis of venereal disease and suspected of prostitution. Results show that the two groups studied did not differ significantly in their motivation for prostitutional behavior.

1760. Newton, R.L., and M.M. Handelsman. "Jungian Feminine Psychology and Adolescent Prostitutes." *Adolescence* 21(84) (Winter 1986):815-25.

Explores Jungian feminine psychology and its application in the treatment of adolescent prostitutes, based on prior concepts formulated by Wolff (1956) and Leonard (1982).

1761. Offenkrantz W., A. Tobin, et al. "An Hypothesis About Heroin Addiction, Murder, Prostitution, and Suicide: Acting Out Parenting Conflicts." *International Journal of Psychoanalytic Psychotherapy* 79(7) (1978):602-8.

Examines unique characteristics of murderers, prostitutes, heroin addicts, and attempted suicides. Concludes that some aspects of their experiences of exploitation and deprivation with their own parents may have resulted in difficulty with their capacity for reciprocal tenderness and eventually led to a fear of perpetrating their own childhood experiences upon their children.

1762. Polenz, J.M. "New Therapy." (Letter) *American Journal of Psychiatry* 127(6) (December 1970):844.

1763. Pospiszyl, K. "Prostitution and Psychological Determinants of the Sexual Behavior of Women." (Polish with English Abstract) *Studia-Socjologiczne* 3(66) (1977):303-324.

Provides a review of various conceptual frameworks (i.e., those of Freud, Deutch, Eysenck, and Rosenblum) that relate a woman's psychosexual features to prostitution. Theorizes that women who become prostitutes do so because of an interaction between environmental conditions and a special personality type.

1764. Potterat J.J., L. Phillips, R.B. Rothenberg, et al. "On Becoming A Prostitute--An Exploratory Case-Comparison Study." *Journal of Sex Research* 21(3) (1985):329.

A comparative study of characteristics and experiences of female prostitutes who were interviewed in a venereal disease clinic in Colorado Springs. Results indicate three variables between the groups; birth order, educational attainment, and the characteristics of male sexual partners, although they cannot be viewed as major contributing factors because of the methodological flaws in the design of the study.

1765. Ross, S.D. "The Limits of Sexuality." *Philosophy and Social Criticism* 9 (Fall/Winter 1982):319-336.

Discusses the absence of limits of sexuality and prostitution.

1766. Rubin, T.I. *In the Life*. New York: Macmillan, 1961.

Presents the dialogue between a prostitute, named Jenny, and a newly appointed staff psychiatrist in a prison setting. She is serving a six-month sentence for prostitution. She is the daughter of a prostitute, has grown up in an urban area, and never known her father. Jenny's verbalizations and silences provide a vivid look at the realities of prostitution. A clinical case report.

1767. Rubinstein, R. "Female Prostitution: Relationship of Early Separation and

Sexual Experiences." (Ph.D. Dissertation) California School of Professional Psychology, Los Angeles, 1980.

This study attempts to determine whether or not there are significant differences in early separation and sexual experiences between prostitutes and nonprostitute women. Utilizes the attachment theory as a means of understanding the early separation experience. Two groups of matched subjects (32 prostitutes and 32 nonprostitute women) were adminstered the MMPI, the Early Sexual Behavior questionnaire and the Hansburg Separation Anxiety Test. Results indicate that the prostitutes had experienced more inaccessibility of an attachment figure and separation experiences than the comparison group. Results also indicate that the prostitute did experience sexual encounters earlier than the comparison group. The attachment process appears to be impaired in prostitutes.

1768. Saslavsky, L. *Psicoanálisis de una prostituta.* Buenos Aires: Falbo Librero Editor, 1966.

1769. Schmitt, L., G. Lefranc, et al. "De l'agressivité au suicide chez les sujets porteurs du virus de l'immuno-déficience humaine." (From aggressiveness to suicide in patients with serological evidence of HIV infection.) *Annales Medico Psychologiques* 146(3) (March 1988):237-240.

Presents four clinical cases of other and self-directed aggression, expressed by deliberate transmission of the acquired immunodeficiency syndrome (AIDS) to sex partners or to offspring and by suicide attempts. Two of the individuals involved in the study were female prostitutes.

1770. Scott, E.M. "Therapy with Female Offenders." *International Journal of Offender Therapy and Comparative Criminology* 21(3) (1977);208-220.

Describes therapy experiences with female offenders, including prostitutes, over a 10-year period. Includes major problem areas encountered in working with this group and suggests therapy approaches.

1771. Shoham, S.G., G. Rahav, R. Markovski, et al. "Family Variables and Stigma Among Prostitutes in Israel." *The Journal of Social Psychology* 120 (1983):57-62.

This study explores the relationship of deviant behavior, such as prostitution, to the development of a negative identity applied to a person by his (or her) social environment. Findings tend to confirm that prostitution is associated with negative images cast by the father, feelings of powerlessness, and social isolation.

1772. Shoham, S.G., et al. "Family, Stigma and Prostitution." (Hebrew) *Megamot* 28(1) (1983):74-82.

1773. Sipova, I., and K. Nedoma. "Family Setting and Childhood in Socially and Sexually Depraved Women." (Czechoslovakian with Russian and English Abstracts) *Ceskoslovenska-Psychiatrie* 68(3) (June 1972):150-153.

Reports of a study on the importance of family background and childhood experience in 100 prostitutes. Concludes that family milieu and childhood influences contribute significantly to the development of prostitutional behavior.

1774. Southwell M. "Counseling the Young Prison Prostitute." *Journal of Psychiatric Nursing* 19(5) (May 1981):25-6.

Examines prostitution in prison facilities.

1775. Spalt, L. "Sexual Behavior and Affective Disorders." *Diseases of the Nervous System* 36(12) (December 1975):644-647.

Three groups of patients diagnosed with affective disorders were studied to test the hypothesis that they are involved more frequently in prostitution and promiscuous behaviors. Results show that personal involvement in prostitution was not significantly different between the groups studied.

1776. Stoller, R.J. "Asthetik der Erotik." *Zeitschrift für Sexualforschung* 1(4) (December 1988):351-364.

Presents several case examples of erotic aberrations, such as prostitution; suggests that such aberrations are the result of aesthetic choices based on nuances.

1777. Tamura, M. "A Pattern Analysis of Delinquent Gangs: I. On the Traits of Members' Personality." *Reports of the National Research Institute of Police Science* 25(1) (July 1984):34-41.

Investigates the correlation between personality and type of delinquency involvement. Divides crime-related involvement into 10 delinquency categories, including female prostitution. Self-image destruction appears to be directly related to the degree of adaptation to school and the type of offense committed. Involvement in drug abuse and prostitution contributes to a marked deterioration in self-image, but violent offenses do not.

1778. Tastevin, H., and A. Horassius. "L'éthique psychiatrique face à un internement pour refus d'investigation médicale." (Psychiatric ethics in a case of institutionalization for refusal to submit to medical investigations). *Psychologie Médicale* 20(10) (October 1988):1497-1498.

This is a case study of a twenty-two-year-old bisexual male prostitute, confined to a psychiatric hospital after refusing further diagnostic or treatment measures related to a diagnosis of human immunodeficiency virus (HIV) infection. This case raises several ethical and medico-legal issues related to a possible diagnosis of acquired immunodeficiency syndrome (AIDS).

1779. Thorneloe, W., and E. Crews. "Manic Depressive Illness Concomitant with Antisocial Personality Disorder: Six Case Reports and Review of the Literature." *Journal of Clinical Psychiatry* 42(1) (January 1981):5-9.

Describes 6 cases of young adults (aged nineteen to twenty-nine) with manic depressive illness, manic type, who also meet research criteria for antisocial personality. One of the resultant clinical findings was an unusually high rate of homosexual prostitution among the group studied.

1780. Townes, B., B. James, and J. Martin. "Criminal Involvement of Female Offenders--Psychological Characteristics Among Four Groups." *Criminology* 18(4) (February 1981):471-480.

Investigates the relationship between psychological characteristics and type of criminal involvement, including prostitution and addiction. No differences between criminal activity characteristics and personality traits were found for any group.

1781. Uchiyama, A. "A Study on Juvenile Prostitution: I. The Attitude of Panders and Customers Toward Prostitution." *Reports of the National Research Institute of Police Science* 30(1) (July 1989):124-129.

Examines the attitudes of clients of prostitution toward the prostitute; based on interviews with prostitutes and customers following arrests. This article is Part I of a 2-part paper (1989).

1782. Uchiyama, A. "A Study on Juvenile Victims Sexually Abused: II. Social Background and Behavioral Characteristics of Victimized Girls by the Type of Victimization." *Reports of National Research Institute of Police Science* 30(2) (December 1989):151-164.

Studies the relationship of victimization to social background, personality, and behavioral characteristics; includes commercialized sex, such as prostitution, as a type of victimization.

RELIGION, PHILOSOPHY, AND MORALS

1783. Addams, J. *A Challenge to the Contemporary Church.* [S.l.: s.n.].
Reprint: The Survey. (Microform) New Haven, CT: Research
Publications, 1977.

1784. Annas, G.J. "The Prostitute, the Playboy, and the Poet: Rationing
Schemes for Organ Transplantation." *American Journal of Public Health*
75(2) (February 1985):187-9.

1785. Beck, H.G. *Byzantinisches Erotikon: Orthodoxie, Literatur, Gesellschaft.*
München: Verlag der Bayerischen Akademie der Wissenschaften: In
Kommission bei C.H. Beck, 1984.

1786. Benton, J.W. "Can Prostitutes Be Helped?" *Urban Miss* (November
1985).

1787. Bristow, E.J. "British Jewry and the Fight against the International White
Slavery Traffic, 1885-1914." *Immigrants and Minorities* 2(2) (1983):152-
70.

Describes the Jewish involvement in European-based international
prostitution and the efforts of the British Jewish community against it,
which resulted in the Jewish Association for the Protection of Girls and
Women.

1788. Bristow, E.J. "The German-Jewish Fight against White Slavery." *Leo
Baeck Inst. Year Book* 28 (1983):301-28.

During the period from 1880 to 1910 Jews were involved in white
slavery, both as procurers and victims, which served as additional
evidence of Jewish criminality for anti-Semites. Explores the German
effort to involve the Jewish community in combating white slavery.

1789. Bristow, E.J. *Prostitution and Prejudice: The Jewish Fight against White Slavery, 1880-1939.* Oxford: Clarendon, 1982; also New York: Schocken, 1983.

Examines all aspects of prostitution.

1790. Brunet, G. "L'hébreu Keleb (N'était pas 'Temple Paederast': C'était un 'éromène')." *Vet Test* (October 1985).

Discusses biblical citations 1 Sam 17:42; 1 Kngs 14:11; Isa 56:10; Ps 22:17, 2 Kngs 8:13; Judg 7:5-6.

1791. Chauvin, C. *Les chrétiens et la prostitution.* Paris: Éditions du Cerf, 1983.

1792. Couturier, G. "Rapports culturels et religieux entre Israël et Canaan d'après Osée 2, 4-25." *L'alterité, vivre ensemble differents: approches pluridisciplinaires: actes du Colloque pluridisciplinaire tenu à l'occasion du 75e anniversaire du Collège dominicain de philosophie et de théologie, Ottawa, 4,5,6 octobre 1984.* Edited by M. Gourgues and G.D. Mailhoit. Montréal: Bellarmin; à Paris: Cerf, 1986.

Discusses biblical citations Hos 2:4-25.

1793. Cox, D. "Justice and Philosophical Method as an Illustration." *J Soc Phil* 11 (March 1980):10-15.

1794. Deissler, A. "Die Interpretation von Hos 1,2-9 in den Hosea-Kommentaren von H.W. Wolff und W. Rudolph im Kritischen Vergleich." *Wort, Lied und Gottespruch.* Edited by J. Schreiner. [Würzburg]: Echter Verlag: Katholisches Bibelwerk, 1972.

1795. Dion, P.E. "Did Cultic Prostitution Fall into Oblivion during the Post-Exilic Era--Some Evidence from Chronicles and the Septuagint." *Catholic Biblical Quarterly* 43(1) (1981):41-8.

1796. Doerfler, B. "Gottes Liebessklaven (Children of God; photos)." *Die*

Himmlischen Verführer: Sekten in Deutschland. Edited by H. Nannen. Hamburg: Grüner und Jahr, 1979.

1797. Duff, F. *Baptism of Fire.* Edited by D. McAuliffe. Bombay: St. Paul, 1961.

1798. Ericsson, L.O. "Charges against Prostitution: An Attempt at a Philosophical Assessment." *Ethics* 90(3) (April 1980):335-66.

Assesses the view of prostitution as an undesirable social phenomenon that should be eradicated. Finds that the charges against prostitution (also discussed in the article) do not incriminate prostitution but instead incriminate the hostile attitudes toward promiscuity and prostitution. Argues that prostitution should be reformed, not eradicated. Elicited a number of comments which are listed in the section on feminism.

1799. Fagundes, A.A. *As santas-prostitutas: um estudo de devoção popular no RS.* Porto Alegre, RS, Brasil: Martins Livreiro, 1987.

1800. Flannery, M. "Ex Nun Now Decoy Hooker." *Criminal Justice Digest* 4(9) (Sept. 1976):7-9.

1801. Gartner, L.P. "Anglo-Jewry and the Jewish International Traffic in Prostitution." *AJS Review* 78 (1982-3):129-78.

Examines white slavery trafficking and the role of young independent Jewish women in East Europe as unwilling victims between 1881 and 1914. Discusses the efforts of the Anglo-Jewish and international Jewish communities against this trafficking.

1802. Godden, J. "Sectarianism and Purity within the Woman's Sphere: Sydney Refuges during Late Nineteenth Century." *Journal of Religious History* 14(3) (1987):291-306.

Explores Protestant and Catholic refuges for reformed prostitutes in Sydney 1870-90 to establish the "social consensus." Finds that women assumed much of the administrative responsibility for the facilities. Describes these women as strict disciplinarians as well as role models of ideal womanhood for the reformed prostitutes. Finds that in these refuges, the attitude toward prostitution was one that emphasized redemption.

1803. Goldern, J. "Immanent Grace" (A Methodist Seminarian Encounters a Prostitute). *Other Side* (June 1985).

1804. Golod, S.I. "Prostitution in the Context of the Sex Morals Changes." (Russian) *Sotsiologicheskie Issledovaniya* (3) (1988):65-70.

1805. Goren, A.A. "Mother Rosie Hertz, The Social Evil, and the New York Kehillah." *Michael on the History of the Jews in the Diaspora*, v.3. Edited by L.P. Gartner. Tel-Aviv: Diaspora Research Institute, 1975, pp. 188-210.

Discusses the Jewish community anti-crime campaign launched in New York City in 1910, which included the establishment of the Bureau of Social Morals to gather evidence.

1806. Gruber, M.I. "Hebrew Qedesah and Her Canaanite and Akkadian Cognates." *Ugarit-Forschungen*. Edited by K. Bergerhof, M. Dietrich, et al. Kevelaer: Verlag Butzon & Bercker, 19??.

Discusses biblical citations Gen 38:21, 22; Deut 23:18; Hos 4:14.

1807. Hayman, A. "Prostitution in the Pulpit (Sex Crimes Addressed in Sermons)." *J Preachers* (1986).

1808. Isou, I. *Histoire philosophique illustrée de la volupté à Paris*. Alger, Société de publications et éditions; distributor: Book Mart, Los Angeles, 1960. (Microform) New York: New York Public Library, 197-.

1809. Johnson, E.C. *In Search of God in the Sexual Underworld: A Mystical Journey*. New York: Morrow, 1983.

1810. Kapelrud, A.S. "Amos og Hans Omgivelser: Opposisjonsinnlegs ved Hans M. Barstads Doktordisputas." *Norsk Teologisk Tidsskrift 84(3)*

(1983):157-166.

1811. La Tourette, A. "Esprit de corps." *Sex and God: Some Varieties of Women's Religious Experience*. Edited by L. Hurcombe. New York: Routledge & Kegan Paul, 1987.

1812. Leab, D.J. "Women and the Mann Act." *Amerikastudien/American Studies* 21(1) (1976):55-65.

Explores the growing hysteria regarding white slavery during the Progressive Era. Finds this movement ignored economic causes for prostitution focusing instead on finding scapegoats.

1813. Leonard, C., and I. Wallimann. "Prostitution and Changing Morality in the Frontier Cattle Towns of Kansas." *Kansas History* 2(1) (Spring 1979):34-54.

Discusses the changes in attitude toward prostitution in cattle towns as they grew. Considers demographic composition and economic activity in determining causal factors.

1814. Metzger, D. "Re-vamping the World (The Holy Prostitute, Feminism; Photo)." *Anima* (Spring 1986).

1815. Mirelmann, V.A. "The Jewish Community Versus Crime: The Case of White Slavery in Buenos Aires." *Jewish Social Studies* 46(2) (1984):145-68.

Traces the ultimately successful efforts of the Jewish community to combat white slavery in Buenos Aires. This group defeated the Zwi Migdal, the association of white slave traders, in the 1930s.

1816. Nadeau, J.-G. *La prostitution, une affaire de sens: étude de practiques sociales et pastorales*. Montréal: Fides, 1987.

1817. Oraison, M. *La prostitution...et alors?* Paris: Seuil, 1979.

1818. Pequignot-Desprats, C. "Une Figure Obscène: Baubo. (An Obscene Figure: Baubo)." *Psychologie Médicale* 19(8) (June 1987):1393-1398.

Explores female sexuality, through the symbolism of the obscene goddess, Baubo. Includes the conceptualization of the female as whore.

1819. Phipps, W.E. "Masturbation: Vice or Virtue?" *Journal of Religion and Health* 16(3) (July 1977):183-95.

Discusses the pros and cons of masturbation from a philosophical perspective.

1820. Pilosu, M. *La donna, la lussuria e la Chiesa nel medioevo.* Genova: Edizioni culturali internazionali Genova, 1989.

1821. Presbyterian Church (USA), General Assembly. *Violations against the Image of God: Report of the Focus Group on Sexual Exploitation of Women, the Committee on Women's Concerns, Council on Women and the Church of the Presbyterian Church (USA) to the 198th General Assembly, 1986.* New York: Office of the General Assembly, 1986.

1822. *Prostituição: desafio à sociedade e à Igreja.* São Paulo: Ediçoes Paulinas, 1976.

1823. Roekaerts, M. and K. Savat. "Mass Tourism in South and Southeast Asia: A Challenge to Christians and the Churches." *Pro Mundi Vita* Asia--Australasia Dossier (1983).

1824. Rohner, T.H. *Prostituição e libertação da mulher: pastoral da mulher marginalizada: subsídios para a formação de agentes.* Petrópolis: Vozes, 1987.

1825. Rose, D.W. "The Committee of One Hundred." *Upper Ohio Valley Historical Review* 15(1) (1985):2-11.

Describes the anti-prostitution campaign in Wheeling, West Virginia during the early twentieth century which was led by a religious citizens' group.

1826. Schottroff, L. "Die grosse Liebende und der Pharisäer Simon." *Verdrängte Vergangenheit, die uns bedrängt: feministische Theologie in der Verantwortung für die Geschichte.* Edited by L. Siegele-Wenschkewitz. München: Kaiser, 1988.

Discusses biblical citations LK 7:36-50.

1827. Schram, P.L. "Wichern und Heldring in Beziehung zum Pietismus." *Pietismus und Reveil.* Hrsg. von J. van den Berg und J.P. van Dooren. Leiden: E.J. Brill, 1978.

1828. Setel, T. "Prophets and Pornography: Female Sexual Imagery in Hosea." *Feminist Interpretation of the Bible.* Edited by L.M. Russell. Philadelphia: Westminster, 1985.

Discusses biblical citations Hos 1:2; 2; 9:12-14.

1829. Sexton, R., O. Maddock, and C. Richard. "The Prostitutes' Syndrome." *Journal of Religion and Health* 19(3) (Fall 1980):226-230.

Indicates that promiscuous sexual behavior may result in guilt, which will often be exhibited clinically as Depressive Neuroses or Psychosomatic Illness. Includes case histories and implications for treatment.

1830. Shrage, L.I. "Should Feminists Oppose Prostitution?" *Ethics* 99 (January 1989):347-61.

Considers the organization of the sex industry based on culturally ingrained beliefs about gender and sexuality. Focuses on what can be done to change these beliefs that legitimize the commercial sex industry.

1831. Stahl, A. "Prostitution among Jews as a Symptom of Cultural Transition." (Hebrew) *Megamot* 24(2) (1978):202-225.

1832. Stone, L.A. *The Story of Phallicism; With Other Essays on Related Subjects by Eminent Authorities.* New York: AMS, 1976.

Reprint of 1927 edition.

1833. Takasato, S. "Eine strukturelle Invasion in Asien; zur Frage der Touristenprostitution." (German) Translated by R. Hetcamp. *Brennpunkte in Kirche und Theologie Japans: Beitrage und Dokumente.* Edited by Y. Terazono, et al. Neukirchen-Vluyn: Neukirchener Verlag, 1988.

1834. Van De Veer, D. "Death, Sex, Odysseus and the Sirens." *Paternalistic Intervention: The Moral Bounds on Benevolence.* Princeton, NJ: Princeton University Press, 1986, pp. 224-310.

1835. Ward, R.B. "Porneia and Paul." *Proceedings, Eastern Great Lakes and Midwest Biblical Society, v.6.* Edited by P. Redditt. [Grand Rapids, Mich.]: The Society, [1986?].

Discusses biblical citations 1 Cor 6:12-20; 7:2; 10:20-1.

1836. Weatherford, J. M. *Porn Row.* New York: Arbor House, 1986.

1837. Wicclair, M.R. "Is Prostitution Morally Wrong." *Phil Res Arch* 7 (1981):1429.

Argues that the conviction that prostitution is morally wrong is not obvious.

1838. Wilcox, K.W. "Can Prostitutes Be Christians?" *Engage/Soc Act* (May 1975).

1839. Wright, D.F. "Homosexuals or Prostitutes--The Meaning of Arsenokoitai (1 Corinthians 6, 9; 1 Timothy 1, 10)." *Vigiliae Christianae* 38(2) (1984):125-53.

SOCIOLOGY

1840. Ackelson, J.J. *Sex for Sale, Improve Your Health: Advertisement of Prostitution Services.* (Association Paper) North Central Sociological Association, Ohio State University, Columbus, Ohio, 1977.

Investigates the extent to which prostitutes advertise their services to the public. Describes development and communication patterns of several types of prostitute organizations, including call-girl operations and massage parlors. Determines means of advertisement, terminology used in soliciting, range of services being offered, and precautionary measures taken in behalf of the prostitutes.

1841. Adler, F., and R.J. Simon. *The Criminology of Deviant Women.* Boston: Houghton Mifflin, 1979.

This collection of essays on women in crime, including several on prostitution, is intended for use in courses in sociology, psychology, criminology, and criminal justice as well as in the area of women's studies.

1842. Antebi, E. and A. Florentin. *Les filles de Madame Claude: un empire qui ne tient qu'à un fil.* (French) Paris: Julliard, 1975.

1843. Armstrong, E.G. "Massage Parlors and Their Customers." *Archives of Sexual Behavior* 7(2) (March 1978):117-125.

Examines massage parlors objectively, from the perspective that not all are institutions of prostitution. Suggests that the motivation for patronizing massage parlors is not solely sexual satisfaction as previously believed.

1844. Armstrong, E.G. "The Sociology of Prostitution." *Sociological Spectrum* 1(1) (January-March 1981):91-102.

Concentrates on the sociological definition and different aspects of prostitution. Concludes that there is no basis for a distinction between

311

conventional behavior and prostitution.

1845. Atkinson, M., and J. Boles. "Prostitution as an Ecology of Confidence Games--The Scripted Behavior of Prostitutes and Vice Officers." *Sexual Deviancy in Social Context* by Clifton D. Bryant. New York: Franklin Watts/New Viewpoints, 1977, pp. 219-234.

Describes the interaction between prostitutes and vice officers as one of mutual goal attainment and minimum interference. Interactions between prostitutes, clients, vice officers, and the general public are analyzed as successful confidence games.

1846. Bell, R.R. *Social Deviance--A Substantive Analysis*. Rev. Ed. Chicago, IL: Dorsey, 1976.

Explores sexual deviancy, including prostitution, following the social-deviance approach, a combination of the scientific approach and the traditional social-problems approach. Develops the concept of subcultures to aid in the discussion of each deviance.

1847. Belorgey, J.M. "Problems of the Family and Sexuality: The Evolution of the Attitude of Government." *Évolution Psychiatrique* 40(3) (July-September 1975):501-512.

A review of laws and public attitudes which affect sexuality, focusing on laws specific to divorce, contraception, prostitution, abortion and concubinage.

1848. Bowers, T.D. *Urban Problems - Prostitution - Blacks, Urbanization and Crime*. Rockville, MD: National Institute of Justice/National Criminal Justice Reference Service Microfiche Program, 1981. Microfiche.

Discusses in the first section the patterns, criminology, and psychology of prostitution. Includes analysis of political, social, and psychological influences, the difficulty in rationalizing the criminality of prostitutes, and demographic patterns.

1849. Boyer, D., and J. James. "Prostitutes as Victims." *Deviants--Victims or Victimizers*. Edited by Donal E.J. MacNamara and Andrew Karmen.

Beverly Hills, CA: SAGE, 1983, pp. 109-46.

Discusses the victimization of prostitutes by their past, their position in the social structure, their lifestyle. Maintains that catagorizing prostitutes as offenders is an injustice and serves only to promote inequities between males and females. Suggests decriminalization of prostitution, licensing, and mandatory health care as means of dealing with this situation.

1850. Bridge, R.G. *Methodological Issues in Self-Disclosure Research: 'Would You Like Being a Prostitute: Why or Why Not?"* Paper presented at the Western Psychological Association Meeting, April 12, 1973, Anaheim, California.

Catagorizes and identifies problems in the methodological approaches in self-disclosure research. Identifies six factors frequently ignored in research.

1851. Bryan, J.H. "Apprenticeships in Prostitution." *Social Problems* 12(3) (Winter 1965):287-97.

Based on a study of 33 prostitutes in the Los Angeles area, provides information concerning induction and training into the call girl occupation. Argues that personal contact either with another prostitute or a pimp gives entrance into the profession and that the primary intent of apprenticeship is to develop an adequate clientele.

1852. Bryan, J.H. "Occupational Ideologies and Individual Attitudes of Call Girls." *Social Problems* 13(4) (Spring 1966):441-450.

Examines the ideological position of the professional prostitute and its impact upon the individual practitioner. Finds that most prostitutes believe that their occupation serves important social and psychotherapeutic functions, that the customer can and should be exploited, and that the role of the prostitute is no more immoral than the role of the "square."

1853. Bryant, C.D., and C.E. Palmer. "Massage Parlors and 'Hand Whores' Some Sociological Observations." *Journal of Sex Research* 11(3) (August 1975):227-241.

Looks at massage parlors as institutions which often offer sexual gratification in addition to relaxation and physical therapy. After studying massage parlors in one area, concludes that there are several norms which are then discussed in some detail including client and masseuse characteristics, possible motivating factors, and attitudes toward labeling.

1854. Bushnell, K.C. *Take Warning!* (Microform) New Haven, CT: Research Publications, 1977. (1 microfilm reel, 35 mm.)

1855. Carmen, A., and H. Moody. *Working Women: the Subterranean World of Street Prostitution.* New York: Harper & Row, 1985.

Records experiences, observations, and attitudes of prostitutes based on eight years of work with prostitutes in New York. Raises the concepts of humanity, individuality and women's rights as major issues to be considered in the discussion of prostitution. Argues that prostitution is just another trade and that most of prostitutes freely choose the profession.

1856. Carmichael, K. "New Directions in Social Policy .6. A City and Its Prostitutes." *New Society* 59(1000) (1982):53-5.

Based on a study in Glasgow, discusses prostitution, including the prostitutes themselves, their clients, logistics and motivating factors. Argues that prostitutes must be accepted by society as people and individuals. Questions the illegality of prostitution and supports demystifying and civilizing the practice.

1857. Chang, D.M., and C.M. Janeksela. "The Subjective Factor in the Perception of Social Problems." *International Journal of Offender Therapy and Comparative Criminology* 21(1) (1977):66-78.

Surveys various social groups to determine what they consider the top ten social problems in America. Interviews college students in criminology related courses, police officers, prison inmates, and security guards. Finds that prostitution is not considered a serious social problem and that there are similarities between the choices of police officers and security guards and between the choices of students and inmates.

1858. Cole, W.E., and C.H. Miller. *Social Problems: A Sociological Interpretation.* New York: David McKay, 1965.

Relevant chapter provides a broad definition of prostitution and examines its social patterns in various contries. Focuses on possible causes and addresses the problems of prevention and rehabilitation.

1859. Davidson, J. *The Stroll: Inner City Subcultures/John Davidson as Told to Laird Stevens.* Toronto: MC Press, 1986.

1860. Defreitas, R.S. "Prostitutes, Madams, and Cops--The Dialectics of Opposed Orders." (Portuguese) *Dados-Revista de Ciencias Socialis* 27(2) (1984):199-214.

1861. Desai, M., and M. Apte. "Status of Prostitutes and Deprivation of Family Care Among Their Children." *Indian Journal of Social Work* 48(2) (1987):171-80.

Presents the findings of a study on the deprivation of family care among children of prostitutes using health services. Recommends a variety of preventative and rehabilitative programs for prostitutes and potential prostitutes. Calls for programs to bolster the physical and emotional condition of their children.

1862. *Deviants--Voluntary Actors in a Hostile World.* Morristown, NJ: General Learning, 1977.

Deals with prostitutes, pimps, and clients. Prostitution is here treated as a voluntary deviancy and the responsibility for deviance is carefully considered.

1863. Dorais, M. "The Politics of Sexual Marginalization or Deviant Identity: The Case of Male Homosexuality and Female Prostitution." *The Social Worker / Le Travailleur Social* 56(2) (Summer 1988):54-9.

Observes that prostitution, in spite of so-called modern liberal attitudes, is still stigmatized by traditional values. This maintenance of the sexual deviant label in turn legitimizes violence against prostitutes. Offers suggestions for countering this sexual modernization.

1864. Earls, C.M., and H. David. "Male and Female Prostitution: A Review."

Annals of Sex Research 2(1) (1989):5-28.

Focuses on the psychosocial characteristics of prostitutes. Identifies variables that differentiate between prostitutes and nonprostitutes, making a distinction between adult and juvenile prostitution. Discusses motivating factors and proposes classification systems of prostitutes.

1865. Ebaugh, H., and R. Fuchs. *Becoming an Ex: The Process of Role Exit.* Chicago, IL: University of Chicago Press, 1988.

Looks at role changes in deviants, including prostitutes, to establish a common pattern and identify specific stages in the process.

1866. Eltzroth, M. "Vocational Counseling for Ghetto Women with Prostitution and Domestic Service Backgrounds." *Vocational Guidance Quarterly* 22(1) (1973):32-28.

Examines two groups of black women over age twenty-five, twenty former prostitutes and twenty domestics, entering vocational training in 1971. Only four from the first group completed the program while all of the second group were successful. Includes characteristic studies of each group, counseling problems, and suggestions for improving the success ratio.

1867. *Female Sexual Slavery and Economic Exploitation: Making Local and Global Connections.* Report of a Consultation Organized by the Non-Governmental Liaison Service (New York) San Francisco, California, October 25, 1984. (1985).

1868. Foltz, T.G. "Escort Services: An Emerging Middle Class Sex-for-Money Scene." *California Sociologist* 2(2) (Summer 1979):105-133.

Explores the process of becoming a prostitute, motivating factors, types of prostitution, organization of escort services, and service transactions. Finds that women engaged in prostitution through escort services interviewed in one town had previously maintained nondeviant occupations.

1869. Forsyth, C.J., and L. Fournet. "A Typology of Office Harlots:

Mistresses, Party Girls, and Career Climbers." *Deviant Behavior* (84) (1987):319-328.

Discusses women who use sex to climb the corporate ladder and attain higher positions in their organization. Develops a typology of office sex and relates this type of activity to prostitution.

1870. "French Nun Advises Saigon on Aiding Prostitutes." *Victimology: An International Journal* 1(4) (Winter 1976):614-5.

Reports on the request of the Communist Vietnamese government for the assistance of a Roman Catholic nun in dealing with the problem of prostitution of Vietnam. Finds that, according to this nun, Vietnamese prostitutes are generally peasant women who were forced into prostitution by the economics of war. Compares these prostitutes with those in Paris and finds the Vietnamese prostitutes "typical" not "exceptions." Fails to provide input on how to deal with the continuing problem.

1871. Geyer-Kordesch, J., and A. Kuhn. *Frauenkörper, Medizin, Sexualität: auf dem Wege zu einer neuen Sexualmoral.* (German) Düsseldorf: Schwann, 1986.

1872. Girtler, R. "Die Prosituierte und ihre Kunden." (The prostitute and her clients). *Kölner Zeitschrift für Soziologie und Sozialpsychologie* 36(2) (June 1984):323-341.

Studies client types of prostitutes in Vienna, using interviews with prostitutes and procurers. Discusses the various reasons that clients contact prostitutes, and the methods prostitutes use to distance themselves personally or internally from their clients.

1873. Goldstein, P.J. "Occupational Mobility in the World of Prostitution: Becoming a Madam." *Deviant Behavior* 4(3-4) (April-September, 1983):267-279.

Suggests that prostitution is more of an occupation than a social problem and argues that prostitution offers the same mobility as more "legitimate" occupations.

1874. Goode, E. *Deviant Behavior--An Interactionist Approach.* NJ: Prentice Hall, 1978.

Explores deviant behaviors in terms of formative processes and the resulting interaction with the normative attitudes and laws established by dominant social groups.

1875. *Hard Work.* (Film)   Durrin Productions, Inc., Washington, DC. Northbrook, Illinois: MTI, 1977.

Advocates the nationwide decriminalization, as opposed to legalization, of prostitution. This film was taken at COYOTE convention, an organization of prostitutes meeting in Washington, D.C., which attracted prostitutes and feminists from all over the country. The pros of decriminalization and the cons of the current illegal status are discussed.

1876. Hawkesworth, M.E.   "Brothels and Betrayal--On the Functions of Prostitution." *International Journal of Womens Studies* 7(1) (1984):81-91.

Presents a feminist analysis of prostitution. Argues that the exploration of the consequences of prostitution on the individual prostitute indicates skepticism about the concept of prostitution as serving a social function.

1877. Heyl, B.S.   "The Madam as Teacher: the Training of House Prostitutes." *Social Problems* 24(5) (June 1977):545-55.

Discusses the role of the madam and the social organization of house prostitution. Includes description of the training procedures and techniques, as well as hustling in general and the values of the world of prostitution.

1878. Heyl, B.S.   "Prostitution--An Extreme Case of Sex Stratification." *The Criminology of Deviant Women.* Edited by F. Adler and R.J. Simon. Boston, MA: Houghton Mifflin, 1979, pp. 196-210.

Explores male domination and social stratification in prostitution. Pimps, police, landlords, politicians, even bell-hops and taxi drivers have power over or in some way benefit from prostitution. Reveals prostitution as an extreme case of sexual stratification, especially at the lower levels. Finds that the economic background of the prostitute often determines which level of prostitute she will become.

1879. Hicks, B. "The Future of Prostitution in Our Society." (Thesis) California State University, Long Beach, 1980. Ann Arbor, MI: University Microfilms International, 1983. Microfilm.

1880. Hirschi, T. "The Professional Prostitute." *Berkeley Journal of Sociology* 7(1) (Spring 1962):33-50.

Views the life of a professional prostitute from an occupational perspective. Focuses on various aspects of the profession, including necessary skills, social relations inside and outside the profession, and measures job satisfaction and occupational ideology.

1881. Hoffman, D.E., and C.E. Marshall. *The Unionization of Prostitutes: Tertiary Deviation or Cognitive Liberation?* (Association Paper) Omaha: Society for the Study of Social Problems, University of Nebraska, 1981.

Explores the social history of the unionization of prostitutes as well as the increasing trend in prostitute activism. Links these developments to general economic forces, the particular working conditions of prostitutes, and the rise of the feminist and labor movements.

1882. Ingle, J.L. *The Streetwalker Turned CB Talker.* (Association Paper) Edmond, OK: Society for the Study of Social Problems, Central State University, 1980.

Examines female prostitution solicited by CB radio and transacted at interstate rest areas. Focuses on prostitutes and trucker clientele, sex transactions, and both trucker and prostitute perceived safeguards.

1883. International Abolitionist Foundation. *Society and Prostitution Today: Rome Congress, May 6-10, 1966.* Geneva, 1967.

1884. Jackman, N.R., R. O'Toole, and G. Geis. "The Self-Image of the Prostitute." *The Sociological Quarterly* 4(2) (Spring 1963):150-61.

Preliminary study on the self-respect of prostitutes. Based on interviews with 15 prostitutes finds that isolated individuals more readily accept patterns of behavior condemned by general social values, that violation of these values must be rationalized, and that other values such as financial success are exaggerated in the process.

1885. James, J., and N.J. Davis.   "Contingencies in Female Sexual Role
       Deviance: The Case of Prostitution."   *Human Organization* 41(4)
       (1982):345-50.

       Reports the results of a study which explores the association between adult
       female prostitution and juvenile experiences, especially home life, sexual
       experience and criminal involvement.

1886. James, J.   "Motivations for Entrance into Prostitution."   *Female Offender*
       by L. Crites. Lexington, MA: DC Health, 1976.

       Argues that motivations for becoming a prostitute parallel motivations for
       joining other "legitimate" occupations. The motivating factors discussed
       here include conscious factors, situational factors, and psychoanalytical
       factors. Based on the findings of this study, the article supports the
       decriminalization of prostitution.

1887. James, J., N.J. Davis, and P. Vitaliano.   "Female Sexual Deviance: A
       Theoretical and Empirical Analysis."   *Deviant Behavior* 3(2) (January-
       March 1982):175-95.

       Examines early sexual experiences and influential factors that shape later
       sexually deviant behavior, including prostitution.

1888. James, J., and P. Vitaliano.   "Modeling the Drift Towards Sex Role
       Deviance."   University of Washington Department of Psychiatry and
       Behavioral Sciences, Seattle, Washington. US Department of Health,
       Education and Welfare National Institute on Drug Abuse.   Arlington,
       Virginia:Eric Document Reproduction Service, 1978. (Microfiche)

       Suggests there is a correlation between deviant life experiences and
       prostitution. The experiences discussed include early home life, sexual and
       pregnancy history, and criminal involvement. Develops three models to
       aid in the understanding of the development of a deviant sexual identity
       and consequent commitment to prostitution.

1889. James, L.   "On the Game."   *New Society* 24(555) (May 24, 1973):426-9.

       Interviews prostitutes about their backgrounds, life-styles and value
       systems. Presents a more favorable picture of prostitution than is generally

accepted but admits the survey is not a representative sample.

1890. Jeffers, H.P., and D. Levitan. *Sex in the Executive Suite.* Chicago: Playboy, 1972.

Attempts to cover the whole spectrum of American business and to determine what impact sex has on it. Based on personal interviews, the authors examine the motives, needs, and objectives of the people involved. Concludes that sex is as important to the way Americans do business as the computer, the telephone, and the assembly line.

1891. Khalaf, S. "Correlates of Prostitution, A Comparative View on Some Popular Errors and Misconceptions." *Sociologia Internationalis* 5(1) (1967):110-122.

Explores popular errors and false assumptions regarding prostitution, including common personality traits of prostitutes, socio-economic conditions associated with the profession, and the social-professional life of the licensed prostitute.

1892. Kiyonaga, K., S. Tsukimura, et al. "A Study on Juvenile Prostitution: I. The Attitude of Juvenile Prostitutes toward their Behavior." *Reports of National Research Institute of Police Science* 30(1) (July 1989):124-129.

Studies the demographic characteristics, educational level, family relationships, past history of juvenile delinquency, and involvement in prostitution of 92 female Japanese adolescents. This article is Part I of a 2-part paper to determine preventative measures that might be effectively implemented.

1893. Klein, L., and J.L. Ingle. "Sex Solicitation by Short Wave Radio." *Free Inquiry in Creative Sociology* 9(1) (May 1981):61-63, 68.

Describes a recent development in prostitution--the use of a Citizens' Band radio in soliciting clients. Analyzes data compiled over a two year period including transactions initiated using CB radio.

1894. Leonard, T.L., M. Freund, and J.J. Platt. "Behavior of Clients of Prostitution." (Letter) *American Journal of Public Health* 79(7) (July

1989):903.

1895. Liss, M. "Prostitution in Perspective: a Comparison of Prostitutes and Other Working Women." (Thesis) Northern Illinois University, DeKalb, 1981. Ann Arbor, MI: University Microfilms International, 1983. Microfilm.

1896. Luxenburg, J., and L. Klein. "CB Radio Prostitution: Technology and the Displacement of Deviance." *Journal of Offender Counseling, Services and Rehabilitation* 9(1-2) (Fall-Winter 1984):71-87.

Discusses prostitution solicited using a Citizens' Band radio. Relates this type of prostitution to the wagon yard prostitution of the nineteenth century and establishes the similarities and differences between CB prostitution and more conventional types of prostitution. Differences emphasize communicative abilities. Also addresses the role of the CB pimp and interstate rest areas as sites for transactions.

1897. Maffesoli, M. "Prostitution as a Form of Sociality." (French) *Cahiers Internationaux de Sociologie* 76 (January 1984):119-33.

1898. Merry, S.E. "Manipulating Anonymity: Streetwalkers' Strategies for Safety in the City." *Ethnos* 45(3-4) (1980):157-75.

Argues that prostitutes are able to exercise social control over their pimps and clientele and therefore do not live in fear. Suggests that cities are not as dangerous as they appear if proper strategies for control are adopted.

1899. Miller, G. *Odd Jobs: The World of Deviant Work.* Englewood Cliffs, NJ: Prentice Hall, 1978.

1900. *Nice Girls Aren't Naughty--Papers from a Conference on Female Deviance.* Colchester, England: University of Essex, 1979.

The relavent paper addresses the existing parallels to Victorian attitudes in the conflicting views of prostitution and modern sexuality and in the differences between promiscuity and prostitution.

1901. *The Participants in Prostitution. Proceedings of the 22nd International Congress of the International Abolitionist Federation, held in Athens, Greece, September 9-12, 1964.* Geneva: International Abolitionist Federation, 1964.

1902. Pomeroy, W.B. "Some Aspects of Prostitution." *Journal of Sex Research* 1(3) (December 1965):177-87.

Provides a preliminary report on a study of 175 white prostitutes. Concludes that prostitutes are more sexually responsive with their customers than previously believed. Also notes motives for entering prostitution and measures degrees of professional satisfaction among prostitutes.

1903. *Prostitution Styles.* (Audiocassette) National Public Radio, 1983.

Explores the class and caste structure of prostitutes and pimps.

1904. Prus, R.C., and S. Vassilakopoulos. "Desk Clerks and Hookers: Hustling in a 'Shady' Hotel." *Urban Life* 8(1) (April 1979):52-71.

Discusses prostitution in the hotel community, in particular the relationship between desk clerks and prostitutes. The mutual support systems that develop are considered important in the study of deviant behavior.

1905. Prus, R.C., and S. Irini. *Hookers, Rounders, and Desk Clerks: the Social Organization of the Hotel Community.* Toronto: Gage, 1980.

Defines the "hotel community" and discusses prostitution as a central activity in this community. Describes all aspects of the process, from making "dates" to dealing with clients, pimps, families, and other men. Attempts to promote a greater understanding of "working girls."

1906. Rasmussen, P.K. "Massage Parlors: Sex for Money." (Dissertation) San Diego: University of California, 1979.

1907. Rasmussen, P.K., and L.L. Kuhn. "The New Masseuse: Play for Pay."

Urban Life 5(3) (October 1976):271-292. Also reprinted in *Crime in Society*, by L.D. Savitz, and N. Johnston. New York: John Wiley and Sons, 1978.

Examines the employees, clientele, services, operation, marketing, and the relationship with law enforcement agencies of the massage parlor. Profiles the masseuse as a well-paid professional with a positive self-image instead of the more traditional view of a desperate prostitute.

1908. Reichert, L.D., and J.H. Frey. "The Organization of Bell Desk Prostitution." *Sociology and Social Research* 69(4) (1985):516-526.

Describes the organization of hotel prostitution as a social network. Shows how this type of organization protects the prostitute and the client from law enforcement officials.

1909. Rosenblum, K.E. "Female Deviance and the Female Sex Role: A Preliminary Investigation." *The British Journal of Sociology* 26(2) (June 1975):169-85.

Suggests prostitution should be dealt with as a female deviance instead of a sexual deviance since prostitution is almost exclusively female. Addresses the complexities of prostitution, the weakness of previous analyses of prostitution, and uses the call-girl pattern to discuss the female sex role.

1910. Savitz, L.D., and L. Rosen. "The Sexuality of Prostitutes: Sexual Enjoyment Reported by 'Streetwalkers'." *Journal of Sex Research* 24 (1988):200-8.

Examines the sexual satisfaction of the working and private life of the prostitute. Based on the findings, this study suggests that a motivation for entering prostitution could be a high potential for erotic enjoyment.

1911. Schur, E.M. *Labeling Women Deviant: Gender, Stigma, and Social Control.* Philadelphia, PA: Temple University Press, 1984.

Examines the social origins for labeling women as deviant and the implication of this labeling for prostitution. Suggests that the definition of female deviance will change as a consequence of the changing balance between male and female social power.

1912. Seabrook, J. "The Prostitute." *New Society* 67(1111) (1984):359-60.

Documents the way of life of a street prostitute in a small English town. Places particular emphasis on social and economic forces which led to the prostitute's choice of profession.

1913. Sheehy, G. *Hustling--Prostitution in Our Wide-Open Society.* New York: Delacorte, 1973.

Provides overview of the problems of prostitution and prostitution law enforcement. Depicts prostitute subculture in New York City. Follows the class ladder of prostitution and discusses motivation. Reveals the types of people who profit financially from prostitution.

1914. Silbert, M.H., and A.M. Pines. "Early Sexual Exploitation as an Influence in Prostitution." *Social Work* 28(4) (July-August 1983):285-98. Also published in *Child Abuse.* Edited by M.C. McClellan. Bloomington, IN: Hot Topics Series, Phi Delta Kappa, Center on Evaluation, Development, Research, 1987.

Tries to determine a causal relationship between sexual exploitation during childhood and prostitution. This study shows that 60% of prostitutes interviewed suffered early sexual abuse. Explores the long-term effects of early sexual exploitation as well as implications for treatment of victims.

1915. Silbert, M.H., and A.M. Pines. "Occupational Hazards of Street Prostitutes." *Criminal Justice and Behavior* 8(4) (December 1981):395-9.

Documents the high levels of victimization experienced by prostitutes on the job. Discusses this problem including physical abuse, rape, forced perversion, nonpayment, robbery, and exploitation. Describes the endless cycle of victimization which ultimately becomes part of the working conditions of prostitutes.

1916. Sibert, M.H., and A.M. Pines. "Victimization of Street Prostitutes." *Victimology* 7(1-4) (1983):122-33.

Documents the cycle of victimization. Details the types and extent of victimization. Argues the need to provide services for victimized juveniles before they enter prostitution as well as for victimized prostitutes.

1917. Simpson, M., and T. Schill. "Patrons of Massage Parlors: Some Facts and Figures." *Archives of Sexual Behavior* 6(6) (November 1977): 521-5.

Discusses in depth the clientele of massage parlors: socioeconomic background, religious beliefs, motivation, self-concept, values.

1918. Snyder, P.W. *A Proposal toward the Socialization in Orange County, Florida.* (Association Paper) Daytona Beach, FL: Mid-South Sociological Association, 1985.

Creates a typology of prostitutes and argues that socialization is the best way to deal with the problem of prostitution. In addition, revenues earned can be used to benefit the municipality.

1919. Staats, G.R. "Stereotypes and Their Importance for Labeling Deviant Behavior." (Dissertation) Washington State University, 1976.

Examines the impact of stereotyping on deviant behavior, including prostitution. Indicates that social distance increases as the intensity of dislike grows. Includes suggestions for future research.

1920. Sternberg, D. "Prostitutes as Victimizers." *Deviants--Victims or Victimizers.* Edited by D.E.J. Macnamara and A. Karmen. Beverly Hills, CA: Sage, 1983, pp. 77-107.

Lists eleven contexts in which prostitutes can be viewed as potential victimizers. Determines that neither continued criminalization, decriminalization, or regulation would have any effect in reducing the victimization by prostitutes in most of these cases.

1921. Tollison, C.D., J.G. Nesbitt, and J.D. Frey. "Comparison of Attitudes Toward Sexual Intimacy in Prostitutes and College Coeds." *Journal of Social Psychology* 101(2) (1977): 319-20.

Suggests that prostitutes have a more conservative view of sexual intimacy than either college coeds or women of a similar socio-economic background.

1922. Van Haecht, A. "Sociology of Deviance and Sociology of Prostitution."
(French) *Recherches Sociologiques* 8(3) (1977):301-22.

Approaches prostitution from a sociological, rather than criminological,
view. Considers prostitutes to be a professional group, not a victim group.
Asserts that prostitution is an institution of society and accordingly serves
a specific function, correlating to trends in the balance of general male-
female relationships.

1923. Vaught, C.   *The Sexual Enclave: A 'Loose-Leaf' Work System.*
(Association Paper) Lexington, KY: Mid-South Sociological Association,
University of Kentucky, 1980.

Depicts the structure of prostitution as an enclave where loosely associated
enterprises base their operations on the processing of sex or sexual
illusions.

1924. Velarde, A.J.   "Becoming Prostituted: the Decline of the Massage Parlour
Profession and the Masseuse." *British Journal of Criminology* 15(3) (July
1975):251-63.

Examines the development of self-identity in a masseuse and assesses the
effect of labeling. Concludes that the labeling process reinforces sexual
deviance through the publicity generated by double standards.

1925. Visano, L.A.   "Generic and Generative Dimensions of Interactionism:
Towards the Unfolding of Critical Directions." *International Journal of
Comparative Sociology* 29(3-4) (September-December 1988):230-44.

Explores the relationships between male prostitutes and socializing
agencies as well as the culture of prostitution. Looks at prostitution from
the perspective that it is work and business, rather than crime, and
discusses the perception of prostitution as exciting and challenging.

1926. Wells, J.W.   *Tricks of the Trade: a Hooker's Handbook of Sexual
Technique. Intimate Confessions by a Girl Who Should Know.* New York:
New American Library, 1970.

1927. Wieking, D. (Producer) *We're Here Now--Prostitution.*   1984
Distributor: New York: Filmakers Library, Inc. (Video cassette.)

Focuses on testimonies made by seven former prostitutes about their
lifestyles, the pressures that led them to become prostitutes, and the
problems trying to reenter the mainstream of society.

1928. Winn, D. *Prostitutes.* London: Hutchinson, 1974.

1929. Winslow, R.W. *Emergence of Deviant Minorities--Social Problems and
Social Change--Selections from Commissions on Crime, Campus Unrest,
Causes and Prevention of Violence, Marijuana, Homosexuality and
Prostitution, and Obscenity.* US: Consensus Publishers, 1972.

Explores societal reactions to many social problems, including
prostitution. Discusses prostitutes as a deviant minority. Describes the
tolerant approach to treatment of deviant minorities in San Francisco
which has resulted in a breakdown of stereotypes and a reduction in the
crime and aggression of these deviants.

1930. Withers, J. *Prostitution, Fact and Fiction.* Seattle: ERA, 1973.

Contains a study of prostitution undertaken by the Seattle-King County
Chapter of the National Organization for Women, a resolution on
prostitution passed by the 6th Annual Conference of the National
Organization for Women and an analysis of the practice of prostitution in
Seattle. Also included is an essay which addresses common myths
concerning the connection between prostitution and venereal disease, law
enforcement and organized crime.

1931. Cashman, V., and E. Coleman. *Prostitution.* (Audiocassette) Presentation at Chemical Dependency and Family Training Project, University of Minnesota, 1981-82. Minneapolis, MN: CDFA Resource Center, Program in Human Sexuality.

1932. Cleckner, P. "Jive Dope Fiend Whores: In the Street and in Rehabilitation." *Women in Ritual and Symbolic Roles.* Edited by J. Hoch-Smith. New York: Plenum, 1978.

1933. Costa, J.A. da. *Droga e prostituição em Lisboa.* Lisboa: Dom Quixote, 1983.

1934. Cushman, P. "Relationship between Narcotic Addiction and Crime." *Federal Probation* 38(3) (September 1974):38-43.

Describes three phases of narcotic addiction, and discusses the correlation between addiction and arrest for prostitution.

1935. Datesman, S.K., and J.A. Inciardi. "Female Heroin Use, Criminality, and Prostitution." *Contemporary Drug Problems* 8 (Winter 1979):455-473.

Reports on interviews in 1978 with 153 female heroin users about their criminal activity. Finds less reliance on prostitution than had been assumed. Statistics are given of arrest histories, and nature and frequency of crimes. Data analyzed according to user/prostitutes and user/nonprostitutes. Presents suggestions for further research.

1936. File, K.N., T.W. McCahill, and L.D. Savitz. "Narcotics Involvement and Female Criminality." *Addictive Diseases* 1 (2) (1974): 177-88.

Compared the criminal patterns of female addicts to determine if prostitution, among other activities, was used to support their drug habits.

Finds that prostitutes had a significantly higher instance of narcotics abuse than non-prostitutes. Indicates that most of these addicted prostitutes are involved in a variety of other crimes.

1937. Goldstein, P.J. *Prostitution and Drugs.* Lexington, MA: Lexington Books, 1979.

Studies the interrelationship of prostitution and drug use. Finds that a high percentage of prostitutes use drugs and that regular use is more common among the lower paid prostitutes. Discusses the effect of drug abuse on prostitution as an occupation.

1938. Goldstein, P.J. "Relationship between Prostitution and Substance Use." (Ph.D. Dissertation) Case Western Reserve University, 1978.

Explores the relationship between prostitution and drug use, finding that this relationship varies depending on the level of prostitution. Determines that different drugs are associated with different classes of prostitution. Establishes the causal connection between prostitution and drug use.

1939. Inciardi, J.A. "Women, Heroin, and Property Crime." *Women, Crime, and Justice* by S.K. Datesman and F.R. Scarpitti. New York: Oxford University Press, 1980.

Argues that female drug addicts should not be stereotyped as prostitutes. Finds that, historically, it cannot be easily determined if prostitution preceded and/or caused drug addiction or vice versa. Determines that female addicts today are involved in a variety of crimes, not just prostitution, to support their habits and that their histories and records indicate a long pattern of drug abuse.

1940. James, J. "Prostitution and Addiction--An Interdisciplinary Approach." *Addictive Diseases* 2(4) (1976):601-18.

Reviews past research on the relationship between addiction and prostitution and the current research of the author. Presents an interdisciplinary framework which combines four approaches to prostitution and addiction, and concludes that changes in prostitution laws cannot be made in isolation from changes in the narcotics laws unless the addict-prostitute is recognized as an offender separate from the prostitute.

1941. Kreuzer, A. "Parasitical Forms of Delinquency in Drug Addicts."
(German) *Kriminalistik* 28(6&7) (June-July 1974):269-73, 309-13.

Discusses prostitution as one of many activities used by young habitual
drug users in West Germany to support their habit.

1942. Lange, W.R., J.C. Ball, M.B. Pfeiffer, et al. "The Lexington Addicts,
1971-1972: Demographic Characteristics, Drug Use Patterns, and Selected
Infectious Disease Experience." *International Journal of the Addictions*
24(7) (1989):609-26.

Studies the demographics, drug habits, and medical complications of a
group of addicts, over one third of which were involved in prostitution or
pimping.

1943. Lentini, J.R. *Vice and Narcotics Control.* Encino, CA: Glencoe, 1977.

Covers consensual crime, including prostitution. As part of the broader
issue, provides basic knowledge of prostitution and various methods of
suppressing it. Offers both a practical and philosophical viewpoint.
Discusses consensual crime in the context of organized crime activity.

1944. Marshall, N., and J. Hendtlass. "Drugs and Prostitution." *Journal of
Drug Issues* 16(2) (1986):237-48.

Studies the relationship between prostitution and drug use as part of a
larger investigation on prostitution. Finds that prostitutes are more likely
to use drugs--tobacco, alcohol, and narcotics--than non-prostitutes.
Suggests that the high frenquency of drug use among street prostitutes
could stem from associations during adolescence with others prone to
deviant behavior.

1945. Milivojevic, Z., V. Milic, and M. Milisavljevic. "Seksualnost
Narkomana (The Sexuality of Drug Addicts)." (Serbo-Croatian with
English Abstract) *Psihijatrija-Danas* (Psychiatry Today) 12(1)
(1980):19-26.

Studies 30 male and 10 female drug addicts with signs of opiate-type
dependence treated in outpatient services in Belgrade health centers.
Results show marked hyposexuality, decreased erotic interest as well as

sexual power, and the existence of prostitution induced by the fear of abstinence.

1946. "Panel Workshop: Violence, Crime, Sexual Abuse, and Addiction." *Contemporary Drug Problems* 5(3) (Fall 1976):385-440.

Explores the powerlessness and subsequent victimization of women and children. Finds that prostitution and narcotic use are related only for younger women.

1947. Philpot, C.R., C.L. Harcourt, and J.M. Edwards. "Drug Use by Prostitutes in Sydney." *British Journal of Addiction* 84(5) (1989):499-506.

Reports on a comparative study of drug consumption by 277 female prostitutes and 95 non-prostitutes in 1985 and 1987. Finds that marijuana was the drug most used by both groups, followed by amphetamines, cocaine and heroin. Prostitutes were more likely to smoke cigarettes than non-prostitutes, and although fewer drank alcohol those who did were more likely to drink at a harmful level. Concludes that where differences in drug consumption exist they are mainly work related.

1948. Reiman, J.H. "Prostitution, Addiction and the Ideology of Liberalism." *Contemporary Crises* 3(1) (1979):53-68.

Discusses the degradation and subsequent harm of prostitutes and heroin addicts. Finds that degradation, and not the traditional liberal conception of harm, supports the decriminalization of prostitution and heroin.

1949. Rosenbaum, M. "Work and the Addicted Prostitute." *Judge, Lawyer, Victim, Thief.* Edited by N.H. Rafter, and E.A. Stanko. Boston, MA: Northeastern University Press, 1982. pp. 131-50.

Examines the pattern for heroin addicts entering prostitution. Of 100 addicts interviewed, 62 were prostitutes who turned to prostitution to support their drug habits. Suggests that due to their addiction they are additionally vulnerable. Shows that these women are able to maintain a positive self-image because they view prostitution only as a temporary means of supporting their drug habit.

1950. St. James, M. *Prostitution and Addiction.* From Proceedings of First International Action Conference on Substance Abuse 3 (Intervention and Prevention)(November 1977). Phoenix, Arizona: Do It Now Foundation, 1977.

Discusses numerous issues related to drug addiction among prostitutes. Determines that street prostitutes have the highest incidence of drug use. Finds that most addict prostitutes were addicts before they became prostitutes and that they turned to prostitution to support their habits. Observes that addict and non-addict prostitutes are two distinct groups. Also discusses general issues such as life experiences and case studies, treatment of prostitutes by law enforcement institutions, and the expected effect of the legalization of prostitution and the decriminalization of drugs.

1951. Silber, M.H., A.M. Pines, and T. Lynch. "Substance Abuse and Prostitution." *Journal of Psychoactive Drugs* 14(3) (1982):193-7.

Investigates use of drugs, prior to and following entrance into prostitution. Suggests that prostitution and drug abuse result from the cycle of victimization, self destructive tendencies, and negative self-concept.

1952. Sterk, C.E. *Upon Realizing Who You Are--Narratives of Heroin Prostitutes.* (Association Pater) Rotterdam, Netherlands: International Sociological Association, 1986.

Stresses the importance of collecting life histories and using ethnolinguistic research methods. Focuses on how these women talk about their lives as "heroin prostitutes."

1953. Suffet, F. and R. Brotman. "Female Drug Use: Some Observations." *International Journal of Addictions* 11(1) (1976):19-33.

As part of a much broader discussion, finds that female addicts are often involved in deviant activities such as prostitution.

1954. Thom, B., et al. *Pathways to Drug Abuse Amongts [i.e. Amongst] Girls in Britain and Holland.* (Conference Papers) Florence: European University Institute, 1987.

WAR AND THE MILITARY

1955. Butler, A.M. "Military Myopia--Prostitution on the Frontier." *Prologue-Journal of the National Archives* 13(4) (1981):233-50.

1956. Christian, G.L. "Newton Baker's War on El Paso Vice." *Red River Historical Review* 5(2) (1980):55-67.

Describes the cancellation of military training in El Paso, Texas, during the war years of 1917-1918 by the Secretary of War Newton Baker who opposed prostitution and liquor in this areal.

1957. *Frauen in Vietnam.* 2. Aufl. Edited by M. Peters. Köln: Initiativkomitee fur Deutsch-Vietnamesische Kulturbeziehungen, 1976.

1958. Greenberg, J.H. "Venereal Disease in the Armed Forces." *Medical Aspects of Human Sexuality* (March 1972).

1959. Masterton, R.G., P.W. Strike. "Sexually Transmitted Diseases in a British Military Force in Peace Time Europe, 1970-1983." *Genitourinary Medicine* 64 (1988):54-58.

The role of prostitutes at a military base in the Federal Republic of Germany in spreading sexually transmitted disease.

1960. Moselina, L.M. "Olongapo's Rest and Recreation Industry: A Sociological Analysis of Institutionalized Prostitution with Implications for a Grassroots-Oriented Sociology." *Philippine Sociological Review* 27(3) (July 1979):181-93.

Discusses the relationship between the emergence of prostitution in Olongapo, the Philippines, and the establishment of an American Naval base in nearby Subic Bay. Focuses on three main factors: The economic deprivation of the women; the "rest and recreation" ideology; and the profit motive. Considers the implications of this exploitative/dependent economy for a grassroots-oriented sociology.

1961. Pivar, D.J. "Cleansing the Nation: The War on Prostitution, 1917-21." *Prologue--Journal of the National Archives* 12(1) (1980):29-40. Describes the effort during World War I to stop the spread of venereal disease and eliminate prostitution to protect the health of U.S. servicemen. Traces the efforts of the American Plan and various federal laws adopted and institutions established for this purpose.

1962. Richard-Molard, G. *Avec les prostituées: l'enjeu d'un combat.* Lyon: Châlet, 1976.

1963. Sandos, J.A. "Prostitution and Drugs: The United States Army on the Mexican-American Border, 1916-1917." *Pacific Historical Review* 49(4) (1980):621-45.

Provides an effective method for reducing drug use and venereal disease in the armed forces. Uses the example of General Pershing, commander of the US Punitive Expedition into Mexico 1916-17. Instead of prohibiting prostitution he regulated it, provided other means of diversion, and isolated the troops from civilians. As a result troop morale was increased and the ban on drugs was more effective.

1964. Stoltzfus, B. "Olongapo's Trap: The Women Outside Subic Naval Base." *Sojourners* (August-September 1986).

1965. Villiers, G. de. *Dossiers roses de la Brigade mondaine.* Paris: Presses de la Cité, 1973.

INDEX OF PERSONAL NAMES
Numbers in index refer to entries